St. Charles Borromeo

St. Charles Borromeo
200 Years of Faith

Jo Ann Brown

The Patrice Press
St. Louis

**Library of Congress
Cataloging-in-Publication Data**

Goetzcraft Printers 20,515 12-5-91
Phone: 973-7636
Tape A

OP 1

Brown, Jo Ann 1954-
   St. Charles Borromeo : 200 years of faith / Jo Ann Brown. p. cm.
   Includes bibliographical references and index.
   ISBN 0-935284-95-8
   1. St. Charles Borromeo (Church : Saint Charles, Mo.) — History.
   2. Saint Charles (Mo.) — Church history.   I. Title.
   BX4603.S32B76   1991
   282' .77839—dc20

                                                    91-43169
Printed in the United States of America   CIP

To the people of
St. Charles Borromeo

Contents

Foreword

Simply and affectionately, it has been called Borromeo. The official title given it some two hundred years ago by the Spanish — St. Charles Borromeo Church — has always been too stiff and formal for most of the local people. The more popular abbreviation speaks of a closeness that is rarely found between the institutional parish and its members.

In its lengthy history, this Borromeo has actually been the title of four churches. From a rugged, primitive log hut to the classic, twin-spired limestone edifice that we identify with today, Borromeo has been a place where early frontier residents and their twentieth-century descendants have come to worship. At its present site, children have skipped rope, acolytes have processed piously, and women have prepared meals for hungry souls at parish festivals. The front steps of the church have been posed with classes of first communicants in their finest apparel, with post-war couples on their wedding day, and with young men on their first Mass day. In all, Borromeo has been an intricate part of the lives and times of the community with which it shares its name. It has been a place where the young have been born in Christ, and others have been placed at death into the loving, tender hands of God. Borromeo for two hundred years has been a bridge from this world into the next.

We should not, however, so easily glamorize or romanticize the past. The church has been as much a home for errant sinners as an honor role of saints. One should not be surprised if the story here told bespeaks weakness as much as glory.

Priests are certainly not perfect — Christ died for them as well — and the flock that they guide also steps off the path at times. Yet to continue for two hundred years in the face of such difficulties as the early years without a resident priest, or natural calamities as the storm of 1915 which destroyed the brick church — it is evident that God had a very special plan for this parish, and that the grace to persevere was in abundance.

The history you are about to read has never been told before. For a parish as old as Borromeo, it would seem that someone would have brought the story to light long before this anniversary celebration. Short summaries have been written. Stories have been passed along, and sometimes facts have been created. Yet nowhere has there been found a complete telling of our rich past. It is appropriate therefore that we tell it now, not as a perfect recollection, but as an honest attempt to recall the major character and events that have made us who we are today.

The motto of St. Ignatius of Loyola, whose disciples shepherded this parish for 134 years, is expressed as *"ad majorem Dei Gloriam,"* "for the greater glory of God." This motto should continue to be the proud goal of the Borromeo community as we reach out into the third century of service. God's will is not always easy, but God's grace is always sufficient. As we do His will, and recall our past, let it be under the shadow of His tender, loving guidance.

Rev. Stephen F. Bauer
St. Charles, 1991

Acknowledgments

Translations

Sara Gaylor, Mary Buschmeyer, Ruth Ann Walendy, William Barnaby Faherty, S.J., Nancy Merz

Archivists

William Barnaby Faherty, S.J., and Nancy Merz, Jesuit Missouri Province Archives; Dr. Martin G. Towey and Teresa Eagan, C.S.J., Archdiocese of St. Louis; Carol Wilkins, Bob Schultz, and the staff of the St. Charles County Historical Society; John Waide, St. Louis University; Richard Salmons and Patsy Luebbert, Missouri State Archives; the staff of the Missouri Historical Society; Marie Louise Padberg, R.S.C.J. and Elizabeth Farley, R.S.C.J., National Archives of the Society of the Sacred Heart; Margaret Caire, R.S.C.J. and Jane Cannon, Academy of the Sacred Heart, St. Charles; Marie Louise Martinez, R.S.C.J., New Orleans; Aurelia Ottersbach, S.L., Archives of the Sisters of Loretto, Nerinx, Ky.; Laura Northcroft, S.S.N.D., Archives of the School Sisters of Notre Dame, St. Louis, Mo; Catholic Cemeteries of St. Louis; Emmons Title Company

Special Thanks

William Barnaby Faherty, S.J., and Nancy Merz, Jesuit Missouri Province Archives; Alfred Lemmon and John D. Barbry, Historic New Orleans Collection; Robert Archibald, Director, and Bryan S. Thomas, Pictorial History Archivist, Missouri Historical Society; Colleen Hamilton and Joe Harl, University of Missouri—St. Louis Archaeological Survey; Abraham P. Nasatir, San Diego State University; Bernard Fontana, Southwestern Mission Research Center; Vivian C. Fisher, Bancroft Library, University of California, Berkeley; Dr. Carl J. Ekberg, Illinois State University; Jack Holterman, West Glacier, Montana; Dr. Elizabeth A. H. John, Austin, Texas; Dr. Marc Simmons, Cerrillos, New Mexico; Marley Brant, Burbank, California; Mimi Jackson, Lewis and Clark Center, St. Charles, Mo.; Richard Watkins, U. S. Postal Service, St. Louis, Mo.; Sam Taylor & Associates; Dave M. Arnold; Garrett Graphics; Monsignor Donald Rau; Theresa Tighe; Richard L. Vinson; Lucille Wiechens; Mark Whealen; Marge Smaglik; the late Reinhart Stiegemeier; Gene and Mary Buehrle; the family of Carl Ueberle; Charlotte M. Thompson; Tom Hayden; Eugene and Billy Williams; Peggy Dupree and Gerry Lanigan; Glenn and Virginia McGuire; Lee and Bea White; Jean Dickens; Kathleen Netsch; Rory and Sue Riddler; our Bicentennial Committee: Chairman Richard Johannesman, Evo Malpiedi, Aggie Graveman, Larry Ohlms, Doug Boschert, Sharon Schnarre, and Joan Bruening; and all the other parishioners and friends whose photographs, remembrances, and support have made this book possible.

Finally, the author wishes to thank her husband, family, and friends for their unfailing support during the writing of this book.

St. Charles Borromeo

Introduction
Before the Founding of the Parish

The First Explorers and Settlers

The Catholic history of St. Charles, Missouri, started long before the 1791 founding of St. Charles Borromeo parish, and even before French Canadian trappers and traders first settled the area around 1769. It began one hot June day in 1673 when Father Jacques Marquette and his companion Louis Jolliet, while exploring the placid Mississippi, were nearly thrown out of their canoes by a frightening turmoil of floodwaters that spewed from an unknown river into the Mississippi. Marquette wrote, "I have seen nothing more dreadful. An accumulation of large and entire trees, branches, and floating islands was issuing from the mouth of the river . . . with such impetuosity that we could not without great danger risk passing through it."

Deciding not to venture up the turbulent river, the pair continued on their journey. Marquette suspected that the river led to the Pacific Ocean and hoped to return someday, "in order that I may preach the gospel to all the peoples of this new world who have so long groveled in the darkness of infidelity," but died before he could. The name of this river (whose territory Father Marquette claimed for God) became the Missouri, and soon other whites explored it. By 1700 the Osage and Missouri Indians, who lived over a hundred miles up the river from its junction with the Mississippi, regularly did business with French Canadian fur traders. So profitable was the commerce in pelts along the rivers that a slow exodus from Canada began.

France owned the lands along both the upper Mississippi River and the Missouri, but for many years did little to develop either section, both of which it called the "Illinois Country." These lands were only a part of France's holdings in central North America, which it called "La Louisiane."

In the 1760s, forces were set in motion that led up to the founding of the first white settlement on the north side of the

Father Jacques Marquette, first priest on Missouri soil

Missouri Historical Society

Missouri River and its parish, St. Charles Borromeo. First, France transferred its entire territory west of the Mississippi River to Spain. This assured that the vast tract would remain Catholic. Protestant England then took France's lands to the east of the Mississippi as its reward for winning the French and Indian War. The river became the political and ecclesiastical boundary between two frequently hostile countries.

On both sides of the Mississippi, most people were French-speaking Catholics (hereafter called Creoles: a term that designated a person of French or Spanish ancestry born in the New World). They cared little about the political transfer, but considered the religious change alarming. Shortly after the founding of St. Louis in 1764, many residents of Cahokia and other villages to the east of the river migrated across the Mississippi to Catholic territory.

In 1767, Spain asserted its right to this land by building at the junction of the Mississippi and Missouri Rivers a fort named for its own King Carlos (Charles) III. This installation was meant to protect the Missouri River territory and its fur trade, from the English. In a short time the entire operation failed. Floodwaters regularly swamped the fort, located on the Missouri River in what is now St. Louis County. A blockhouse named for young Carlos, the crown prince of Spain, stood across the river in present-day St. Charles County. Located on lower ground, it fared even worse than the fort.

So quickly did the buildings deteriorate that soon they became useless. Dissent broke out among local Creoles and Indians who resented Spain's attempts to regulate their commerce in furs. Unrest also seized the Spanish soldiers garrisoned at the fort, and they mutinied against their commander, Francisco Rui. Another Spanish officer named Pedro Piernas eventually replaced Rui, but before he could straighten things out at Fort Don Carlos, a rebellion against Spanish rule in New Orleans forced him to return south.

Later, in 1769, Spain reasserted control over all of its Mississippi valley holdings by sending to govern the area an Irishman named Alexander O'Reilly. One of O'Reilly's first acts was to partition the valley into north and south, and to send Pedro Piernas back to St. Louis as lieutenant governor of the northern tract.

At about the same time, a French Canadian hunter named Louis Blanchette established a settlement which he called "Les Petites Cotes" (the Little Hills), below the first bluffs to rise back from the north bank of the Missouri River. Like many other roving French Canadian traders (called *voyageurs),* Blanchette lived with an Indian woman, by whom he had three children. His cousins and perhaps other emigrés from Canada settled at the little village. At some unknown time, Blanchette became commandant of the settlement. Tradition holds that he built the first Catholic chapel in the village and helped establish the parish of St. Charles Borromeo.

King Charles III of Spain. During his reign (1757-1788) the village later named St. Charles was settled.

Spanish Roots

At first, Spain was probably not aware of Petites Cotes. Before Rui was replaced by Piernas as commander of the Spanish troops, he described the area he called "Ylinois" to Governor O'Reilly. His report sketched the villages, tribes, and streams of the Mississippi and Missouri valleys, but failed to mention any permanent settlement along the Missouri River. In describing the population of St. Louis, however, Rui stated that his census figures did not include mention of the *voyageurs,* "because most of the time [they] are either out hunting or trading among the Indian tribes." Perhaps Blanchette and the other earliest settlers of St. Charles, all hunters and traders according to tradition, were

purposely overlooked as well.

A year later, in 1770, Spanish documents hinted at the existence of some settlement along the Missouri when O'Reilly sent to Lieutenant Governor Pedro Piernas instructions for governing St. Louis, Ste. Genevieve, "and all the districts of the Missouri River. . . . " But for a long time there was no specific mention of a village along the river; early government reports concerning the area now known as Missouri named only the settlements of St. Louis and Ste. Genevieve.

These reports also fail to mention Louis Blanchette. Some very old church archives from the St. Louis parish, however, mention him and his family as having received various sacraments between 1775 and 1790 at the hands of St. Louis's pastors. Because these records do not state that the Blanchettes were "residents of this Parish," as do most entries concerning the early residents of St. Louis, it is possible that the ceremonies were performed at St. Charles. The records also state that Blanchette's cousins—the Michous, Moreaus, and Malbeoufs, according to tradition all early residents of Petites Cotes—served during these ceremonies as godparents and witnesses. These church archives offer the best evidence that Blanchette and his relatives lived somewhere in the vicinity of St. Louis before the Spanish government recognized St. Charles.

During this time, Spanish census and military records named many other residents of the area who eventually moved to St. Charles: Charles Tayon, Blanchette's successor as commandant; Alexis Cote, whose land along the Missouri River was later platted as Block 6 and conveyed to the Jesuits; Joseph Chancellier and his wife Elizabeth Becquet, who conveyed their land grant along Main and Jackson Streets to the embryonic church at St. Charles; Antoine Gautier, later to become Tayon's second-in-command of the St. Charles militia; Joseph Thebeau, a Canadian rower who married a Pawnee woman; Louis Barada, a shoemaker who eventually owned a number of slaves in St. Charles; Marie Louise Quebec Langevin, who married Etienne Bernard of Montreal before the first resident pastor of St. Charles Borromeo; Jean Baptiste Brugiere, chosen as contractor by the parishioners in 1817 to replace the crumbling log church; and Pierre Troge, later chanter and sacristan of the parish and lieutenant of the village's militia.

It is not clear from the civil records exactly when the Spanish government recognized Petites Cotes. The validity of Blanchette's commandancy of the area is not provable until a few years before his

---

Commandants of St. Charles until 1804
Blanchette, Louis
            from an undetermined date until 1793
Tayon, Charles 1793-1801
Mackay, James 1801-1804

---

death in 1793, and the first Spanish census for St. Charles, prepared in 1787, says nothing about the age of the settlement or the role of its reputed founder. It seems, however, that once the royal government became aware of this first white settlement along the Missouri River, it administered the village exactly as it administered the other settlements within its jurisdiction.

When O'Reilly split "La Louisiane" into two tracts, the northern section became known as "Ylinois" as well as "Upper Louisiana." He granted Piernas great discretion in governing the area, but insisted that Piernas further Spain's three goals: "that the dominion and government of His Majesty be loved and respected; justice administered promptly, impartially, and according to the laws; and that commerce be protected and increased as much as possible." Piernas put his previous experience with the area and its residents to work, and soon had in place the machinery for running the government.

To the outsider, Upper Louisiana's lieutenant governors might have seemed to embody all-encompassing powers; not only did they command the citizen militia, they acted as judge and jury in difficult lawsuits and decided the fate of the few accused of crimes. They also collected taxes, promoted the fur trade, and regulated the surveying and conveyance of lands.

In a region populated mostly by laborers who could neither read nor write, good surveyors were hard to find. Usually dedicated but unqualified men were employed to locate land grants, relying on such nebulous boundaries as piles of stones or marks slashed on trees. Sometimes the surveys raised as many questions as they settled.

After the Louisiana Purchase many were hotly contested, but during the Spanish regime they helped further the settlement of the seemingly endless land. In 1797 the official surveyor for Upper Louisiana, Antoine Soulard, surveyed the St. Charles area with the assistance of an uneducated but prominent Borromeo parishioner named Gabriel Latreille.

Another function of the Spanish government was to regulate such pleasures as liquor, games of chance, and billiards. Although the law strictly forbade trafficking in alcohol with the native tribes, such dealing was expected and sometimes demanded by the Indians as the price of doing business. An alcohol tax coupled with a tavern license fee served to limit the amount of liquor sold in Creole villages and the

Lieutenant Govenors of Upper Louisiana, 1764–1803	
St. Ange de Bellerive, Louis	1764-1770
Piernas, Pedro Joseph	1770-1775
Cruzat, Francisco (first term)	1775-1778
Leyba, Fernando de	1778-1780
Cruzat, Francisco (second term)	1780-1787
Pérez, Manuel	1787-1792
Trudeau, Zenon	1792-1799
Delassus, Carlos Dehault	1799-1803

number of taverns in each. The government used the liquor revenues in different ways. Tavern taxes from St. Charles normally helped support the Borromeo parish, but in 1798 the lieutenant governor ordered that the $700 collected that year from the village's drinking establishments be given to the poor.

Catholicism in the Spanish Era

As lieutenant governor, Piernas also commanded the militia and oversaw relations with the many Indian tribes in Upper Louisiana. One of his greatest concerns was the advancement of the Catholic faith. No Constitution drew a line between Church and State in Upper Louisiana; the civil government was expected to cooperate with the clergy for the promotion of religion. Since the 1500s the Spanish crown had controlled church revenues and appointments, and it extended this "Royal Patronage" to its New World holdings. From his headquarters in St. Louis, the lieutenant governor could supervise the construction of churches, oversee the payment of expenses and the salaries of priests, and regulate the collection of tithes.

In 1772 Governor Luis de Unzaga issued a report on religious matters. Opening with a roster of the seven officially functioning priests of the Mississippi valley, he called for at least eleven more to serve the growing population, then described the state of parish administration from New Orleans to St. Louis. In doing so, Unzaga mentioned that the area's priests received a "sufficient" stipend from the government, along with a house and various fees from their parishioners. Additional revenues, Unzaga reported, came from pew rentals as well as from fees for burials inside the church, "the rate decreasing from the nearest [perhaps to the altar] to the most remote."

Then Unzaga detailed the different functions of the laity on whom the area's many priestless parishes relied, starting with *marguilliers* (later called trustees or churchwardens). At St. Charles Borromeo, a board of three such laymen took care of the parish's property, paid bills, and collected tithes and pew rents. In some places, *marguilliers* also provided candles for their churches and tools for burials. Unzaga's report then mentioned lay singers called chanters, and added that these laymen usually attended services in cassocks and surplices, and received small fees for their singing.

Last, he explained the role of the beadle, "... a man dressed in a blue uniform, with a scarlet scarf. He carries a pike, and in this guise attends the divine service. His function is to prevent irreverence in the sacred edifice, and to repress conversation." Although Borromeo's records mention a beadle only rarely, they frequently mention another minor lay official called a sacristan. In St. Charles, one of the most important functions of the parish's sacristans was to preside at burials. Like chanters, beadles and sacristans received small fees for their services.

As a result of the transfer of "La Louisiane" to Spain, religious authority passed from the archbishop of Quebec to the archbishop of Havana in 1772. One of the earliest records from the Borromeo archives is a schedule of burial fees known as the Tariff of Havana. Although listed in *dolares* and *sous*, the currency referred to is probably the French *livre*:

> Burial of a white over 7 years, [the fees going] to the Priest, the Chanter and the Sexton [Sacristan]
> in silver or deer skins   60
> A white under 7 years   20
> A slave over 7 years   40
> A slave under 7 years   15
> A mulatto, Indian or free negro—
> the same as a white.

Besides their governmental salary (officially 600 pesos per year, although letters from Spanish officials in Missouri suggest that priests there received substantially less), priests in the Mississippi valley re-

<table>
<tr><td colspan="2">Currencies and Values</td></tr>
<tr><td colspan="2">French livre equivalent to .20 American dollar, Spanish peso, Spanish piastre (also called gourde)</td></tr>
<tr><td colspan="2">French sou (or sol) equivalent to .05 livre, .01 Spanish peso or piastre (also called gourde), .01 American dollar</td></tr>
<tr><td colspan="2">Spanish piastre (also called gourde) equivalent to Spanish peso, American dollar, 5 French livres</td></tr>
<tr><td colspan="2">Deer hides, frequently substituted for currency, were worth roughly between 20-40 sous (20-40 cents) per pound.</td></tr>
</table>

ceived small sums for baptizing, marrying, and burying. For tithes, they made do with about one-twenty-sixth of each parishioner's harvest, payable in bushels of wheat or corn, deerskins, or very rarely, in cash. Depending as it did on the climate, this tithe amounted to a considerable second income for a priest during "good weather" years, but amounted to much less during years of drought or flood. Spanish harvest figures for the settlements in Upper Louisiana show that St. Charlesans, per capita, sometimes out-produced residents of larger villages. Nevertheless, for many years Blanchette's settlement had a hard time attracting, and then keeping, a resident pastor.

One of the problems was an acute shortage of priests, caused in part by France's 1763 suppression of the Society of Jesus, which had forced most of the Jesuit missionaries in the Illinois Country to leave North America. Although Spain continued the suppression, it tried to compensate for the lack of priests by recruiting young men for Spanish seminaries from staunchly Catholic Ireland, in the hope of one day attracting more Catholics from east of the Mississippi with these English-speaking clergymen. Fathers James Maxwell and Thomas Flynn, missionaries who visited St. Charles during its early years as an American town, were examples of this Irish connection.

The first priests who had any connection, direct or indirect, with St. Charles were not Irish. The earliest priest who spent any time in the area was Sebastian Meurin, a Jesuit missionary who gained a special permission to return to the Upper Louisiana after the expulsion of his order. Although Meurin's connection with St. Charles is difficult to prove, he did visit St. Louis as a missionary outpost regularly from about 1766 until 1769, when questions about his jurisdiction forced him to leave the area for several years. In 1772 he returned and again ministered to the town as a visiting missionary for three years. Among his last recorded acts was the 1775 baptism of Blanchette's sons. Whether Meurin traveled to Petites Cotes or ministered to its inhabitants who made the journey to St. Louis is not clear, but by 1775 he was in his sixties and worn out by years of illness and life on the frontier.

In 1767 Father Meurin asked the bishop of Quebec for an assistant, adding that serving the spiritual needs of Upper Louisiana was too much even for "the most robust man." The next year his request was answered. Quebec sent Father Pierre Gibault to Meurin's home parish at Kaskaskia on the east bank of the Mississippi, and over time the two priests worked out an arrangement in which Gibault took over many of Meurin's travels to the outlying missions.

Like Meurin, Gibault stopped regularly in St. Louis while riding the mission circuit—Kaskaskia, Ste. Genevieve, Cahokia, St. Louis, Prairie du Rocher, even distant Vincennes. From June 1770 until January 1772, he baptized in St. Louis thirty whites, eighteen blacks, and sixteen Indians, and signed the register "Parish Priest of the Immaculate Conception of Our Lady of Kaskaskia and Vicar General of My Lord, the Bishop of Quebec," although as such he lacked jurisdiction in Spanish territory. Whether he traveled to St. Charles during this time is not proven; on one hand no more than a few families lived there, and according to tradition all the men regularly left the area to hunt and trade; but on the other hand St. Charles then was probably one of the few settlements within a reasonable distance from St. Louis.

Father Gibault was certainly energetic. His name appears in parish registers as far away as Peoria, Detroit and Sault Ste. Marie during this period. He traveled on horseback and foot and occasionally by canoe. Like Meurin, he spent his life "attending so many villages, so distant from each other, in all weathers, night and day, snow and rain, windstorm or fog on the Mississippi, so that I [Gibault] never slept four nights in a year in my own bed . . ." And like Meurin he had little success getting along with authorities. Sent by the bishop of Quebec to Kaskaskia, he voluntarily ministered to the people across the Mississippi as well, and won the affection of many. As a young priest he differed sometimes with the infirm Father Meurin, but their common goal—the spiritual well-being of all the inhabitants of the upper Mississippi valley—made for a high degree of cooperation.

Father Gibault is the earliest priest to be

mentioned in St. Charles Borromeo's archives, though as vicar general, not as a ministering priest. In this capacity he passed along an undated schedule of fees from the bishop of Quebec (who technically had no say over the parish), detailing such things as the costs of saying a High Mass ($8.50) or a Low Mass (.50); of burying in the cemetery an adult ($5.50), or a child (1.50); of digging a grave in the church floor ($30); of publishing the three banns of matrimony ($2.50) or dispensing the banns ($5 for the first, $10 for the second and $40.00 for the third).

After Gibault's last missionary visit to the area, the first of several Capuchins arrived and set up housekeeping in St. Louis. Father Valentine de Neufchateau, who quite possibly accompanied the Spanish troops to St. Louis in 1767 as the soldiers' chaplain, stayed three years. During this time he officiated at numerous baptisms and funerals and blessed the new bell for the church at St. Louis. Whether he had any direct contact with the village called Petites Cotes is unprovable, because the records kept by the church of St. Louis (now in the care of the Old Cathedral) did not regularly mention locations. Still, it is likely that Father Valentine visited the settlement, as he was probably connected with the nearby Spanish fort. He left the area in 1775 under mysterious circumstances.

The next priest in the area was the controversial Capuchin, Hilaire de Geneveaux, who announced during a visit to St. Louis in the spring of 1776 that a resident pastor for that town was on his way. Whether Father Hilaire visited St. Charles is unrecorded. During his brief stay in St. Louis, he administered various sacraments, then returned to his parish at Ste. Genevieve, where he was engaged in a battle with his parishioners for a literal one-tenth of their harvest instead of the customary one-twenty-sixth. He eventually lost, and was transferred by the government.

The priest heralded by Father Hilaire was another Capuchin, Bernard de Limpach, who arrived in St. Louis in May 1776 and stayed nearly thirteen years. French customs and celebrations flourished during this time. Because most holidays were religious in nature, a typical year included the communal observance of Epiphany, Ash Wednesday, Easter, All Saint's, Advent, and a gala celebration of Christmas with midnight Mass, altar decorations, and as many candles as could be afforded. New Year's Eve was primarily a holiday for the young, who received presents then instead of on Christmas Day. That night the young men of the villages donned costumes and traveled from door to door singing *La Guignolée* and seeking donations for a large community party, a custom which gave way in general interest over the years to the Veiled Prophet ball. Birthdays as such were not celebrated, but the feast days of patron saints were. The moveable feast of Corpus Christi acquired special significance in Spanish territory around this time, and it was celebrated with the procession of the Blessed Sacrament through the village streets. Across the Mississippi in American territory, religious parades were forbidden.

Although the custom of conducting business and socializing on Sunday predated Father Bernard's tenure, it continued in the area without much opposition until his successor arrived. Traditionally, Sunday was reserved for a High Mass, followed by auction sales at the door of the church. Weddings most often occurred on this day. Parties and dances began Sunday afternoon and sometimes went on well into the night, livened with music and liquor imported from New Orleans.

Father Bernard played an important role in preparing the village of Petites Cotes to be one of the earliest canonical parishes in Missouri. As pastor of St. Louis he assumed responsibility for the outlying settlements—Carondelet, Portage des Sioux, Florissant, and St. Charles, and even crossed the Mississippi occasionally to minister outside his jurisdiction in Cahokia. It is known that he maintained a hectic schedule in St. Louis, performing over 600 baptisms, 119 weddings and 326 funerals. Perhaps his exertions or the climate took a toll on his health; in 1787 he wrote his superiors for a less strenuous assignment, noting that his parish at St. Louis "has four villages depending on it, and these increase daily by the emigration of French families that establish themselves here, to be free from the vexations of the Americans, who are on the eastern side of the river."

Political Priests

Being a priest during the Spanish regime was a political statement, forcing even the most unwordly men into making difficult choices and involving some in controversies not of their own making. All six priests responsible for the Catholics of St. Charles before the dedication of Borromeo parish found themselves caught up in the larger struggles going on around them.

Sebastian Meurin: Originally a Jesuit missionary to the Indians east of the Mississippi, Meurin won special permission from the Superior Council of Louisiana to return upriver after the 1763 suppression of his order, promising to accept the authority of the Capuchin superior. For the rest of his life he remained an unwilling pawn in the struggle for power between English forces to the east of the Mississippi and Spanish forces to the west, as well as in the related struggle for spiritual jurisdiction of the Mississippi valley between his former superior, the Bishop of Quebec, and the Capuchin order.

Pierre Gibault: Sent from Canada to assist Father Meurin, Gibault lived for several years on the east side of the Mississippi, but traveled secretly to Spanish territory on the west side to serve the residents of St. Louis, Ste. Genevieve, and possibly St. Charles. During the Revolutionary War, he persuaded residents of the eastern side to support George Rogers Clark's American forces, but later became disillusioned with American ways and moved across the river. For many years he ministered unofficially to the residents of Upper Louisiana, but because of the ongoing dispute over ecclesiastical authority, he was denied the standing and salary of a parish priest until 1793.

Valentine de Neufchateau: Probably the chaplain who accompanied Spanish forces to the St. Louis area in 1767, Valentine was living proof of Spain's determination to establish the Catholic faith throughout the territory. He returned in 1772 as St. Louis's first resident priest, but left hastily in 1775 under mysterious circumstances.

Hilaire de Geneveaux: A Capuchin friar sent to Ste. Genevieve, Hilaire refused to cooperate with the much-loved Father Gibault, then alienated his civil superiors as well as his parishioners by demanding increased financial support. Eventually Governor Bernardo de Gálvez recalled the unruly priest to Louisiana.

Bernard de Limpach: Eight years before becoming St. Louis's first canonical pastor in 1776, the Capuchin Father Bernard was allegedly involved in an unsuccessful mutiny against the Spanish government in New Orleans.

Jean Antoine Le Dru: Shortly after being appointed by the bishop of Baltimore to Cahokia in 1789, Le Dru abandoned his parish on the eastern side of the Mississippi for Spanish territory. Documents in the General Archive of the Indies suggest that Le Dru thereafter failed to live up to the Spanish government's expectations of its priests, and was reprimanded by Lieutenant Governor Zenon Trudeau.

Preparing for a Parish

During the pastorate of Father Bernard, the system of *marguilliers* developed at St. Charles Borromeo, where it lasted until the 1820s. The system worked like this: each January 1 the adult males of the parish elected one of their numbers to serve as third *marguillier,* thus "bumping" the previous year's third *marguillier* to the office of second *marguillier,* and the previous year's second *marguillier* to the office of senior *marguillier.* These men acted as trustees of the parish's material goods, auctioning the pews of the church to the highest bidding parishioners, enforcing the repair of the fences which surrounded the church and cemetery, and keeping track of revenues and expenses. From their special pew in church the *marguilliers* enforced respect during services.

Before Bernard de Limpach left the area, he petitioned Lieutenant Governor Manuel Pérez for official authorization of a parish for Petites Cotes. On October 13, 1789, he and Pérez visited the town to look things over. After celebrating a High Mass, Father Bernard and Pérez visited the house of Commandant Blanchette, where the future parishioners had assembled. "Being desirous to build a church," the group "agreed among themselves unanimously to erect a log church, forty feet in length by thirty in width" by the proposed deadline of late spring, 1790. To supervise construction they then elected an early resident, Maturin Bouvet. After the people affixed their marks to the written resolution, Bouvet was granted the power "to summon those who refuse to lend their labor or furnish materials, he having received the plurality of the votes of the citizens." The document closes on a wistful note: "May many good people settle here in the future, and contribute a like just share of aid on their part."

The construction deadline was not met. On June 16, 1790, Father Bernard's successor at the St. Louis parish, the Dominican Jean Antoine Le Dru, traveled by way of St. Ferdinand (Florissant) to Petites Cotes, "where they intend constructing another church which will be the second branch of this one [St. Ferdinand of Florissant]."

On September 10, 1790, Lieutenant Governor Pérez wrote to his superior in New Orleans about the new parish of St. Ferdinand and its counterpart across the river, "There is no doubt that these two towns needed to have a church and a cemetery, on account of their great distance from those of St. Louis. At the present time it would not be too much to have one priest between the two of them, so that they could with greater frequency have someone to attend to them and say Mass, because the priest at St. Louis cannot do so himself as long as it is necessary for him to go everywhere." This proposed sharing of a pastor was just one creative way in which Spain tried to deal with the shortage of priests. It soon became a reality.

Part 1
The Log Church Era

Chapter 1
1792-1804

Legends and Facts

The log church was dedicated on November 7, 1791. On hand to do the honors were Lieutenant Governor Manuel Pérez and Father Jean Antoine Le Dru. Afterward, both Pérez and Le Dru attested to the event in the parish archives, but recorded little else about the dedication or the new parish. Stories grew up over the years to fill in this gap of information, but these stories are partly refuted by surviving records in the custody of the Spanish government.

The first of these stories is that during the dedication, Pérez suggested the name "St. Charles" for both the parish and the settlement, taking the residents by happy surprise. In a letter to his superior dated September 10, 1790, however, Pérez wrote, "The inhabitants of the small hills on the other side of the Missouri [from St. Ferdinand] have also agreed to build a church of their own, and have already begun to work on it. The people have decided to choose as patron, St. Charles, in the name of our August Sovereign."

This same letter describes a similar rationale behind the name given to the St. Ferdinand. "As patron of the said town and church," wrote Pérez, "they [the residents] have chosen St. Ferdinand in honor of His Royal Highness, the Most Serene Señor Prince of Asturias, which has greatly pleased [them]. . . ." The naming of a village for a royal personage and his patron saint was probably a common method for the Spanish government to dignify that village, and it likely gained the residents a measure of official approval as well. In addition, the name "Charles" had already been associated with the area, dating from the 1767 construction of the Spanish military buildings named for King Carlos III and his son.

Another notion which later developed about the early parish concerned the architecture of the church. Although the structure was built of logs, it did not resemble the modern notion of a log cabin, one of horizontally-placed logs with interlocking grooves at the corners. Horizontal log cabin construction reminiscent of Abraham Lincoln was typical of the eastern "Anglo" United States, but not of the Creole Mississippi valley, where for years people had erected their houses, churches and trading posts of upright timbers. Two types

Manuel Pérez, lieutenant governor, 1787-92

A conception of the first church in St. Louis, by Sheila M. Harris

of construction had evolved over the years: *poteaux en terre,* in which the bottom ends of the timbers were planted in the ground; and *poteaux sur solle,* in which they rested on a rock or wooden sill so as to discourage termites. Cedar, being pest-resistant, was preferred to other types of wood but commanded a higher price. The 1789 resolution drawn up by Pérez, Father Bernard, and the people of Petites Cotes to build the church mentions white oak as the construction material of choice, a cheaper but sturdy alternative to cedar.

The resolution also specifies *poteaux en terre* as the type of architecture. Although burying the ends of the oak timbers in the ground ensured rapid decay of those ends, it also facilitated repair. When decay had progressed enough to endanger a structure, each side of the structure was laid on the ground and the rotten ends were sawed off. Then the timbers, three or four feet shorter than before, were raised and re-fitted into the ground. If the original timbers

of the log church were very long—and an unidentified source from the Jesuit Archives in St. Louis states that those of the log church measured eighteen feet—the building might provide adequate head room through up to three cycles of repair. Spaces between the upright logs were chinked with an earth-based mortar, and later, clapboards were probably fastened to the outside of the church so that it resembled a frame building. Although no illustration of the structure exists, it may well have looked like the log church of that period in St. Louis, with twin galleries running along each side of the building to provide some additional shelter, and a belfry in front. The same uncredited source cited above states that one of the church's sacristies doubled as the pastors' living quarters.

Another persistent mystery concerns a previous building or buildings used for church purposes and their location. Father James Conway, in his centennial monograph "History of St. Charles Borromeo," states that the 1791 building replaced a "rude chapel" but fails to mention the location of the chapel. Tradition holds that Blanchette, upon settling at what is now Block 20 (bounded by the Missouri River and McDonough, Riverside, and Main streets) erected several log buildings, one of which was used as a chapel. Over the years three possible locations for this chapel have been presented. The first, on Block 20, is nearly impossible to document but comports with Blanchette's reputation as a devout Catholic and a generous community leader.

The second possible location for an early church building was on Block 15, bounded by the Missouri River and Main, Jackson and Tompkins streets. An 1817 lawsuit over a lot claimed by the parish on Block 15 stated that this land was granted by Spanish authorities to Joseph Chancellier, one of the earliest residents of St. Louis. Sometime after burying a child on the land, the suit continued, Chancellier conveyed it to the parish. Frederic L. Billon, in his *Annals of St. Louis in its Early Days Under the French and Spanish Dominations,* stated that Chancellier married in 1782 and died in 1784. Although the suit did not mention a church building on the site, it referred to a cross which stood there in 1817.

In examining this question, Father W. B. Sommerhauser (whose attempt to write the history of the parish during his 1932-1944 pastorate was abandoned due to ill health) dismissed the possibility of a church building on Block 15. He reasoned that the donation must have occurred between 1782 and 1784, and that any church on the site would have been in reasonably good shape by 1789, when the parishioners agreed to build a new one. And in years of normal weather his assumption would be correct. But 1784 and 1785 were years of extreme flooding; any building located near the Missouri River (as most buildings in town

then were) would have been severely damaged, if not swept away. Therefore, the chance that a church stood on Block 15 before 1791 cannot be overlooked.

The third possibility is that Block 28, the site of the 1791 church, was also the site of an earlier building. Given the somewhat higher elevation of Block 28 from that of Blocks 15 and 20, and the eighteenth century custom of burying next to the church, it seems reasonable that an earlier church building, farther from the floodplain, may have stood here. If so, it probably lay paral-

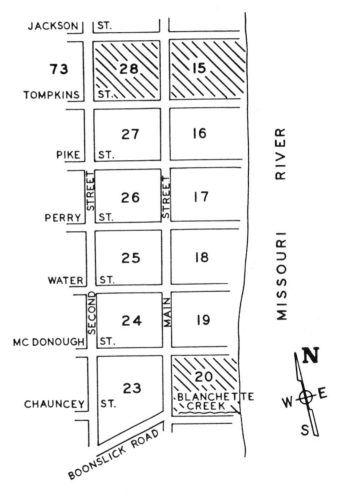

\\\\\\ = POSSIBLE LOCATIONS OF CHURCH BUILDINGS BEFORE 1791.

Dave M. Arnold

Map of possible locations of a church before 1791

lel with Main Street, so that its builders would not have had to excavate much into the hill to the west.

A fourth possibility is that more than one structure was used between the time of the town's earliest settlement and 1791. Perhaps a rude chapel built by Blanchette did stand on Block 20, to be replaced in the 1780s by another on Joseph Chancellier's land on Block 15, which in turn gave way to a third building on the higher ground of Block 28. From the existing records it is impossible to tell.

The exact location of the 1791 log church is also a mystery. An archaeological dig by the University of Missouri-St. Louis during the summer of 1990 attempted to determine whether it stood next to the intersection of Main and Jackson streets, on Block 28. After digging many holes of up to six feet in depth, the archaeologists found no reliable evidence of any structure ever standing on the site.

A private excavation in 1981 behind a nearby store at 407 South Main Street turned up a human hip socket, leg bones, and casket fragments, all of which, it was decided, remained from the original cemetery near the log church. Evidence of this cemetery sheds further light on where the 1791 log church may have stood. As the sources agree that the church was built on Block 28, and that the cemetery was adjacent to the church, it is possible that the 1990 dig missed the remains of the cemetery and the church by a narrow margin.

A document dated 1815 in the Jesuit Archives of St. Louis concerns repairs of the fence surrounding the log church's cemetery. It suggests that the cemetery was roughly rectangular in shape, and that it ran from near the church on the east, well up the bluff on the west, perhaps taking up some of Block 73 (bounded by Second, Third, Jackson and Tompkins streets). As Second Street was not laid out until some time after the 1789 dedication of the cemetery, there may very well have been burials west of the present Block 28. This document also suggests that the log church faced south.

UMSL students sift for evidence of the log church in 1990.

Borromeo's First Pastors

In December 1789, before the Capuchin friar Bernard de Limpach retired from the St. Louis parish, he visited Petites Cotes one last time and blessed the cemetery in the yard of the church then under construction. In October 1791, Father Le Dru blessed the first burial register, into which he wrote a stern injunction against working on the Sabbath (except during harvest season). He then named Louis Blanchette to arrest and punish offenders, "in an exemplary manner as he will deem proper, for the maintenance of religion, and good order and public edification." Afterward, Lieutenant Governor Pérez wrote into the book an order setting up perhaps the first Sunday School west of the Mississippi, by directing parents to pay sacristan Pierre Troge a minot of wheat (between five and ten pounds) annually for teaching catechism to their children.

These guidelines laid down by Le Dru and Pérez were very specific, probably because the parish lacked a pastor. Despite the November 7, 1791, dedication, no priest regularly served the members of St. Charles Borromeo until July of the following year, when a Benedictine priest named Pierre Joseph Didier arrived. On July 21, 1792, Father Didier baptized Pierre Belland, the first recipient of the sacrament in the log church, then noted the event in the parish new baptism register. That September he celebrated the first wedding in the log church, between Jean Baptiste Prevot and his Sioux bride, Angelique.

Pierre Joseph Didier was a French nobleman. During the French Revolution he had quartered the king's troops in the Abbey Church of St. Denis, of which he was procurator. This drew a furious response. Revolutionaries soon ransacked the Abbey, where generations of French royalty had been buried, but missed avenging themselves on Didier because he had escaped to America. He found his way to the west side of the Mississippi and went to work for the Spanish government as the pastor of Borromeo and St. Ferdinand, prompting Governor Carondelet to write to his superior:

> In accord with the Señor Vicar General of these provinces we have, after the necessary examinations and investigations, permitted Don Juan Bautista Didier . . . and Don Pierre Gibault . . . to exercise temporarily the functions of parish priests, the former at the new settlements of San Fernando and San Carlos. The inhabitants of these places, clamoring for a long time for priests to administer spiritual guidance to them, have erected the two churches of San Fernando and San Carlos at their own expense and have promised to support the priest, Don Juan Bautista Didier, until His Majesty is pleased to approve him and allot him a suitable stipend.

> I cannot fail to call . . . attention, in this connection, to the abandon and lack of spiritual instruction in which these provinces find themselves. The pious heart of His Majesty would doubtless be moved to know that so many souls, so well-disposed and who yearn for pastors to guide them on the road to salvation, are being lost miserably through lack of ministers. . . .

Carondelet then pointed out the usefulness of priests in adding to the Catholic population by converting Protestants, and asked his superior to approve a stipend of 240 pesos for Didier. The stipend must have been approved, because the priest spent the rest of his life in the employment of the Spanish government. From 1792 until 1794 he divided his time between St. Charles and St. Ferdinand, but in 1795 was assigned to the larger parish of St. Louis. Afterward he made occasional missionary visits to St. Charles.

Didier's entries in the parish archives reveal him as an aristocrat who complied to the letter with formalities. In recording the first "society" wedding in St. Charles, that of the wealthy Toussaint Cerre and Marie Roi, Didier made careful mention of the illustrious guests in attendance, styling them "Sir" and "Lady," but did not overlook the rest of his flock. In all the registers he carefully enumerated the required information about his parishioners, most of whom were poor, and took pains to have all necessary parties sign or scrawl their cross-shaped marks in the books.

Didier was also a sort of apothecary, stocking the St. Louis hospital with prepared red coral, distillation of stag horn, powdered rhubarb, prepared crawfish eyes, and most importantly, a form of quinine which was probably used to treat malaria. When he died in 1799 his library of nearly 300 volumes, including over two dozen on medicine and botany, was sent down the river to be sold in New Orleans.

Although his superiors regarded him as a well-educated, moral priest with a streak of impetuousness, there is no direct evidence of how he got along with his parishioners. But the fact that they cooperated with him in maintaining parish records, especially of burials, which were performed by laymen after he left for St. Louis, suggests that relations were good. Unlike Father Le Dru, Didier did not record any opposition he may have felt to prevailing customs, such as dancing and conducting business on Sunday.

After Didier left in 1795, the parish was once again without a priest. Lieutenant Governor Zenon Trudeau pondered what to do in a letter dated April 30, 1795: "I also gave a passport to . . . the Abbot Flagier [Flaget], priest of Vincennes Post, whom I know particularly and who has been coming frequently here [St. Louis] where there was no difficulty in inducing him to remain, either for the parish of St. Charles or that of Ste. Genevieve. . . ." But Benedict Flaget, a relatively young Sulpician emigré from the French Revolution, did not stay on the Spanish side of the Mississippi despite the evident welcome and promise of a guaranteed income. He had already earned a reputation to the east as a generous, dedicated missionary and there he returned. Many years later, as bishop of Bardstown, Kentucky, he helped St. Louis's Bishop Dubourg prepare St. Louis to become a diocese.

On September 26, 1795, Trudeau explained the ongoing need for a priest in a long letter to Governor Carondelet:

> St. Charles is too distant from St. Louis for Don Didier to offer to go there; the customs are so depraved there due to its being in a most out-of-the-way location and its residence of the savages, mongrels and the worst scoundrels in Illinois. A curé would be for them a God who would restrain them in their vices, and would insensibly fix them to the work of the land, thus rendering them all the more happy. St. Ferdinand is

practically in the same condition but the population is small, while on the contrary St. Charles is increasing every year.

How Trudeau arrived at his opinion of St. Charles one can only guess. An early French spy, Georges-Victor Collot, echoed this opinion of St. Charlesans after he visited their village that same year: "it would be difficult to find a collection of individuals more ignorant, stupid, ugly and miserable. Such are the side effects of extreme poverty. . . ." Perhaps the rude settlement had been too much for the cultured, well-educated Didier, or perhaps Le Dru before him had made his feelings known about the village where people danced and worked on the Sabbath.

In the fall of 1795 St. Charles still lacked a priest, but the town's Catholics got a unique opportunity to request one. Visiting St. Louis was Don Manuel Gayoso de Lemos, who succeeded Carondelet as governor. Gayoso de Lemos had traveled up the Mississippi on *La Vigilante*, a state-of-the-art war vessel bristling with bronze cannons and swivel guns. On October 31 he dispatched *La Vigilante* to St. Charles, waited until November 3, then set out for the village on horseback. At the Missouri River he boarded the ship and crossed over to St. Charles.

His visit, made for the purpose of demonstrating Spain's might and inspiring loyalty to the king, happened to coincide with the birthday of King Carlos IV and the feast day of his and the town's patron saint, Charles Borromeo. Gayoso de Lemos listened sympathetically to the residents' requests for a priest. "This town is already too big to be without a permanent priest," he wrote later. "The people are naturally devout and it pains them to be deprived of spiritual aid." In his official report he spoke highly of St. Charles, but the village did not get a resident priest for another three years.

In 1798 the much-awaited pastor arrived, a Recollect priest named Charles Leander Lusson. Like Father Le Dru, Lusson had abandoned his parish east of the Mississippi for the favorable conditions offered by the Spanish government to the west. His former superior, Bishop John Carroll of Baltimore, complained without success to the bishop of Havana about Lusson's unauthorized departure. Like Le Dru, Lusson had experienced disrespect east of the river, as well as poverty and seemingly impossible, thankless work. It is no wonder that he and so many others succumbed to the attractions of working for the Spanish king—a guaranteed income, a rectory of sorts, some adjoining land for farming, the right to certain ministerial fees, and freedom from harassment.

Lusson's arrival freed Didier, then pastor of St. Louis, from the duty of ministering to St. Charles as a visiting missionary. Lusson wrote with an exceptionally elegant, legible penmanship, and took pains to include all the customary information in the parish records, but his phonetic spellings of many names suggest that he did not speak the hybrid French of St. Charles very well. Civil records of the area frequently bore his signature as witness; probably he was one of the few men around who could read and write more than minimally. As did most other men of standing in the community he owned slaves.

Lusson served the parish until the Louisiana Purchase made St. Charles an American town and erected a wall between church and state. In 1804 he and the twenty-six other priests of the Mississippi valley received a circular from the bishop of Havana, advising them of their options: to stay with their parishes and try to survive on occasional fees and whatever charity the people could afford, or to follow the banner, and pesos, of Spain. Lusson and twenty-one others left.

He took with him all the goods in the log church that had been furnished by the Spanish government, but had a hard time telling these from objects previously owned by Father Didier. His last recorded act was to leave the baptism register with Antoine Janis, the senior *marguillier*. After Lusson's departure there were no more entries in the parish records for many months.

Mission Stations

Late in the 1700s the district of St. Charles stretched without boundaries to the north and west. By extension, so did the jurisdiction of the district's parish, St. Charles Borromeo. Just as the residents of Petites Cotes had once depended on visits from St. Louis's priests, so later did the residents of the newer villages springing up in the wilderness to the north and west of St. Charles rely on Borromeo's priests to baptize, marry, and bury them.

In 1799, a St. Charlesan named Francois Saucier moved to the narrow strip of land between the Missouri and Mississippi Rivers, laid out a grid of streets, and called the settlement Portage des Sioux. According to instructions from the Spanish government, he persuaded people from east of the Mississippi, as well as other St. Charles residents, to move to his village. Portage des Sioux did not get its own pastor until 1818; in the meantime, Borromeo's priests ministered to the village while riding a large circuit of mission stations.

Another frequent stop on the circuit was Dardenne, near present-day St. Peters. Settlement of the town began around 1796 when St. Charlesan Jean Baptiste (Drezi) Blondeau began cultivating the land along Dardenne Creek. Eventually enough Catholics moved to Dardenne to qualify the village as a "dependency" of the Borromeo parish, and it remained dependent on Borromeo's priests until well into the 1800s.

Another village probably served by Borromeo's priests was La Charette, the site of a Spanish fort located up the Missouri River near present-day Marthasville. Borromeo's records occasionally mention a colony of Catholics at Marais Croche ("Crooked Swamp") north of St. Charles, later called Boschertown. As Borromeo pastors, Fathers Didier and Lusson frequently married non-Catholics living on the other side of the Missouri River, especially at Marais des Liards ("Cottonwood Swamp," later called Bridgeton) and Post St. Andre, near present-day Chesterfield.

Everyday Life

A visiting French engineer named Nicolas de Finiels recorded his impressions of St. Charlesans late in the 1790s. Like Georges-Victor Collot, he described the people as poor and indolent, and blamed their lack of "civilization" partly on the Missouri River, which impeded communication between St. Charles and St. Louis, and partly on the *voyageur* way of life, which drew most men up the river to hunt, trap, and trade during warm weather months.

Like Collot, De Finiels was an outsider who judged the people of St. Charles after only a short visit. A more detailed glimpse into the lives of Borromeo's early parishioners comes from the pages of the first baptism, marriage and burial registers.

These confirm that many of the earliest settlers of the town migrated from nearby St. Louis, Cahokia, Kaskaskia, and Prairie du Rocher, as well as from the more distant settlements of Vincennes, Prairie du Chien, New Orleans, and Quebec. Because parish records were not routinely kept until 1792, they are not helpful in determining the date of St. Charles' founding or the role played by Blanchette. They rarely mention his cousins surnamed Michou and Moreau, but frequently note the weddings, baptisms, and burials of Blanchette's other cousins, the Malbeoufs.

A historical account written by Father Peter Verhaegen, superior of the missionary Jesuits in the 1830s, mentions the family names of Quenelle, Bayotte, and Vivaron as belonging to some of first settlers of the town. All three names appear in the archives (allowing for variable spelling, such as "Quenel" for Quenelle and "Buat" for Bayotte), although Vivaron appears only rarely. Some names from the Spanish census records of St. Charles have disappeared completely over the years, but others persist in identical, or nearly identical form: Thebeau, Langevin, Pettit, Dubois, Laffleur, Pallardy, and Conoyer.

The parish records prove that by the end of the Spanish era, there were quite a few enslaved blacks and mulattoes living in the St. Charles area, and even a few enslaved Indians. Slaves probably did not assist at the earliest settlement of St. Charles; hunters had little use for their services. They likely appeared when farming began to replace hunting.

Lured by the prospect of cheap land in the Mississippi valley, French Canadians in the 1700s fled their homeland to take up farming, but found that they could not work the fields without additional help. At first they turned to their fellow settlers (the Spanish census of St. Charles for 1787 shows that many households included French-speaking hired hands), but even these did not provide enough help. Immigration lagged. Forcing Africans to come and work as the French had been doing for decades in the Caribbean seemed the best solution. Slave traders responded by funneling some Africans northward and charging high prices. French farmers bought the few they could afford and set about protecting these prized human "possessions." As Catholics they may have felt qualms about trading in human beings, but they also looked upon slavery as an opportunity to bring heathens to the light of the true faith. The parish records demonstrate that slaveowners in St. Charles took this responsibility seriously.

Relatively well-to-do white parishioners frequently stood as godparents for slave babies, who were almost always given Christian names. This indicates that the Creoles recognized slaves as more than mere property. Under the Spanish regime, slaves enjoyed more rights than they later did as Americans; they were allowed by law to purchase their freedom and were protected, at least in theory, from family breakups. How well these rights were protected in rural villages like St. Charles is not known.

The Borromeo archives prove that there was a small population of emancipated slaves in town before the Louisiana Purchase. One of them came to St. Charles as the property of newlyweds Francois Duquette and Marie Louise Bauvais, then probably gained her freedom and married Marie Louise's uncle, Antoine Janis.

Racial intermarriage was rare, but less formal unions were not. The baptism registers note several instances when "black" mothers presented "mulatto" babies for baptism. As in most other cases of illegitimacy, the records do not name the fathers, but paternity was irrelevant concerning the financial support of children born to slave mothers. Sometimes slave babies were baptized along with the white babies of their masters, as were Charles "Mulatto" and Elizabeth Couns, slave baby and baby daughter respectively of Jean Couns and his wife. Charles' mother is named as "Rebecca, Negro slave" but his father is left unnamed.

Fathers Didier and Lusson carefully distinguished between full-blooded blacks and mulattoes, and in so doing reflected the attitudes of their day, when dark-skinned Africans generally fared worse than those with lighter skin. On June 2, 1799, Lusson baptized a child named Francois Antoine, adding that he was a "Negro slave," then baptized the child's brother Noel Francois, noting that he was a "mulatto slave."

Despite the slavery of Africans, there was still a need for more laborers. Soon a variation of the "peculiar institution" evolved to fill it. Although Indians were kept as slaves only rarely, the Borromeo archives prove that a few local people did indeed have Indian slaves. On November 8, 1802, Father Lusson buried an "Indian-Creole" slave named Joseph, who had belonged to former Commandant Charles Tayon. This Joseph was a double oddity. Not only was he part French, he was also part Indian, and most enslaved Indian men considered captivity and field work so unbearable that they usually ran away or died trying. Indian women generally fared better than men, if allowed to work indoors.

Indians had practiced slavery among themselves before the French arrived, and generally did not object to it when it involved rival tribes. Pawnees were enslaved so often that "Pawnee" became another word for slave. Fathers Didier and Lusson used this term frequently in the registers, but it is unclear in which sense. Another mystery concerning Indians is the mention in the archives of the "Courte-Oreille" (Short-Ear) nation, which may refer not to an actual tribe but to ear-docking, a horrendous punishment inflicted on runaway slaves and sometimes on captured Indians.

Between 1792 and 1795, nearly half of the weddings celebrated at the log church joined white men with women of at least some native American blood. Many such "weddings" were really validations of earlier civil unions, which may have begun in St. Charles when Father Le Dru in 1790 joined Louis Blanchette and Tuhomehenga, a woman of either Osage or Pawnee origin, although by then the couple had three adult children. As did many other Indian brides, Blanchette's took the Christian name Angelique.

After 1795 such weddings and validations of unions between whites and full-blooded Indians dropped off quickly, probably indicating that a sizeable number of marriageable white women had moved to town. But for a long time weddings between whites and "half-breeds" persisted, probably because so many local people had at least some Indian blood. There is also reason to believe that eventually white St. Charlesans considered certain Indians to be more or less assimilated into their society.

Early in its domination of Upper Louisiana, Spain tried to restrict settlement of the area to Catholics, but this policy kept villages like St. Louis and St. Charles small and vulnerable to Indian raids. In 1787 Spain tried another tack: allowing Protestants to settle the area, providing that they marry and have their children baptized in the Catholic church.

An arm of the government, St. Charles Borromeo implemented this policy. Father Lusson kept a special register of weddings performed between 1798 and 1801 between local Protestants. These weddings were not celebrated in the log church but in Lusson's quarters, a private home, or across the river at the ferry landing.

The priest used a unique service devised by the Spanish government. After having sworn the bride and groom to answer truthfully, he asked which faith they professed, and then inquired whether they

Non-Catholic Marriages

Between 1798 and 1801, Father Leander Lusson married many non-Catholic couples, using a special wedding rite that asked the brides and grooms to state their religious affiliation. This list of their answers comes from the Register of Mixed Marriages.

Protestant	10
Anabaptist	10
Presbyterian	9
Anglican	6
Lutheran	2
Calvinist	1
Free Thinker	1
Roman Catholic marrying outside the faith	3

would bring any children born from their marriage to a Catholic church for baptism. If the answer was yes, he proceeded with the marriage.

The "register of mixed marriages" is a *Who's Who* of English-speaking families in the St. Charles area. Among the couples married were Daniel Morgan Boone, son of the explorer, and Sara Griffin Lewis. Other well-known people from the book are Francis Howell and Commandant James (Santiago) Mackay, and the family names Zumwalt (spelled "Sommewalt" and "Somwat"), Musick, Spenser, Price, Graham, Bell, Hodges, James, Brown, and Long.

Despite its high intentions, Spain only discouraged further settlement with this policy. Not just fear of Indians kept Protestant "Americans" from east of the Mississippi away; in 1798 Lieutenant Governor Zenon Trudeau noted that many were leaving the St. Louis area for their homes back east, "because they are obliged to celebrate their marriages and baptisms by means of our Catholic priests."

Marriage normally occurred earlier for women than for men. Most brides were at least eighteen, and most grooms were in their twenties when they entered into their first marriage. Children usually followed a year or two later. Although cohabitation without benefit of clergy was common (due in large part to the scarcity of priests), the law did not recognize common-law marriage until 1804. The parish archives of this era do not even mention divorce.

Fathers Didier and Lusson routinely inquired whether brides and grooms were "legitimate" or "natural" (illegitimate) children of their parents, but apparently treated both groups equally in administering the sacraments. The sheer numbers of illegitimate children, including Blanchette's, made bias unlikely. The question of paternity surfaced during infant baptisms, when unmarried fathers sometimes stepped forward to acknowledge their relationship and responsibility.

Most married women in St. Charles continued giving birth as long as their health held out. For many, this was not long. Regardless of a woman's race or economic status, childbearing took a high toll.

Therese Valle, for example, was a full-blooded Aricara Indian who married a Creole man and bore four children between 1794 and 1802. Six months after the burial of her youngest child, Therese joined the little one in the parish cemetery. Another bride who died after producing several children was Victoire Coussot, wife of St. Charlesan Pierre Coussot. Unlike Therese Valle, who came from the wilds of the upper Missouri, Victoire grew up in St. Louis and thus may have been better nourished, but her life was equally short: in December of 1798, Lusson entered into the records the baptism of baby Pierre Chalifour, "born yesterday to Pierre Chalifour and the deceased Victoire Coussot."

Even Louis Blanchette's daughter Marie may have met a similar fate, although she gave birth six months before dying in January 1796. Probably the wealthiest woman to die shortly after giving birth was Marie Roi, wife of Toussaint Cerre. The couple had little but grief in their married life, as three of their four children died in infancy.

Marie died on her sixth wedding anniversary, having just given birth to the youngest.

The burial register usually does not mention causes of death, and therefore it is not absolutely certain that the mothers described above died from childbirth. But considering the relatively high number of parish women who died shortly after giving birth, it seems likely that childbirth or resulting infections killed a high percentage.

Most residents, male as well as female, lived short lives, but a few men listed in the burial register died at remarkably old ages. Pierre Yvon, for example, died in 1800 at the reported age of 100. The next year another long-time resident, Joseph Rivard, was entered into the burial register as being around eighty years old. Even slaves occasionally became elderly; Jean Baptiste, Negro slave of Jean Baptiste Hubert La Croix, died in 1803 at the reputed age of ninety.

In cases of foul play or accidental death, the author of the burial entry sometimes elaborated about the cause. When a little Osage girl named Celeste died in 1816, the sacristan who buried her noted in the burial register that the child had been "killed by mistake," and that some sort of an inquest had followed. The next spring, the parish records imply that this same sacristan lost a close relative to a bolt of lightning.

Although most early burial entries do not name the cause of death, other sources can sometimes fill in the missing information. A tripling of Borromeo burials in 1801 over those performed in 1800 suggests an epidemic. Spanish records for St. Louis indicate that in 1801, smallpox devastated that town. Better record-keeping in later years indicates that epidemics, especially of smallpox and cholera, spread quickly from town to town.

There was no school in St. Charles until Philippine Duchesne and the Religious of

Early Creole drawing, Woman carrying bucket with child, *by Anna Maria von Phul*

the Sacred Heart arrived in 1818. During the Spanish era, few parishioners had much reason to read or write, and few knew how. Page after page in the marriage register show that many of the parish leaders, including Louis Blanchette, never mastered the art of signing their own names. Commandant Charles Tayon was one who did, but his characteristic scrawl "Charletaijon" casts doubt on the extent of his literacy.

Nearly every marriage witness in the 1790s marked a sign of the cross in the register instead of writing his or her name. Those who could sign well usually appeared often in the records, suggesting that they were sought out as witnesses. In the earliest years most residents with French names, especially women, could not sign their names. Parishioners who could included Jean Baptiste (Drezi) Blondeau, Noel Antoine Prieur, Francois Duquette and his wife Marie Louise Bauvais, Antoine Janis, and Antoine Reynal.

Even those who could write, including Father Lusson, could not agree on how to spell many names. Borromeo records illustrate that uniform spelling did not exist until long after the Spanish years of the parish. The surname Hunault, for example, appears variously in the archives as "Hunaut" and even as "Uno." Thebeau appears as "Thibault" and "Thibaut." Even Blanchette shows up as "Blanchet." The spelling of tribal names probably gave the pastors difficulty. Lusson rendered the Iowa tribe "Ayovoise" and the Kaw, "Cau." Didier before him called the Aricara the "Ritava."

Even more confusing than spelling were the many nicknames which substituted for surnames in Creole St. Charles. Blanchette himself used "Chasseur" (Hunter) so often in civil matters that many years later there was still some doubt over which was his family name. Sometimes the word *dit* (called) was used between surname and nickname, as when Marie Louise Sorin dit La Rochelle married Jean Baptiste Le Sage in 1799. But generally, nicknames appear only rarely in the parish books; it seems that most parishioners used theirs more frequently in civil matters. Occasionally they came in handy for filling in gaps of information about outsiders, like the thirty-six-year-old man of unknown surname who was buried in June of 1798 simply as "Joseph dit Le Allemand," or "Joe the German."

Louis Blanchette: A native of the Quebec province, Blanchette spent most of his life in the Mississippi valley. According to Ben Emmons's "The Founding of St. Charles and Blanchette, its Founder," he appeared in the area around 1758 with his Indian wife, who came from one of the tribes along the Missouri River. Thus Blanchette was probably at least familiar with the St. Charles area years before the reputed founding of his settlement. He and his wife had three known children. Sons Pierre and Louis, who may well have been twins, were born around 1759, and daughter Marie was born probably a few years later.

Blanchette owned various tracts of land in and around St. Charles, as well as farm buildings and tools, when he died in the summer of 1793. Together with his wife, who died in February of that year, he was buried under the floor of the log church.

Charles Tayon: Born at Fort Chartres around 1760, Tayon served in the St. Louis militia in 1780 as a sub- lieutenant. He succeeded Blanchette as commandant of the St. Charles post in 1793. As such, he attested to the dedication of the Borromeo marriage register, and as a layman he frequently witnessed weddings and served as a godparent.

The Spanish government considered Tayon a zealous but unintelligent commander, "who gives himself to drink. . . ." In his article on early St. Charles, Ben Emmons suggested that Tayon destroyed many of Blanchette's records after Blanchette died. If so, perhaps Tayon removed the page in the burial register containing the entry of Blanchette's interment under the log church floor; that leaf has been missing since the early years of the parish.

Pierre Troge: One of Tayon's lieutenants at St. Charles, Troge served as *huissier* (court bailiff) in Cahokia before moving to town in 1791. For many years the parish sacristan, Troge conducted funeral services and kept information in the burial register. His penmanship was sometimes nearly illegible and his spelling almost as bad. At his funeral in 1812, he had the rare (and expensive) honor of being buried under the church floor.

Noel Antoine Prieur: Commandant Tayon's secretary during the Spanish era, Prieur had fine handwriting and an elegant, swirling signature. He and his family moved to St. Charles from New Madrid in the late 1790s. At some later date, Prieur lost a leg when a house given him by Francois Duquette fell on him. He served the parish as a chanter and occasionally as a sacristan, and performed lay baptisms when the parish lacked a priest.

Antoine Reynal: St. Charles' first resident physician, Reynal was in his late fifties when he moved to St. Charles in 1799, having earned a reputation as a rabble-rouser when he refused to allow Spanish authorities to build a road over his land near St. Louis. In St. Charles he prospered. For the parish he witnessed many weddings and served as godparent.

Isidore Savoye: Like Troge, an emigré from Cahokia, Savoye and his family moved to town around 1791 and grew wheat. He served the parish in many capacities, and in 1800 agreed to launder and mend the church's linens for 62.10 livres.

Jean Baptiste (Drezi) Blondeau: A newcomer from Prairie du Chien, Blondeau was one of Borromeo's first laymen whose name is recorded as having assisted at a burial. He continued renting his pew in the log church until 1800, when he perhaps settled permanently in Dardenne.

Chapter 2
1804-18

From Spanish to American Rule

During the tenure of Father Lusson the parish achieved stability, thanks in large part to the support of the Spanish government. But by the end of the 1700s, Spain found the vast Louisiana Territory prohibitively expensive to govern. Unlike Mexico and Peru, the area produced no gold or silver. Its main value was as a buffer zone between Spain's richer Latin American holdings and the English-speaking colonies along the east coast. In 1800, by means of a secret treaty with France, Spain sold its holdings west of the Mississippi River to Napoleon.

When the people of the valley learned of the transfer, they did not rejoice in the return of French rule: they disliked Napoleon because he symbolized the hated French Revolution. Also, life as Spanish subjects had not been unpleasant. Land had been readily available, taxes unknown, and the Catholic faith upheld. To ease the doubts of his new subjects, Napoleon retained Spain's public servants to continue administering the valley. A few years later, news of a more upsetting political change arrived: Napoleon had sold the entire Louisiana Territory to the revolu-

tionary, non-Catholic government of the United States.

A boom in immigration was the ultimate result, but for the first few years after 1803, towns like St. Charles received a steady trickle of newcomers from east of the Mississippi. Many were non-Catholics who did not speak French. Unlike the Creole majority, almost all could read and write at least a little, including the women. Many objected to the Creole customs of dancing, drinking, and conducting business on the Sabbath, but the newcomers introduced their own favorite vices, especially dueling and drinking whiskey.

The experience of Protestant minister Timothy Flint in St. Charles during the second decade of the 1800s typifies the differences between American and Creole notions of morality. Flint's first public sermon was prophetic of his career in the town. Forced to preach next to a racetrack, he found himself competing unsuccessfully for attention with the horses. After he publicly condemned Sunday trading and recreation, local people simply stayed away from his services. He tried to supplement his meager income with a secular job but

National Park Service
Meriwether Lewis

National Park Service
William Clark

found himself further ostracized. " . . . there is in the very atmosphere, which we respire here," he wrote from St. Charles, "a moral miasma [poisonous vapor] fatal to religious sensibility."

Meriwether Lewis and William Clark also noted the fundamental differences between their world and the Creole world of St. Charles. In May of 1804, the explorers came to town to prepare for their voyage up the Missouri River. In his unique spelling, Lewis described the village as having about 100 houses and 450 inhabitants, most of whom were poor, illiterate, and easy-going to a fault. "They live in a perfect state of harmony among each other; and plase an implicit confidence in the doctrines of their spiritual pastor, the Roman Catholic priest, as they yeald passive obedience to the will of their temporal master the commandant."

That harmony among villagers and nearly all traces of Creole culture would erode under the coming tide of immigration. Although Lewis poked genteel fun at the early parishioners' obedience to Father Lusson and Commandant Mackay, Clark pragmatically gave the expedition leave to attend Mass at the log church. In the evening both explorers dined with former commandant Tayon, and the next day with Francois Duquette, then embarked with their party into the unknown.

During their two-year-long expedition,

St. Charles began adapting to American rule. One of the first changes in town was Father Lusson's departure, brought about by the end of governmental support for Catholic priests. But Lusson demonstrated his commitment to the parish by staying until all hope of even a subsistence income was gone. As late as June 1804, the American government was seriously debating whether to offer the remaining priests of the Mississippi valley an annual salary of $300. "I know these clergymen well," argued Captain Amos Stoddard, the American officer who assumed command of Upper Louisiana for the United States, "they are learned, and liberal in their principles; they have great influence among the Catholic people, and speak the English as well as the French and Spanish languages."

Constitutional problems soon proved insurmountable, though, and Lusson left St. Charles in October. To have remained in the poverty-stricken town with no firm source of income would have surely proven disastrous, and to have attempted supporting himself through a secular trade would have been out of the question. As Timothy Flint learned, Creoles expected their spiritual leaders to confine their efforts to spiritual matters, even if doing so led to financial ruin.

Without a pastor, St. Charles Borromeo again fell back upon its parishioners. A gap in some of the records shortly after 1804 may seem to indicate that for a while sacramental activities ceased, but a closer look suggests that during this time the laity were regrouping. By giving the baptism register to *marguillier* Janis, Lusson was probably preparing the laity to baptize without him, just as they had on previous occasions.

The burial records prove the growing importance of the laity. Most lay interments before 1804 were performed by a sacristan or chanter whose name was not recorded in the register. After 1804, burial entries specified the name and title of the officiant. In various capacities, Noel Prieur and Pierre Troge alternated burial duties during the first years after 1804.

No such arrangement was possible for marriages. Then as now, only an ordained minister could witness a Catholic wedding. From 1804 until 1807 not even one couple repeated their vows in the log church, although an average of ten per year had done so previously during the pastorate of Father Lusson. The law of the land now recognized marriages performed by civil officials as well as common-law marriages, and it is reasonable to assume that a certain number of parishioners entered into such unions, perhaps intending to marry someday before a priest. As justice of the peace in 1807 and 1808, Francois Duquette married a few parishioners, then recorded the acts in the parish's obsolete register of mixed marriages.

Sometimes missionaries came to town. The first, Father James Maxwell, was an Irishman educated and sent by Spain to the Mississippi valley, where he became vicar general after 1804. He appeared in St. Charles for a few days in 1806 and 1808, baptizing by the dozen each time.

The next missionary to visit was a rootless Capuchin named Thomas Flynn, whose desertion of the Baltimore diocese for Missouri after 1804 made the mission field east of the Mississippi look even less desirable than that of the west. Like Lusson, Flynn found work almost at once. He contracted in November of 1806 with the *marguilliers* of St. Louis to act as pastor for one year, agreeing to make occasional visits to St. Ferdinand and St. Charles Borromeo. During that year he appeared several times in St. Charles, where he baptized and performed weddings. When his contract with the St. Louis parish expired, he left the area for good.

A Trappist Comes to Borromeo

The next priests in the St. Louis area were Trappist monks who had fled Kentucky after an epidemic ravaged their monastery. They included Abbott Urban Guillet, Bernard Langlois, and Joseph Marie Dunand, all of whom eventually ministered to St. Charles. The little band settled for a time in Florissant, then moved to quarters on top of one of Cahokia's Indian mounds.

On Christmas Eve 1808, Father Dunand walked across the frozen Mississippi to St. Louis. He found religion there "in a pitiful state" because, he reported, of the lack of priests and the influx of non-Catholic newcomers. To his shock he found Catholicism even more imperiled in the surrounding villages, one of which may well have been St. Charles:

> On my arrival I established myself in one of the parishes well known for the excesses and scandals of its people. They danced seven days a week and nearly every night was passed in balls

and other kinds of debauch. Their un-
bridled passions knew no law; and
young persons and even young married
women became the prey of libertines.
A certain man was so lost to all sense of
decency (can one believe it?) as to
barter his wife as one sells a horse or
beast of burden, and for a bottle of
brandy. The man who bought her sold
her for a horse and this second pur-
chaser resold her to a third party for a
pair of oxen. But I will draw a veil over
these horrors which make modesty
blush and which my hand refuses to
write down.

   Astonished at these debaucheries,
I remained for a time quiescent,
deeply touched by the unfortunate
state of these poor people. I waited
until heaven should offer a favorable
occasion of speaking to them. This opportunity was not slow in presenting itself. One day a terrific thunder and
lightning storm killed three animals
that were grazing in the meadows.
Nothing is more appropriate to give a
vivid idea of the majesty of God than a
clap of His thunder; above all in these
countries where it breaks with a force
one can hardly describe. I seized the
occasion to make them understand
that if the God of majesty thundered
thus from the heights of the heavens it
was because He was incensed at the
sins which they committed on earth
and above all among themselves. I
pointed out the evil of their ways and
the horror of the crimes by which they
provoked the wrath of this avenging
God. This produced good effects, as I
shortly found myself . . . overloaded
with confessions. . . .

Soon afterward, Father Bernard died and
Abbott Guillet returned east, leaving the
energetic Dunand by himself.
   Joseph Marie Dunand was born in Lorraine in 1774. During the French Revolution he joined the republican army but
deserted when ordered to shoot a priest.
He fled to Switzerland and joined the
Trappists, then fled to America when the
republican army invaded Switzerland.
Henry Brackenridge, a Pennsylvanian who
wrote extensively of his travels in the Creole world, visited the monastery on top of
the Indian mound in 1811 and recorded
one of the only known impressions of Prior
Dunand: "He is a sprightly, and intelligent
man, and, much to my surprise, talked
with wonderful volubility, which excited in
me almost as much surprise as Robinson
Crusoe in his island felt, when his parrot
addressed him."
   Dunand's talkativeness began to manifest
itself in the Borromeo records at about the
same time, when the parish council hired
him to serve as pastor. Unlike Brackenridge, Dunand's rustic flock apparently did
not find him amusing. The archives suggest that not long into his pastorate, his
parishioners broke into opposing camps
with many against the monk. Considering
the large drop in recorded weddings, baptisms and burials during his years at Borromeo, it seems that either Dunand ceased
performing (or at least recording) these
sacraments, or that St. Charlesans simply
avoided his services.
   Tempers flared at a parish meeting in
January 1812 over the sum of $89 owed to
the monk on his salary of $250. Dunand
brought up the matter by reading a letter
from absent Francois Duquette, which
urged that the $89 be paid out of parish
funds. Duquette himself must have owed
the parish a considerable amount; his fellow council members then voted unanimously to solve the problem by collecting
the $89 from him. At this point Duquette
walked in, sensed the general drift of the
meeting, and walked out. Citing the "scan-
dal" that would result if the matter went
unsettled, the council members then voted
that two parishioners would act as special
arbitrators, but tipped the scales of justice
in their own favor by their choice of individuals: Noel Prieur, the chanter who had
lost a leg in the collapse of one of Du-

quette's houses, and Antoine Reynal, the firebrand doctor who had rebelled against Spanish authority.

Two days later, Dunand met with the council and established strict rules for keeping the parish solvent, among them: borrowers were directed to pay their debts within the year, and further lending of parish funds was forbidden. As most parishioners at that time were poor, these rules seem more revealing of Dunand's high ideals than of the realities of the day.

Father Dunand

Father Dunand had an apparent disregard for the feelings of his people. Perhaps hoping to shame certain parishioners into reform, the priest began using the parish registers to record their failings.

Some of these "faults" reveal as much Dunand's scrupulosity as any wickedness of his parishioners, especially his frequent habit of baptizing "under condition," an otherwise rarely used means of correcting any defect which may have occurred in a previous baptism, especially one performed by a layman. Properly performed, lay baptisms were (and are) allowed by canon law. Though usually not recorded in the registers, they probably occurred with some regularity in priestless St. Charles.

Before Father Dunand arrived, priests in the town rarely performed conditional baptisms, but during his time in St. Charles (especially between 1814 and 1816) Dunand performed a majority of baptisms "under condition." Although his motive is unknown, so many such baptisms suggest that the priest doubted the validity of lay baptisms, canon law notwithstanding. And by entering so many baptisms into the records specifically as "under condition," he probably gave offense to his parishioners who could read.

The marriage records suggest that the zealous, white-robed priest disregarded formalities. Unlike Fathers Didier and Lusson, who had written long, careful entries full of information and background about the bridal couples and the ceremonies, Dunand dispensed with many details altogether. Sometimes he omitted having the bride and groom sign or mark the page; sometimes he forgot to sign it himself.

Shock waves must have rippled through St. Charles when Father Dunand's literate parishioners read his entry for the June 29, 1812, wedding of Joseph Poirier and Catherine Uno. For some reason, Dunand had spelled out the embarrassing details of the bride's previous marital history: " . . . said Catherine had [before] been married legally to Pierre Carboneaux. Their marriage was found null by default of consent on the part of the said Carboneau, who was juridically forced to get married."

Not long afterward, the priest delivered what must have been interpreted as an affront to the laity and to chanter Noel Prieur as well. Customarily, banns of matrimony were announced on three successive Sundays before the wedding date, by a layman when a priest was not available. Canon law recommended no more than three readings or publications of the banns. In August 1813, after a long absence from the parish during which Prieur had already announced an upcoming wedding three times, Dunand stood before his parishioners and read the banns a fourth time.

In many cases, Dunand probably had legitimate cause for concern about the spiritual welfare of certain parishioners. But by writing about their errors, real or imagined, he probably defeated his own efforts to bring about their reform. After an 1812 baptism, for example, he referred to a witness as a woman "who frequents too often in beds." On other occasions he named the fathers of illegitimate children. Sometimes he included lurid details, seemingly to dramatize a story. Years after he returned to Europe, Dunand wrote his superior a long report about his ministry in America, and larded it with exaggerations about such things as the wild animals of Missouri (twenty-five-foot long alligators, scorpions and "tigers"), and fanciful stories about tricks played by the impious on priests (floating them down the Mississippi in hollow logs.) Yet his journal also contains many accounts that ring true, particularly those about Dunand's visits to Catholics in remote areas of Missouri and native Americans. With a sensitivity rare for Europeans of his era, the monk appreciated Indians as individuals and mourned their exposure to certain aspects of white culture.

In October 1811, Dunand insulted sacristan Pierre Troge in the burial register. Noticing that for some reason Troge had neglected to write an entry for a service that Troge had performed, Dunand wrote his own, in which he suggested that Troge had purposely removed his. Troge abruptly retired from burying, leaving Dunand to perform most of the services in 1812, including Troge's own burial on December 23.

Soon Noel Prieur picked up the slack, but a standoff developed with Dunand over which man would keep the burial register. Prieur evidently had the book, but Dunand kept his own records and inserted them into the register whenever he could, although by the time he did, they were usually out of order and sometimes included baptism entries. In April 1813 the inevitable occurred: two entries were written for the same burial.

Not long afterward, Prieur and a new layman, Francois Carbonneaux, took over most graveside duties. From November 1813 until July 1814, Father Dunand added nothing to any parish register, indicating perhaps that he had left for one of his many missions.

He returned in July 1814 with a powerful reinforcement, Kentucky Bishop Benedict Flaget, who attempted to mediate Dunand's grievances with the parish, one of which was the deplorable condition of his "rectory" (perhaps a small annex to the ramshackle log church). Flaget managed to extract from the parishioners a promise to build Dunand a new residence. But all was not harmonious for long. A few months later, when his new rectory failed to materialize, the monk moved to Florissant.

Perhaps he was upset over more than the rectory. During his six-month absence, the sacristans had begun writing mysterious entries in the burial register, mentioning that "Extreme Unction" or "all the sacraments of the church" had been administered to certain deceased parishioners. By whom? The entries do not elaborate. There is no evidence in the registers that Dunand was in St. Charles when these alleged sacraments were administered; his journal strongly suggests that he was elsewhere. Priests in Missouri were then almost as scarce as they had been in the days of the Jesuit missionaries. The question of who administered the last rites to the dying members of St. Charles Borromeo is indeed a problem, but the possibility exists that some of the laity may have tried to take over this priestly function.

Without Dunand, parish affairs at St. Charles Borromeo continued in a slump. In 1813 weddings at the log church nearly ceased and did not resume with any frequency for over a decade. Dunand performed occasional baptisms when visiting St. Charles from Florissant, as did Father Francis Savine from Cahokia. By the end of 1816, however, baptisms either ceased or were not recorded for over a year. Prieur and Carbonneaux performed all recorded burials during 1815 and continued noting that some of the deceased had received the last rites, but never specified by whom, although Dunand or Savine may have been in town to do some. The death of his friend Francois Duquette in February 1816

brought Dunand back to St. Charles to celebrate his last funeral at the log church.

Francois Carbonneaux performed the other burials at St. Charles Borromeo that year and most in early 1817. All recorded burials stopped abruptly for nearly a year after a deadly thunderstorm in April 1817 killed the adolescent Louise Carbonneaux and her companion, Celeste Tayon. Perhaps out of kindness to Francois, who may well have been Louise's father, another layman named Antoine Latreille buried the girl. Francois Carbonneaux buried Celeste Tayon that same day, then apparently retired from performing burials. It seems possible that, to his rebellious parishioners, Dunand's sermon about divine judgment in the form of lightning had come uncannily true.

The Lawsuit

The pastorate of Father Dunand coincided with an increase in immigration to the St. Charles area. Easterners, mostly from Kentucky, Tennessee, and Virginia, passed through town for points west along the Salt Lick Trail, but many others settled in St. Charles. Unlike Borromeo's Creoles, these people spoke (and often read and wrote) English, and participated in American culture. One value they shared was an appreciation of land ownership, supported by written title. Before the Louisiana Purchase, land had been considered nearly endless, and was grossly undervalued as well as casually conveyed. As easterners began flooding into the Mississippi valley, however, they drove up land prices and sometimes litigated titles not based on written grants.

In 1817 a case of attempted land fraud pitted St. Charles Borromeo's uneducated

laymen against two Eastern newcomers, Andrew Wilson and Uriah J. Devore. The land in question was the northern half of Block 15, bounded by Main, Jackson, and Tompkins streets, and the Missouri River. This lot had been claimed by the parish since the 1780s, when Joseph Chancellier had orally conveyed it to Borromeo. Only a cross marked it as church property in 1817; by then it was also the site of the public jail.

Since Chancellier's death, his widow, Elizabeth Becquet, had married Antoine Gautier. By 1817 she was a widow again with two married daughters, Therese Chancellier Proulx and Marguerite Gautier Berthelot. The three women were unable to read or write, and spoke only French.

Andrew Wilson was an easterner who had migrated to St. Charles by way of New

Early watercolor, Creole Cart and Driver, *by Anna Maria von Phul. The* charette, *or two-wheeled cart, was a common means of transportation in the early nineteenth century.*

Madrid, where he had served as recorder. In St. Charles he hung out his shingle as a doctor, and also served as justice of the peace and notary public, but probably derived his greatest income from dealing in real estate. In December 1813 he bought the southern half of Block 15, paid $400, and built a house.

Uriah J. Devore was also an entrepreneur, serving at various times as innkeeper, ferryboat operator, sheriff, county treasurer, and postmaster. He owned a lot close to the log church on Block 28. As sheriff, he undoubtedly used the jail on the parish property.

Though probably not practicing Catholics, both Wilson and Devore had each brought a child to the log church for baptism. Both lived close enough to the church to be aware of the uproar in the parish over Father Dunand. And both were business-minded public officials; finding out that Borromeo lacked written title to both Block 15 and Block 28 would probably not have been difficult.

On December 6, 1816, Wilson and Devore visited the three illiterate women. Wilson was then a justice of the peace and Devore was sheriff. Claiming that they wished to confirm Joseph Chancellier's conveyance to the parish, the men then offered the women $40 and asked them to sign at the bottom of a long document written in English. The women accepted, and scrawled their cross-shaped marks. The document was really a deed, granting to Wilson and Devore all the women's right not just to the Block 15 lot, but also to the site of the log church on Block 28. Probably anticipating problems, Wilson and Devore had added a clause allowing the parish to continue using Block 28.

The pair soon conveyed back Block 28, but kept their claim to Block 15. When Borromeo's senior *marguillier,* Gabriel Latreille, learned what had happened, he had the women deed their interest in Block 15 back to the parish. Three days later, Wilson and Devore approached Basil Proulx, husband of Therese Chancellier,

Thomas Hart Benton as he appeared in 1817 to painter Matthew Harris Jouett

Cleveland Museum of Art

and paid him $20 to sign over any interest he might have in the lot on Block 15. Then Wilson built a storehouse on the premises. When Latreille demanded that he leave, he refused.

At some point, Latreille and the other *marguilliers* must have realized that they needed outside help. Although Latreille was a civic leader and enjoyed a fine reputation around St. Charles, he could neither read nor write. Whether he went to St. Louis for assistance or whether his assistance came to St. Charles is not clear, but however it happened, the parish soon retained a young real estate attorney named Thomas Hart Benton.

Benton was not originally from St. Louis. He had arrived four years earlier to find the town a center of litigation involving Spanish land grants. By 1817 he had built up a loyal clientele among local Creoles by defending their technically weak titles. He filed suit in June of that year, seeking to establish Borromeo's good title.

Apparently the parish won the first round. A document dated June 7, 1817, from the parish file at the Jesuit archives in St. Louis, asserts that an Act of Congress in 1812 vested title to the parish land in the inhabitants of the town, leaving the Creole women with nothing to convey to Wilson and Devore. The writer of the document, evidently a judge, suggests that the parish file suit to eject Wilson and Devore.

Unfortunately, the paper trail begins to taper off here. In December 1817 Devore and his wife sold their lot next to the log church. Two years later, Devore deeded back to the parish his controversial claim to Block 15. By this time, Devore was in deep trouble. An abstract of the Circuit Court docket from 1819-1826 reveals that during these years he was sued repeatedly, mostly for debt, trespass, and breach of contract. Most of the suits involved land. Andrew Wilson was one of the few St. Charlesans who did not sue Uriah J. Devore; Devore sued Wilson instead, but the substance of the matter is unknown.

Missouri's entrance into the union in 1821 probably added to the confusion, causing the pleadings (which were filed in territorial days) to be preserved apart from the judgment (which seems to have been issued in 1822, according to a handwritten entry on a fragment of paper in the Jesuit archives) – for which side is not clearly stated. The parish ultimately established clear title to both Blocks 15 and 28, and it demonstrated this in 1825 to United States Recorder of Land Titles, Theodore Hunt.

Nevertheless, Wilson stubbornly retained his claim to Block 15 for the rest of his life. After he died in 1842, his debt-ridden estate was probated and his remaining real estate sold to offset the losses. Among the interests sold at a public auction on May 20, 1847, was his claim to the northern half of Block 15. The buyers were two Jesuits who represented St. Charles Borromeo. Probably because Wilson's claim was so baseless, the sale price was a nominal $35, or $5 less than he and Devore had paid over thirty years earlier to the illiterate heirs of Joseph Chancellier.

As for Benton, his experience with St. Charles seems to have served him well. The town supported him during his long career in the United States Senate, beginning with Benton's first senatorial race in 1820.

Francois Duquette: a French Canadian businessman who amassed large tracts of land in St. Charles. Unlike many other Spanish land grantees, Duquette held provable title, and no doubt relied on his properties to see him through occasional financial reversals. His most famous acquisition was the four-block tract now occupied by the Academy of the Sacred Heart, where he built his residence and moved his wife and slaves in 1795. In the present cemetery a large marker with a bronze plaque memorializes Duquette and his wife.

Marie Louise Bauvais Duquette: Daughter of Ste. Genevieve's richest family, Marie Louise was one of St. Charles' few literate women, and frequently served the people of the parish as matrimonial witness and godmother. She and Francois had no children. During his life, their house served as a meeting place for the parish council. Afterwards she rented out its extra rooms to Timothy Flint and later to Philippine Duchesne and the Religious of the Sacred Heart. Her funeral in 1841 was said to have been the largest until that date in St. Charles.

Antoine Janis: Maternal uncle of Marie Louise Bauvais Duquette, Janis was a pillar

Tombstone of Francois and Marie Louise Duquette

of St. Charles Borromeo, although earlier he had been the object of much criticism by the Spanish government for his involvement with a mulatto slave named Marie Louise, who accompanied the Duquettes to St. Charles. Janis probably succeeded in buying the woman's freedom, as the parish registers seem to indicate that the couple eventually married and had many children. Like Duquette, Janis was a businessman who owned large tracts of land and several slaves. His signature is one of the finest in the early registers. He served as *marguillier* and witnessed many weddings and baptisms.

Marie Louise, Mulatto: Although not an active laywoman in the same sense as her onetime mistress, Madame Marie Louise Duquette, this Marie Louise's name appears frequently in the records at the baptism of her many children and later at their weddings and burials. Her story is unique. As a slave she lacked a surname, but she seems to appear throughout the early registers not only as a slave, but also as a free woman of color, and later as the wife of Antoine Janis.

Louis Barada: a frequent witness and godfather, Louis Barada moved to St. Charles around 1800 from St. Louis, where he had emigrated from Vincennes, married Marie Becquet, and become a shoemaker. Parish records from 1812 reveal that Barada also served as *marguillier* and for a time provided laundry and mending service as well as altar wine to the parish. He prospered in St. Charles, becoming a prominent land owner and businessman, but remained illiterate. He had several children and owned several slaves. In 1828 his family received special recognition from the parish for their large contribution to the construction of the stone church.

Francois Carbonneaux: Originally from Kaskaskia where he served as clerk of the court, Carbonneaux moved to St. Charles in the early 1800s to escape the lawlessness east of the river. Like Noel Prieur and Pierre Troge, he performed many lay burials and was otherwise active in parish affairs.

Jean Baptiste Louis Collin: a Frenchman whose civil union with Louisianan Marie Maureau was legitimated by Abbot Urban Guillet in 1811, Collin began serving the parish during the pastorate of Prior Dunand, after having served St. Ferdinand

U.S. Postal Service

Jean Baptiste du Sable, from 1986 postal commemorative stamp

of Florissant for many years as chanter and sacristan. With Francois Duquette he frequently assisted the monk at burials, and occasionally served as matrimonial witness.

Jean Baptiste Point Du Sable: Haitian-born fur trader of French and African descent, Du Sable was the first non-Indian settler of the Chicago area, where he lived with his Potawatomi wife and children before moving to St. Charles around 1800. He owned farm property and lived at Second and Decatur Street in a stone house that later became the residence of Missouri's first governor, Alexander McNair. Tradition holds that he was a devout Catholic, but his name rarely appears in parish records. Du Sable died in August of 1818 and was buried in the parish cemetery. A marker at the present cemetery commemorates his place in history as the founder of Chicago.

Basil Proulx: A layman who became active in parish affairs soon after settling in St. Charles late in the Spanish era, Proulx furnished the log church with candles in 1804 for the price of three livres. He assisted over the years at numerous weddings, baptisms, and burials.

Gabriel Latreille: A blacksmith who remained illiterate throughout his life, Latreille nevertheless was highly regarded in St. Charles. He assisted Auguste Chouteau in making the original survey of the area, and later testified before U. S. Recorder Hunt as to the ownership of many tracts of land in town.

Gregoire Tiercereau: Uncle of Latreille's wife, Tiercereau was from one of the earliest St. Louis families. His father, Rene, served for many years as chanter of the St. Louis parish.

Pierre and Louis Cornoyer: Natives of France who arrived in St. Charles late in the Spanish era, the Cornoyers served the parish for many years as *marguilliers,* witnesses, and members of the parish council. The surname was later Anglicized to Conoyer.

Jean Baptiste Brugiere: An immigrant to St. Charles by way of St. Louis, Brugiere was elected in 1817 to oversee construction of a new log church, although the effort was later abandoned.

The Chauvin family: Prominent ferryboat operators for many years, the Chauvins lived on the St. Louis County shore of the Missouri River, but considered themselves residents of St. Charles. People from several generations of Chauvins, especially La Freniere and Silvestre, were active in parish affairs.

Chapter 3
1818-23

Bishop Dubourg

While the parish was contending with Father Dunand and the events leading up to the lawsuit were taking shape, a priest unknown in St. Charles was preparing to change the practice and administration of Catholicism up and down the Mississippi valley.

His name was William Louis Valentine Dubourg. Shortly after his birth in Santo Domingo, Dubourg's family moved to France, where William grew up and prepared to join the Sulpician order. During the French Revolution he fled to Baltimore, where he studied English and then took on the presidency of Georgetown College. His friend and fellow Sulpician, Benedict Flaget, served as Georgetown's vice-president. By all accounts Dubourg was affable and polished, but he had a mercurial streak and a tendency to envision grand designs without the practical means to carry them out. His English and French were flawless.

As a priest in Baltimore, Dubourg served Archbishop John Carroll, whose diocese then included the parishes west of the Mississippi. For many years Carroll had needed a bilingual administrator for New Orleans. On August 18, 1812, he appointed Dubourg "Administrator Apostolic of the Diocese of Louisiana and the Two Floridas," in charge of the lands between the Mississippi and the Rocky Mountains, from the gulf to Canada. Too busy to leave New Orleans and visit the rest of his jurisdiction, Dubourg asked his old friend, Benedict Flaget (who was then the bishop of Bardstown, Kentucky,) to travel to Missouri in order to gauge the state of Catholicism. Flaget agreed. In May 1814 he set out for the west, stopping at first at Vincennes, and then at Cahokia and St. Louis. Along the way he met Borromeo's pastor, Joseph Marie Dunand, and visited his congregation at St. Charles. Flaget was upset by the state of the Catholic faith in the town, but several other Missouri parishes concerned him just as much. By the end of his mission it was evident that St. Charles Borromeo was just one of the many dispirited parishes of the upper Mississippi valley. Flaget reported to Dubourg that his old friend faced a herculean job.

Dubourg knew he could not do much by himself. The Missouri Territory was still feeling the effects of the 1804 withdrawal

Bishop William Dubourg

Jesuit Missouri Province Archives

of most of the area's priests. Since then, missionaries James Maxwell and Bernard Langlois had died, and Urban Guillet had returned to France, leaving only Joseph Dunand north of Ste. Genevieve. Taking care of his New Orleans churches demanded all of Dubourg's time and attention, but he realized that his other parishes were suffering from years of neglect. In 1815 he took the matter personally to Rome.

The pope responded by appointing Dubourg bishop of Louisiana and Florida, and consecrated him as such in September of that year. Dubourg then set about gathering priests and nuns for his vast new diocese. He started in Rome at the office of the Congregation of the Mission (or Vincentians, also known as the Lazarists), where the bishop found and recruited an impressive young missionary, Felix de Andreis, to direct the seminary Dubourg planned to build in his new diocese.

De Andreis then set out to gather personnel for the new seminary, recruiting his fellow Vincentian, Joseph Rosati, and another Vincentian named John Baptist Acquaroni, who later became pastor at St. Charles Borromeo, among others. Dubourg stayed for a time in Europe to enlist more help, but sent this first band of missionaries across the Atlantic to work in the St. Louis area.

Meanwhile, Dubourg's friend, Bishop Flaget, was trying to prepare the missionar-

ies' future parishioners. Flaget agreed that St. Louis was a good base for Dubourg; his 1814 visit had convinced him that strong measures were necessary there to rescue Catholicism. But he knew that the region was poor, so in February 1816 he circulated a letter informing all the parishes of Missouri that a new bishop would soon arrive and asked that they select delegates to discuss the financial needs of a diocese, especially the building of a seminary and a residence for the bishop. Having noted that the oldest residents of the Mississippi valley remembered the Jesuit missionary Sebastian Meurin with nostalgia, Flaget then suggested to his superior that missionaries from the reinstated Society of Jesus be sent to the area.

While in France, Bishop Dubourg made another fortunate acquaintance in a Jesuit named Louis Barat, whose sister, Madeleine Sophie, had founded the Society of the Sacred Heart of Jesus in 1800. Barat knew that one of the order's nuns, a middle-aged Frenchwoman named Philippine Duchesne, had pestered his sister for years to send her to the New World as a missionary. He believed that the woman had great potential for mission work, but his sister considered her irreplaceable as a convent administrator and had already tried to discourage her:

> It is simply astonishing that a woman of upright intention and sane judgment like yourself could have concocted any such scheme, fixed her will on it, and then could believe it to be the will of God. What does it amount to? Simply abandoning a solid and lasting good to go in search of one that is uncertain. . . .

Behind his sister's back, Louis Barat recommended to Dubourg that he recruit a band of Sacred Heart nuns, to be led by Philippine Duchesne. The bishop found the idea intriguing and called on Mother Barat. In what must have been one of his

Benedict Joseph Flaget, the first bishop to visit St. Charles

most eloquent feats of persuasion, he convinced the superior to send Philippine and a small group of her nuns to St. Louis. Soon afterward she changed her mind. In May 1817 Dubourg returned to the convent expecting to discuss Philippine's departure for America, but Sophie Barat took him by surprise with her change of plans. The volatile bishop at once grew angry. Just then Philippine, who had been listening outside the room, burst in on the meeting and threw herself at Sophie Barat's feet. The mother general deliberated for just a moment, then told Philippine to begin recruiting other religious to go with her to America.

While Philippine made her preparations, Dubourg set sail for America with yet another band of clergy, some of whom later made their way to St. Charles. The group arrived in St. Louis in January 1818. The bishop's first official act was to call a meeting of St. Louisans to discuss plans for construction of a new church. Among those in attendance were several old Creole families, but also a large number of Protestants, including Thomas Hart Benton and title examiner Theodore Hunt. The meeting netted pledges of over $6,000 and construction began.

In St. Charles, however, church affairs remained in the doldrums. Although Borromeo parishioners had voted to build a replacement to the log church, many ob-

stacles stood in the way. Few parishioners, for example, lived much above a subsistence level. After the events leading up to the lawsuit, they may well have been reluctant to build anything on Block 28, for which the parish still lacked solid, written title.

In April 1818, the parish registers received their first information in over a year, a burial entry written by the visiting Vincentian John Baptist Acquaroni. On the last day of May that year, Bishop Dubourg came to St. Charles and legitimated five civil marriages which united some of St. Charles' leading families: Louis Berthelot and Marguerite Gautier, Charles Bricot and Angelique Penneton (whose grandfather, Pierre Vial, had pioneered the Santa Fe Trail), Antoine Janis, Jr., and Marguerite Thibaut, Michel La Matte and Marie La Ferne, and Auguste Dorlac and Melanie Barada.

In advance of the bishop, a newly ordained priest named Francois Niel had spent several days in St. Charles performing numerous baptisms. Father Niel was the first of Dubourg's seminarians to begin his priesthood in St. Louis and was no doubt intended by the bishop for important work. Although he never reappeared in the St. Charles Borromeo records after the spring of 1818, Father Niel soon received a major assignment in St. Louis: the opening of boys' academy, which later became St. Louis University. A few years later when Felix De Andreis died, Niel took on the pastorship of the St. Louis parish and with it inherited the thankless task of raising money for a cathedral. He alienated would-be donors by preaching against the morals of the local people. His health began to falter. After suffering a stroke in 1823 he returned to Europe to do more fund-raising, but enjoyed little success there, either, and never returned to America.

During his visit to St. Charles, Bishop Dubourg called a meeting of the town's leaders, both Catholic and Protestant, to discuss the construction of "a Seminary for female education on a large scale, for the direction of which he [Dubourg] expects during the course of the present season from France six distinguished Tutoresses" on "a certain vacant ground in our commons, lying back of Dr. Ant. Reynal's lot, and west of third main street. . . ." A document dated June 13, 1818, was drawn up attesting to the group's willingness to donate the land in question, and was signed by over fifty people, including Andrew Wilson and Uriah J. Devore.

The Religious of the Sacred Heart Arrive

The woman Bishop Dubourg had in mind to run the girls' school in St. Charles, Philippine Duchesne, was not notified of this plan until she arrived in St. Louis in August 1818. With her had come four French-speaking nuns, thirty-year-old Octavie Berthold, twenty-six-year-old Eugénie Audé, forty-year-old Catherine Lamarre and forty-year-old Marguerite Manteau.

Though all were Religious of the Sacred Heart, Philippine, Octavie Berthold and Eugénie Audé were "choir religious," in charge of teaching and governing the convent, and were addressed as "Mother"; the others were "coadjutrix sisters," in charge of the household duties and the education of young children, and were addressed as "Sister." This two-tiered system was employed for several reasons: nuns devoted to teaching had little time for the daily chores of convent life; some women lacked the necessary education or desire to teach but felt called to religious life nonetheless; and some, through performing household work, identified with the "hidden" life of Christ—the years before His public ministry. Although this system was eventually abandoned, it served Philippine's group well, probably because the women were well-suited to their roles.

Philippine Duchesne had been born in 1769 in Grenoble, France, to a prominent family. She entered the Visitation convent in Grenoble at the age of eighteen, but was forced to leave in 1792 when the revolutionary government closed the convent. For the next several years she undertook charitable work as sort of a "resistance" worker, caring for the sick and indigent and aiding priests in hiding. By 1801 religious orders were no longer banned, and she reopened the convent, but soon decided to associate it with Sophie Barat's order dedicated to the Sacred Heart. Between 1805 and 1815 she taught and served as administrator of the convent and its school, all the time dreaming of teaching the Indians of North America. In 1815 she traveled to Paris for the Second General Council of the Society of the Sacred Heart and stayed there afterward as Sophie Barat's secretary.

In Paris Bishop Dubourg had explicitly promised Philippine that she would work with native Americans in or near St. Louis. But when they reunited in St. Louis, he claimed that more good would come from the education of white children than of Indians, and insisted that the nuns move twenty miles west to St. Charles. Philippine fought his decision with every argument she could muster, suggesting that the nuns open a school in St. Louis, where they were already well received, or in Ste. Genevieve, which they had visited during their journey from New Orleans. But the bishop refused, leaving them only the choice between St. Charles or Florissant, where building costs were excessive. Philippine reluctantly

Academy of the Sacred Heart

Mother Philippine Duchesne

chose St. Charles.

She expressed her feelings about the little town in a letter to Sophie Barat in which she called St. Charles "a tomb in which [the] enterprise for the Society would be buried." Later she tried to explain the bishop's puzzling decision:

> Monseigneur Dubourg, who looks very far into the future, considers this place quite important, as it is the largest village on the Missouri, about twenty miles from its junction with the Mississippi. American settlers from the eastern states are constantly pouring into this section of the country—restless people, who hope St. Charles will become a great commercial link between the United States and China, for the Upper Missouri rises not far from another river that pours its waters into the Pacific Ocean at a place where the crossing to Asia takes just two weeks.

In September 1818 Dubourg rode out from St. Louis beside the nuns' carriage over the dusty, hot roads to St. Charles. At the Missouri River crossing, Borromeo parishioner La Freniere Chauvin took the travelers, their saddle horses and belongings (including the nuns' prized picture of the Sacred Heart) across in his ferry and declined payment for his services. The little party then trudged uphill to one of the largest houses in town, where widow Marie Louise Duquette lived. After Francois's death in 1816, she had taken in boarders, and one of them, Timothy Flint, had described the surroundings of *Chez* Duquette:

> The town is partly visible from this retirement, although the noise is not heard. The river spreads out below it in a wide and beautiful bay adorned with an island thick set with those regular cotton[wood] trees which so much resemble trees that have been planted for a pleasure ground. The trees about the house were literally bending under their load of apples, pears, and the yellow Osage plums. Above the house and on the summit of the bluff [toward the present site of the Borromeo church] is a fine tract of high and level plain covered with hazel bushes and wild hops, a great abundance of grapes, and red prairie plums.

Madame Duquette's house was of *poteaux sur solle* construction. Larger than most local houses, it measured roughly twenty-five by thirty-five feet, but was still too small for the many uses for which Philippine intended it. The rent, admitted Philippine in her first letters from St. Charles, was "exorbitant," nearly 2,000 francs a year, for "seven small rooms badly in need of repair, a large garden and orchard left uncultivated. . . ." One central room occupied most of the building's interior, with three tiny rooms measuring about five by eight feet flanking each side. Each of these little rooms had its own door to the outside as well as two windows; probably Madame Duquette had modified the house's original layout after Francois's death to accommodate boarders. With its little side rooms

44 † *St. Charles Borromeo*

and large interior room the house provided cramped quarters. The central room served as a convent parlor, schoolroom and studyhall by day and a dormitory by night. Shortly after moving in, the nuns converted one of the little side rooms into a chapel and there Philippine hung a picture of one of her favorite saints, the French missionary Francis Regis.

In explaining their choice of abode to Mother Barat, Philippine mentioned that "the village is willing to give the Bishop a plot of ground for us, 180 feet by 300 feet, but two Presbyterians are withholding their signatures and so preventing the donation. The Bishop is going to take up the matter with them." The dimensions stated in this letter are not similar to those of the land to be granted along Third Street. Andrew Wilson and Uriah J. Devore, perhaps the two uncooperative parties, had already agreed to the donation of the block on Third Street. This passage therefore seems to refer to another tract, perhaps on Block 28 or Block 15. The same letter states that "the parish would build for us near the center of the lot and close to the church, as the pastor will be our chaplain. . . . "

The pastor of whom Philippine wrote was Father Benedict Richard, one of Dubourg's Benedictine recruits, with whom the nuns had traveled north from Louisiana. The bishop directed Richard to move close to the Duquette residence, which probably indicates that the parish lacked a suitable rectory. Soon the nuns' chores included cooking for their confessor/chaplain, whose company proved to be an acquired taste. Philippine found it hard to cover up her disappointment in Dubourg's choice of spiritual father for her community:

> Mr. Richard . . . is a true priest, according to the heart of God. His large and emaciated frame, his meditative and austere face, lend him the appearance of an anchoret [hermit], rendering

him better calculated to inspire respect than to elicit affection. For all that, he is none the less an excellent man, and a full noble character who hides beneath his extreme reserve of words and manner a devoted heart.

Father Richard's ministrations at St. Charles Borromeo began in September 1818 with his first baptism in the log church. Unlike earlier pastors, he did not have to ride the mission circuit to Portage des Sioux and Dardenne; Dubourg had appointed Father John Acquaroni (who earlier that year had spent much time at the log church) to tend to those parishes. Father Richard served as the nuns' confessor and spiritual director, said Mass at the log church on Sunday and holy days, but on other days when attendance was likely to be low, he offered Mass at the Duquette house. In general, he performed most regular pastoral functions at the church and school, but a lack of entries in the burial register for 1819 suggests that he did not perform burials.

The priest's cheerless appearance was deceiving; as Philippine's letter suggested, it hid a generous heart. At one of the nuns' lowest financial ebbs, Father Richard startled the women by promising to reimburse them 600 francs per year for his board, then made good with a hefty installment of 350 francs, enough to rescue the community (at least for awhile) from debt. Letters written after the nuns had left St. Charles reveal that Benedict Richard was a stern confessor, but by then Philippine did not seem to mind; she knew the man's hidden qualities, and he must have known hers. Just before leaving St. Charles in 1819 she described the nuns' last meal with their students, and added that their wasted-looking chaplain, who apparently enjoyed their cooking, was so disturbed by their imminent departure that "he went off without taking his breakfast." A few years later Father Richard was sent back to New Orleans to serve as chaplain of the Ursuline convent and never returned to the Sacred Heart community, despite his requests to the bishop. He died in the cholera epidemic of 1833, and left the nuns a large, unexpected legacy.

Education Begins

By sending both Benedict Richard and the Sacred Heart community to St. Charles, Bishop Dubourg aimed to do more than just shore up Catholicism in the town; he intended nothing less then the improvement of society through the education (both secular and religious) of the upper classes, reasoning that benefits from this arrangement would eventually "trickle down" to the poor. Philippine contested this logic, not only because she longed to work with the poor but also because it further thwarted her dream to live near the Indians: "When we complain to the bishop that we have no savages, he says, 'Indeed you have, and your work among these children will be wider and more lasting because of the influence of the rich over the poor.'" Although there were no truly wealthy families in St. Charles, Dubourg believed that the leading families of St. Louis would send their daughters to a Sacred Heart boarding school in St. Charles, and that tuition from this venture would support a free school for the poor.

This system of a "select" school for the wealthy supporting a free school for the poor originated in America in the early nineteenth century. The first to advertise these schools side by side was St. Elizabeth Seton, whose select school in Emmitsburg, Maryland, supported her adjacent school for the poor. This system was the same as the Sacred Heart system.

On September 14, 1818, the nuns opened at St. Charles the first free school west of the Mississippi. In doing so they planted the seed of what would later become the parish school of St. Charles Borromeo. Soon they had more than twenty pupils. They taught reading, writing, arithmetic, and catechism. From the free school a day school soon developed for pupils who could pay a nominal tuition fee, in part because some parents of children in the free school resented its being called the "poor school." On October 3, three St. Louis girls arrived, Emilie and Therese Pratte and their cousin Pelagie Chouteau, and so the boarding school opened at last. Mother Duchesne described all three classes of pupils, starting with those in the free school:

> These children have never heard of our Lord, of His birth or His death, nor of hell, and they listen open-mouthed to our instructions. I have to say to them continually, "Yes, this is really true." All except two are learning the alphabet. Among the children who pay a little fee there is the same ignorance. . . . We have to combat worldliness as well as ignorance. Some of the boarding pupils have more dresses than underclothes or handkerchiefs; they have embroidered dresses of gaily colored silk, with lace trimmings and fancy sleeves of net or lace. The day pupils who pay tuition dress on Sundays like our boarding pupils in Paris. They scorn black shoes and must have

pink or blue, yellow or green ones, and the rest to match, but they do not use handkerchiefs. We have had to require them to do so at school.

Because poor children from Catholic St. Charles families comprised most of the non-boarding students, most of these students were Borromeo parishioners. Several had at least one Indian parent. Although the nuns had wanted to work with native Americans, they generally did not enjoy teaching Indian children, about whom Philippine wrote: "Their laziness, the freedom of their way of life, which is a barrier to all self-restraint, their slowness in acquiring even a mediocre degree of instruction, point to the most distant hope of ever having them amongst us."

Children of African ancestry presented an even larger problem. Bishop Dubourg advised the nuns that although frontier society accepted, more or less, children with some Indian blood, it stood firmly against acceptance of blacks and even their light-skinned children. Philippine explained his instructions:

Bishop Dubourg has said positively that we may not admit them to the boarding school or free school, and he has appointed a separate day for the instruction of the colored people; otherwise, he says, we should not hold the white children in school were we to admit the others. He told us of an experience he had in the college in Baltimore, which shows that prejudice against people of color cannot be overcome in this country. He consulted the Archbishop of Baltimore on the matter and was told that this prejudice would have to be maintained as the last safeguard of morality and manners in this country.

Accordingly, the nuns admitted children of mixed race to the day school alone.

Performing manual labor without hired help was also a trial for the nuns. Shortly after moving to St. Charles, the women tried to hire local people to work as servants, but discovered that even the poorest Creoles considered such work fit only for slaves.

Difficulties Increase

Observing the rule of cloister made the nuns' everyday lives more difficult, but it was essential to their identity as religious women. When the Society of the Sacred Heart was founded in 1800, the Church did not allow women not enclosed in a monastery to call themselves "Religious." The Society's founders, however, had modeled it on the Jesuit order, which was unified under one director who had the power to send his members anywhere in the world. Because the Church was not ready to allow such autonomy to religious women, it required of the Society of the Sa-

cred Heart a modified form of cloister in order to recognize its members as "true Religious." To have dispensed with cloister even on the frontier would have compromised the status of the Society and ultimately hindered its members from accomplishing their mission.

Philippine Duchesne and her community soon discovered that cloister was a concept foreign to St. Charlesans:

As to cloister, in the whole country for 500 leagues around us there is not a single wall around property. They put

Creole Picket Fence, *drawing by Anna Maria von Phul. A wooden fence surrounded the Duquette property, but provided the nuns little privacy.*

up wooden fences that keep out animals better than human beings. Our cloister consists in staying at home, but people come in as often as they please. They make openings for themselves [in the wooden fence] anywhere. We shall have to be in our own house in order to regularize our life. In this house it is impossible.

Because they were cloistered, the nuns did not go to market or cultivate the common fields or leave the Duquette grounds without sufficient cause. Fetching water from the nearby Missouri River, even after the Duquette well ran dry, was not sufficient cause; the women rationed even drinking water until they could find someone to haul it for them. Because they lacked help they dug their own garden, tended their cow, cleaned out her stable, and hauled manure.

Although records kept during the winter of 1818-1819 prove that the weather was unusually mild, the women suffered nevertheless. They were not accustomed to their wet laundry freezing before the fireplace or the wind whistling through the chinks in their walls. They had logs to burn but no tools for reducing them to kindling, and neither did anyone they knew. Although the Duquette house had four fireplaces, most of the heat produced in them went up the chimneys. Nutrition was also a problem. Philippine's letters speak of the shortages of produce, eggs, butter, and even bread, but these shortages affected many people in town as well. Less palatable foods like salted fish, corn, potatoes, dried apples, and rice tided the community over until the spring.

Having managed the financial affairs of convent life before, Philippine knew soon after moving to St. Charles that the Sacred Heart community could not survive for long in the town without its own house. Not only did the nuns need privacy and more room, they could ill afford another year's rent on the Duquette house. Philippine hoped for a new residence in St. Charles, as she explained to Mother Barat:

So many difficulties make us dream of building elsewhere, but the townsfolk have had a meeting and named a committee with a chairman. They are getting the signatures of all the inhabitants who are willing to chop trees in the common woods and prepare them, so as to erect and roof a house for us. We should have only to finish it off inside and put up the partitions. They plan to make it 36 feet long and 25 feet wide—and that is considered large out here, where there are only log houses plastered with mud, which comes off easily and so lets in light through the chinks.

This letter fails to specify where this convent was to have been built. Another letter dated March 5, 1819, mentions that the building effort was then well underway, "They [the people of St. Charles] have already hauled to the spot huge logs forty feet long to build the house. It will look out over the Missouri. . . ." In just ten days, however, the prospect had changed enough for Mother Duchesne to write:

> As we are in a time of trial, God has allowed that all I wrote about our situation here has changed, and for a new convent we have no resource but the good will of the people of St. Charles, who show some interest in building a skeleton of a house for us. I understand their eagerness is diminishing. Instead of a month, they say it will take them until next autumn. God knows what will happen. . . ."

Why did construction begin and then taper off, so that by the end of March, Bishop Dubourg was able to persuade the nuns to abandon St. Charles in favor of Florissant, where construction costs were even higher? None of Philippine's letters explains exactly what happened; maybe she was not sure herself. Records left by the priests involved in the building effort—Benedict Richard of St. Charles,

John Acquaroni of Portage des Sioux and Dardenne, and Joseph Dunand of Florissant—fail to shed light on this question.

By the spring of 1819, it was clear that the nuns would have to move elsewhere; there simply were not enough potential boarding students in the local population to keep the free and day schools afloat. Despite Bishop Dubourg's rosy projections, the boarding school had drawn only three girls from St. Louis, and prospects for the next year were just as dim. Putting food on the table and paying the myriad expenses of the schools and convent had made the nuns unwilling to take any more risks. While there was still hope for a new convent building in St. Charles, Mother Duchesne had considered splitting up the community by moving Octavie Berthold and the boarders to Florissant while keeping Eugénie Audé behind in St. Charles to run the day school, but she realized that doing this would only slow, not stop, their financial losses. She agonized in a letter to Sophie Barat over abandoning the poor children of St. Charles:

> The section north of the Missouri River can never send us boarding pupils who will pay tuition. The best we can do here is a day school run by a few of us, and it will not support the nuns. Pride tries to hide misery, but we see these poor, hungry children coming barefooted often in the coldest weather and wearing a single cotton garment—a very thin one, too—and nothing under it.
>
> You see, my dear Mother, that though we are forced to give up the boarding school here, it is heartbreaking to leave no help at all for these children, who could be nicely trained. In four months many have learned to read, to write, to know the whole of the little catechism, a number of hymns, and the prayers at Benediction. They do all the singing [in the log church] now, and formerly the priest could not get a single person to say *Amen*.

The Nuns Depart

After construction of the new convent had slowed considerably, Bishop Dubourg made a retreat in St. Charles. During this time he and the nuns discussed the Society's future in the area. From the women's arrival, the bishop (who had no authority in the matter) objected to their order's rule of cloister as well as to their two-tiered system of choir religious and coadjutrix sisters. During his retreat he tried to persuade them to compromise both as well as to move to Florissant, where, he promised, he would spend another 2,000 francs sent by Mother Barat for erection of a new building. The nuns refused to compromise either of their rules, but realized that another year in St. Charles would cause even more hardship and would perhaps endanger the Society's mission in the New World. Reluctantly, they decided to move all operations to Florissant.

For the remainder of the spring and summer the religious worked constantly with the children, trying to leave them with as much education and training as possible. Father Richard gave the children their First Communion in August, and later that month Bishop Dubourg distributed awards to the schools' best students. In early September, nearly one year to the day after moving to St. Charles, the Religious of the Sacred Heart left. Although she had clearly not wanted to move to the little town in the first place, Mother Duchesne had done so in obedience to the bishop. Deeply embarrassed by the failure of her work in St. Charles, she blamed herself, forgetting that she never would have

chosen this location had she been allowed a choice.

Father Benedict Richard remained at St. Charles until 1820, then moved to St. Louis for a time before eventually transferring to New Orleans. Two of Dubourg's other missionary recruits assisted Richard from time to time in St. Charles. The first, Andre Ferrari, was a Vincentian. He appeared just once in St. Charles, but got along well with the Sacred Heart community and later with the people of Florissant. He died in the early 1820s, perhaps of yellow fever. The other, Charles De La Croix, was a favorite of Mother Duchesne. His name appears only once in the parish archives, as a "missionary priest commissioned by the curé [Benedict Richard] of St. Charles" to perform the wedding of St. Charlesans Jacques Platte and Eulalie Mournier, on January 4, 1820. In April of that year Bishop Dubourg appointed the young missionary pastor of St. Ferdinand in Florissant, displacing Prior Joseph Marie Dunand, who soon returned to Europe.

Two years later Father De La Croix traveled up the Missouri River to the Osage Indians, where he performed the first missionary activity among native Americans west of the Mississippi since the expulsion of the Jesuits, and paved the way for Peter De Smet and others. In doing so De La Croix nearly ruined his health. Later he returned to Europe, where he influenced missionary work as treasurer of the Association for the Propagation of the Faith.

John Baptist Acquaroni returned to St. Charles Borromeo in 1820, but split his time between the three largest Catholic communities of St. Charles County—Borromeo, Dardenne, and Portage des Sioux—until about 1822. A whimsical entry dated April 29, 1821, commemorates his baptism of a churchbell for St. Charles Borromeo. Jacques Chauvin, Sr., and Mrs. Marie Reynal served as godparents.

Acquaroni is said to have contracted at Portage des Sioux a chronic illness called scurvy-leprosy and left for Italy in 1824. He never returned to the New World. During his time at Borromeo he performed many baptisms and six weddings, but little evidence remains of his success in guiding the parish. The memoirs of Felix Verreydt, a Jesuit who ministered to the area for many years beginning in 1828, testify to the success of Acquaroni among the people of Portage des Sioux:

> They all must have deeply felt his departure, for he was as their common father of all. How often did I not hear the old people [relate] with what particular care he instructed their children. He was constantly surrounded by them and trained them in the way children ought to be raised. If the tree is known by its fruits, surely Rev. Mr. Acquaroni must have been a very pious priest.

Part 2
The Stone Church Era

Chapter 4
1823-30

The Jesuits Arrive

Bishop Dubourg's recruits helped reverse the inertia and divisiveness that had crept into parish affairs since Father Lusson's departure in 1804. Each of the missionary priests who visited St. Charles between 1818 and 1823 ministered to all levels of society, and most of these priests soon lost their health. Though all of the Sacred Heart nuns survived their first years in the Mississippi valley, they periodically suffered from the same illnesses that afflicted most newcomers to the area, especially debilitating fevers. By the early 1820s, St. Charles Borromeo was again barely functioning, due mainly to the shortage of healthy missionaries.

In 1823 Bishop Dubourg found a way to attract members of the Society of Jesus to the St. Louis area. Learning that a band of Belgian Jesuits was planning to leave their Maryland seminary because of financial hardship, the bishop offered to create an elaborate Jesuit-run network of missionary activities to benefit the tribes of the Missouri and upper Mississippi Rivers, and asked the federal government (which then subsidized various methods of dealing with native Americans) for support. Meanwhile,

Dubourg negotiated with Jesuit Superior Charles Neale and promised to the Society of Jesus exclusive rights to minister to all inhabitants of the Missouri valley. At last all parties agreed, and Dubourg received a federal subsidy large enough to launch the project.

The bishop promptly deeded to the Jesuits a large tract of farmland near Florissant, then set about moving the men. The travelers consisted of two ordained Jesuits, vice-superior Charles Felix Van Quickenborne and Peter Timmermans; three coadjutor brothers, Henry Reiselman, Charles Strahan and Peter DeMeyer; seven young Belgian novices, Felix Verreydt, Francis de Maillet, Judocus Van Assche, Peter J. Verhaegen, John Baptist Smedts, John Elet and Peter Jan De Smet; and three black married couples brought along to till the Florissant farm. Hardly had the group taken possession of the tract when they began expanding the small *poteaux en terre* farmhouse and planning the completion of the seminarians' studies. Soon afterward they built a two-story frame building for an Indian school, with timbers cut by the seminarians from the Missouri River bottomlands and islands.

For Philippine Duchesne, the arrival of their order was a dream come true but she was soon disappointed. Father Van Quickenborne wanted little to do with the Ladies of the Sacred Heart, and refused to serve as their spiritual director until ordered to do so by his superior. Although his attitude toward the nuns eventually mellowed, the priest remained throughout his life a quirky man. Like Dubourg he was zealous and lacked the common touch, and behind his back his own seminarians called him "Napoleon." It is probably fortunate that Van Quickenborne spent more time on the farm teaching the seminarians than he did riding the mission circuit. Peter Timmermans instead took over parochial duties at St. Charles Borromeo and the other mission stations.

Timmermans celebrated Mass at the log church on two Sundays every month, but reviving the faith in St. Charles proceeded slowly. Lay burials continued. Catholic weddings lagged, suggesting that many couples were joined in civil ceremonies or by common-law unions. Nevertheless, the roving Jesuit kept up a demanding schedule caring for the scattered parishes and settlements of the Missouri River valley. He regularly visited Portage des Sioux and Dardenne and came at all hours to hear confessions and give the last rites. Like so many other Europeans who exhausted themselves in the frontier river towns, Father Timmermans soon lost his health, perhaps to a particularly virulent strain of malaria. After saying Mass at the log church on May 30, 1824, the priest rode back to the Florissant farm and collapsed. He died the next day.

Van Quickenborne's duties immediately increased as he tried to add Timmerman's schedule to his own. Soon his own health suffered. Philippine Duchesne wrote of him, "The Father Rector is in very poor health. Now he has four parishes on his

Grave of Peter Timmermans, S.J.

hands, along with several remote missions, the direction of the studies [of the seminarians]. . . . "

Letters between Jesuits suggest than the Father Rector had fallen victim to a less dangerous but more persistent strain of malaria: he suffered on and off for several years with fevers, jaundice, and fatigue. Until he built up enough resistance to resume some of his former duties, Bishop Dubourg revoked his authority to minister anywhere but St. Ferdinand except in an emergency, and added that this ban would be lifted only by the addition of at least two more priests to the Jesuits' operation.

Short of ordaining two seminarians prematurely, Van Quickenborne had no choice but to beg for help, and did so in June 1825. That fall his request was answered in the arrival of another Belgian Jesuit, Theodore de Theux, and Brother John O'Connor. A nobleman who had renounced his title and right of inheritance upon becoming a Jesuit, de Theux later served many years as pastor of St. Ferdinand and for a year in the same capacity in St. Charles. Brother O'Connor was then forty-five years of age, the oldest Jesuit in Missouri. Assigned to cultivate the mission's garden, he stayed on the farm, but his example interested several young men from the area in joining the Jesuits.

Van Quickenborne's convalescence meant that parishioners of St. Charles Borromeo went for about a year and a half without Sunday Mass. During this time, seminarians Peter Verhaegen and John Smedts took turns riding on Sunday out to St. Charles, where they instructed the parishioners and led prayers in French. Some baptisms were performed—by Van Quickenborne when he was able and by de Theux when he was not. Probably lay baptisms, which were not recorded, occurred, too. Catholic weddings were scarce events until 1826, when the first of the seminarians were ordained. Burials, being performed on shorter notice, remained partly the responsibility of layman Louis Collin, but the recording of burials stayed haphazard until 1828. One result of this poor record-keeping is that the cause of death for a unusually high number or St. Charles children who were buried in the parish cemetery in 1824 is not known, although a letter written that year by Philippine Duchesne, who was then stationed in Florissant, mentions that whooping cough was currently ravaging that village and St. Louis.

Father Van Quickenborne aptly summarized all the reasons he needed priestly assistants to take over for him at St. Charles Borromeo, in a letter to the Father General:

St. Charles is a town situated on the left bank of the Missouri River, nearly all the inhabitants being Catholics. There are three other congregations at a distance of 10 or 12 miles from St. Charles. These congregations contain about 300 souls. Our seminary is situated off at one extremity, we are separated by a river, the roads are very bad for six months of the year and it is dangerous to cross the river. At St. Charles we are in the center with respect to the other congregations. A church will be built [to replace the tumbledown log church], the pew rent will amply suffice for the support of two priests and from this place, furthermore, the smaller congregations to be organized can be visited from time to time. The priests now lose all their time in making trips to bring the sacraments to the sick, and also ruin their health for they often have to go through deep water. For the same reason the children in those families cannot be properly instructed. The people complain that they have to come so far to call us for the sick and crossing the river makes these trips expensive both for them and us.

Building a New Church

Peter Verhaegen and John Baptist Smedts were ordained in early 1826. Father Van Quickenborne ordered Smedts to remain in Florissant as his assistant; Verhaegen he sent immediately to St. Charles to serve as visiting missionary for the Borromeo parish as well as for five other more remote stations. The young priest soon complained about the moral conditions of St. Charles:

I do not hear regularly more than twenty confessions a month [the Catholic population of St. Charles then numbered about 500], and I do not see how, without a change in circumstances, this number will increase. The French spend the spring, summer and fall on the river, finding thus their only means of support. During their absence, their wives almost perish of hunger and are often without decent dress, while the children are in a miserable state. When the voyageurs return, a mass of debts contracted during their absence has to be paid. I am convinced it will require a miracle for our missionaries to gather in anything like a spiritual harvest. For if, according to the old saw, occasion makes the thief, here navigation makes the devil. There are few men of genuine piety in this locality. So general indeed is the corruption among the rivermen, that there is little room left for the good seed.

It seems that as long as the *voyageur* way of life persisted in St. Charles, the Jesuits (like their ecclesiastical predecessors) believed the local people to be spiritually barren and unwilling to change.

For several years, Father Van Quickenborne had planned to raise the level of piety in the town by replacing the log church, but his poor health and a lack of funding prevented immediate action. In 1825 the seminarian Judocus Van Assche described the situation:

> The churches of St. Charles and Portage, to put the matter as briefly and accurately as possible, are barns, not of stone but of wood, without foundation of any kind except a few stones placed under the joists to keep them from rotting. . . . Our Superior [Van Quickenborne] has begun to make preparations for a new church of brick; but being still alone, he has so much to do that it will take him long to finish it, for the church will have to be built with alms, which at present he has not time to beg. It is, however, a real necessity as we fear that some fine day the old church will come down on our heads. I do not think that Messrs. Verhaegen and Elet will preach in it during the winter on account of the cold, for the windows are now without glass.

Before he took ill, Van Quickenborne had indeed laid the groundwork for replacing the log church. In January 1825, he wrote Bishop Joseph Rosati (then serving as Dubourg's coadjutor) that if he received a large sum of money from Europe he would buy the nine-acre Duquette tract, including Madame Marie Louise's house, as the site for a new church building. Already the Jesuit Superior had decided not to carry out the parishioners' original resolve to rebuild the church on Block 28; perhaps the lawsuit or the parish's lack of written title to its land had convinced him to rent it out and build elsewhere. A larger structure as well as additional land for further expansion were needed; the Duquette tract offered both plus clear, provable title and an elevation untouched by even the highest floodwaters. In the same letter to the bishop, Van Quickenborne requested permission to lease "the land on which the old church now stands, if your Lordship approves the plan and the parishioners consent."

The parishioners consented. It is unfortunate that the parish records do not contain information of a meeting between Van Quickenborne and the council in early 1825; the only evidence comes from letters written by the Jesuits. In one dated February 28, 1825, to Bishop Rosati, Van Quickenborne fairly crowed over having won over the parishioners to his plan, and also having persuaded them to abandon the old system of marguilliers, as other local parishes were then doing:

> I have the pleasure of informing you that at a parish-meeting in St. Charles the trustees [marguilliers] and all present named me sole administrator of the property of the church, to lease or rent it, the income to go to the curé [pastor], without there being any trustees in the future. The materials of the old church will be utilized in the construction of the new one, which will be built on ground belonging to Mme. Marie Louise Duquette and purchased by me. They have all promised to subscribe. The church will be in brick or

stone 70 feet long and 40 feet wide.

On March 8, 1825, Marie Louise Duquette sold to Van Quickenborne her residence and the surrounding land bordered by Clark, Decatur, Second, and Fourth streets. Although the price of $650 was not excessive, Madame Duquette's terms were hard enough to solidify forever her reputation as a sharp trader: $300 down in cash, the remaining $350 to be secured by the Jesuits' 240-acre farm in Florissant. In placing his entire operation on the bargaining table Van Quickenborne must have felt confident of his ability to repay, and he eventually did without losing his farm. But like Philippine Duchesne, who had complained about the "exorbitant" rent on the widow's house, he must have regarded the canny woman as more than just a model of piety. A few weeks after the sale, title examiner Theodore Hunt came to St. Charles and confirmed the Jesuit's ownership of the Duquette land as well as the parish's ownership of the log church property on Block 28 and the "public square" tract across Main Street on Block 15. Now the building could begin.

To fund it, Father Van Quickenborne placed his hopes in Divine Providence, as well as in the arrival of a large inheritance from Europe. Building the new church, which eventually measured eighty feet by forty feet exclusive of the sacristy, would cost several thousand dollars; pledges from St. Charlesans amounted to a mere thousand. But the parishioners seemed eager and those who could not pay offered to provide labor and materials. Not only Catholics supported the Jesuits's efforts; Protestant St. Charlesans also helped defray the costs of building what Van Quickenborne planned to be the finest church for hundreds of miles around.

Peter J. Verhaegen, S.J.

Making this dream a reality was the first priestly assignment of the Peter Verhaegen. Years of theological study could hardly have prepared the erudite Jesuit for two-and-a-half years as construction supervisor. The young priest, who already had extensive experience chopping wood along the Missouri River bottoms, also provided manual labor. During occasional trips to St. Louis he "cast aside all timidity" and begged for funds, which, strangely, seemed to trickle in when most needed. Verhaegen and the other Jesuits suspected that a lion's share of the funding came from Father Van Quickenborne's Belgian connections, but the taciturn superior neither confirmed nor denied their suspicions.

In a letter dated November 7, 1827, Verhaegen described his troublesome assignment:

> The church is to be roofed in a few days. No one who has never gone through the experience would believe how beset with difficulties is building in the State of Missouri. Now one is without workingmen, now without wagons, now without materials. I bespeak a stock of patience for one who undertakes a similar task in the future. When I think, however, how much this little church is going to do for this town, *ad majorem Dei gloriam,* I make light of past unpleasantnesses and by anticipation rise superior to those which are to come.

Difficulties aside, Verhaegen succeeded so well in his duties that Van Quickenborne relied on him to find a suitable property nearby for a pastoral residence. Unwilling to take on another construction project, the superior directed Verhaegen to find a house already built with enough room for at least two Jesuits and enough land nearby for a school. Again Verhaegen delivered. Through him Van Quickenborne bought the southernmost strip of Block 6, bordering on Main and Lewis Streets and running back to the river. A two-story frame house resting on a solid stone foundation occupied the property. Although the upper story was not then finished, Van Quickenborne deemed the package a good deal for $300. That same day he bought another strip of land on the northern half of Block 6, near Main and Decatur Streets, for the future boys' school. Until a new brick school could be built, the dilapidated log church was uprooted from Block 28 and hauled in pieces over to Block 6, where it was used to build a temporary school for boys and a kitchen.

By the fall of 1828, Van Quickenborne's worries about finishing and financing the church disappeared when he received a large donation from France. Altogether he calculated the cost of the church at $6,455. With Louis Barada and La Freniere Chauvin leading the way, the laity had contributed nearly all of the $1,000 pledged and had furnished $500 worth of labor. The Jesuits and their many contacts had provided the remaining money and manpower. In September, Van Quickenborne asked Bishop Rosati (who, after Bishop Dubourg resigned his position in America and returned to Europe in the fall of 1826, was named the first bishop of the St. Louis diocese) to fix a date for the consecration of the new church. Rosati obliged by choosing October 12, 1828.

Surviving likenesses of the stone church fail to do it justice. Upon its completion it dwarfed the log church and nearly every other church in the diocese, and for a time was the only one with a plastered interior. Facing east from its location near the corner of Second and Decatur, it occupied roughly the same space later taken up by the brick chapel of the Sacred Heart nuns. "The facade was of cut stone," wrote Verhaegen, "surmounted by a pretty cornice, which rested upon four handsome pilasters." Its consecration drew the amazing total of nine priests (not including Bishop Rosati), six Jesuit brothers, two seminarians, and four Sacred Heart nuns, including Mother Duchesne, who wrote Bishop Dubourg in France:

> On the 12th of October . . . I assisted for the first time in my life at the consecration of a church. It was that of St. Charles, built by the Jesuits, who have consumed in its erection all the funds which they had received for their own support. It looks out upon the Missouri. . . . Mgr. [Rosati] performed the ceremony, assisted by all the Jesuits, two Lazarists and several young seminarians. Fathers De Theux and Dusaussoy preached, one in English and the other in French, to a vast concourse be-

Missouri Historical Society

Felix L. Verreydt, S.J., Borromeo associate for about fifteen years.

The stone church, from an 1865 drawing of Sacred Heart Academy

fore the church door. I never saw so grand a spectacle. . . .

Bishop Rosati named St. Charles Borromeo as patron of the church, and as secondary patron named Philippine Duchesne's favorite saint, Francis Regis. During the consecration, relics reputed to be those of martyred Saints Valentine and Dieudonne as well as those of Saints Francis de Sales and Ignatius were placed to rest under the altar. This part of the ceremony apparently made quite an impression; the next day Eulalie Petit presented her two sons for the first baptism in the stone church, requesting for them the names Guillaume Dieudonne and Charles Dieudonne.

Borromeo's new resident pastor, John Baptist Smedts, performed the baptism. He and Felix Verreydt, who was ordained in 1827, replaced Verhaegen in St. Charles and moved into the house on Block 6. Smedts set about furnishing the spacious

rectory and landscaping around it with fruit trees, flowers, and a vegetable garden. He attended to details inside the stone church, too, including the addition of pews, a pulpit, an organ, and an imposing wooden architrave, embellished with the word "Jehovah" in gilded Hebrew letters over the altar. For the first time ever, St. Charles had two priests in residence, although Verreydt's main duty was to care for outlying missions like Dardenne, Portage des Sioux, and those along the Missouri River.

With the Church and rectory underway, the Jesuits turned their attention to education. Shortly after the dedication of the stone church, they opened one of the first parish schools west of the Mississippi, free of charge to St. Charles boys. Within a short time thirty-five pupils had enrolled. Studies included catechism, reading, writing, grammar, arithmetic, and a little geography. The first teacher was Jesuit lay brother Henry Reiselman, who had come to the area as a Trappist in 1809, then left for the eastern United States where he joined the Society of Jesus and Father Van Quickenborne's band of recruits.

The records of the boys' school have apparently not survived. Letters by the Jesuits indicate, however, that the school succeeded from the very beginning, although the precarious health of Brother Henry (who may have suffered from a chronic but comparatively mild strain of malaria) worried Father Van Quickenborne during the early years:

Our dearest Brother Henry began to be troubled again with his old complaint, so that he was unable to teach the boys. . . . Father Verreydt thought himself unqualified to teach the boys English. If the school had been interrupted, all of the boys would have gone over to the Protestant teacher or preacher. I ordered him to teach. He obeyed with alacrity to the great satisfaction of the pupils, and their remarkable progress. Now our good and zealous brother is restored to health. The average daily attendance of his school is never less than twenty-six.

Ladies of the Sacred Heart

In 1828 the Religious of the Sacred Heart opened a free school for the parish girls. During the previous few years Father Van Quickenborne had lobbied Mother Sophie Barat to allow a foundation in St. Charles, but she had initially refused, counseling Philippine Duchesne, "Do not think of St. Charles at present. . . . You might starve to death out there." Undaunted, Van Quickenborne deeded to Mother Duchesne in May 1827 the two northern blocks of his four-block "Duquette" property, reserving only the land occupied by the stone church and sixteen surrounding feet, and the expanse between the entrance and Second Street.

The next year Sophie Barat, fearing another religious suppression in France, reversed her opposition to starting over in St. Charles and explained that such a foundation might soon be needed to shelter French nuns in exile. In the summer of 1828, Philippine Duchesne accompanied Father Van Quickenborne and Bishop Rosati to the little town to inspect the once and future convent—the now empty Duquette house—but renovation of the rundown structure did not commence until

that fall.

Just two days before the October 12, 1828, dedication of the stone church, the Ladies of the Sacred Heart arrived to stay. As the carriage bearing Philippine Duchesne, Octavie Berthold, and two other religious named Lucille Mathevon and Mary Ann O'Connor rolled down Main Street, people waved and called greetings and a group of women got together to cook several meals for the nuns. The Duquette residence was less welcoming; for the past few years its sole occupants had been stray pigs and sheep that had rooted away the house's foundation stones. Glass from the windows had disappeared and the rotted floorboards had partially fallen through. Even the front door needed repairs. Unable to enter their new convent, the nuns had to rely on a neighbor to crawl through a window and force the door open from the inside.

An Indian woman helped sweep, and local carpenters soon closed the gaps in the flooring and foundation, but mice roamed the house at night and bothered the women who, lacking furniture, slept on the floor curled up in rugs. Having brought only sugar, coffee, rice, and vinegar to stock their kitchen, the nuns were delighted by the many generous gifts of food which arrived at all hours from the townspeople. On the morning of October 12, they treated Bishop Rosati and the other men helping dedicate the stone church to a hearty breakfast, served frontier style on top of an empty barrel.

After the dedication, Mothers Duchesne and Berthold returned to Florissant, leaving only Lucille Mathevon and Mary Ann O'Connor to found a school for girls. Lacking another building, the women had little choice but to modify the Duquette house to serve as convent, free school, boarding school, and dormitory for the boarders. Mother Mathevon wrote:

> In order to keep down expenses, we have become masons, carpenters, day-laborers. We have scrubbed and painted the walls, made twelve benches, a table, a chicken house. No one would recognize the convent, it is so much improved. . . . The kind Jesuits who serve the parish send us everything imaginable. Our meals are always ready. We lack nothing, not even a good appetite, which neither of us had before coming here.

Philippine Duchesne had hand-picked Mothers Mathevon and O'Connor for reinstituting the St. Charles foundation. Born in Lyons, France, in 1793, Lucille Mathevon had entered Mother Duchesne's Grenoble convent at the age of twenty and sailed for America nine years later. At Florissant she adjusted to rough frontier conditions with unfailing good humor and optimism, and perfected her English. Her Irish helper, Mary Ann O'Connor, needed no introduction to frontier life. While living with the nuns several years at Florissant, she supervised that foundation's Indian school, taught in the free school and orphanage, and later helped establish a house in St. Louis.

With a capital fund of just eight dollars, the women began operations, and within two weeks opened a day school. Enrollment that first year reached thirty. With so many local girls to instruct, it soon became necessary to attempt offsetting losses with a boarding school, but, as before, paying boarders were scarce. Contributions from other Sacred Heart foundations enabled the nuns to furnish the house and equip the school, but from the beginning the women relied on the small tuition from the day students for their main support. Payment took a variety of forms: sacks of flour, buckets of water, pounds of butter, cheeses, dinner plates, work in the garden, or help with the laundry. No child was refused an education on account of poverty, and some paid nothing at all.

For milk, the nuns brought over a cow from Florissant. In the spring of 1829 they planted a garden which barely supplied their needs; the following year the plot yielded enough extra produce to sell. Soon they began supplementing their income by selling butter and eggs, sewing, and giving occasional retreats. Letters from Lucille Mathevon to Bishop Rosati suggest that for awhile the women even tried to raise silkworms on the leaves of sixteen mulberry trees they planted on their grounds.

Like Philippine Duchesne, Mother Mathevon found the children of St. Charles poorly prepared in catechism as well as in academic subjects, but her praise for the local people suggests that perhaps the old Creole way of life, with its Sunday balls and long forays into the wilderness, was ending:

> The people of St. Charles give the missionaries much consolation. They are very docile folk. It is enough for the pastor, or the "ladies," as they call us, to recommend a thing—it is done at once. [Of the students] eighteen have made their first Communion and six older girls have been baptized. Since their first Communion and Confirmation, they have approached the sacra-

ments every month. When they came to us, they did not even know how to make the sign of the Cross, and were at the "a, b, c," stage in everything. Their companions were not much further advanced. Now the greater number read and write well, and know almost the entire catechism. I have trained a girls' choir for the church. We help them, and on Sunday about three hundred people attend High Mass. They say that in the town now one hears no songs except hymns to the Blessed Virgin and the Sacred Heart.

The nuns occasionally took in orphans and those with special needs, but received the same instructions Mother Duchesne had received a decade earlier concerning racial matters. Lucille Mathevon agonized in 1830 over what to do with a little girl of mixed race, probably an orphan:

Mr. Proux [most likely Basil Proulx, the nuns' neighbor] proposed to me . . . that a little free mulatto girl come here for instruction. I would accept her . . . if I knew where to put her. We have only one room for the religious, boarders, day scholars and an orphan. . . . But I think that in Florissant where there is already an orphan Indian girl, she could go together with Mr. Proux. It would be impossible for her to stay alone and to mix with the others would harm our class. I feel much pain.

An understanding of the Society of the Sacred Heart, its history and apostolic goals, is necessary to understand the curriculum introduced by Mothers Mathevon and O'Connor in 1828. This curriculum mirrored that taught by Philippine Duchesne and her colleagues a decade earlier. When Sophie Barat founded the order in 1800, she sought to stress devotion to Christ himself, using the powerful imagery of his heart as a symbol of God's love and compassion for the world. In order "to glorify" the heart of Jesus, members of the So-

ciety were (and still are) enjoined to imitate, in their thoughts and actions, the virtues of Jesus and to work for the salvation of others.

These two goals—personal transformation along with the sanctification of others—implied a radical shift from the isolated, purely contemplative life of religious women of that era. Maintaining cloister in the early 1800s was necessary to the survival of the Society as a religious order, but it limited its members' involvement in the secular community. Mother Barat dealt with this by establishing schools on the same grounds as her orders' convents. Education, therefore, was one of the Society's means of sanctifying others. By establishing schools for girls, the Society introduced another innovation: female education was rare in France and nearly unknown in America.

Recognizing women as the prime moral and religious influences in the home, the order sought to shape society through the spiritual and academic preparation of future wives and mothers, regardless of whether they attended the free school or boarding school. To this end, girls were to learn Christian doctrine and scripture, with attention to the formation of character, and enough "secular" knowledge to enable them to "live a Christian life in the world according to the requirements of their state and position." For this reason, the classes taught by the Sacred Heart nuns in St. Charles included catechism and preparation for receiving the sacraments, as well as reading, writing, arithmetic, music, and sewing. As testimony of their commitment to education, the French-born nuns struggled to learn and teach in English, which had replaced French as the vernacular of the Mississippi valley.

In 1829 a reinforcement arrived in the form of Mary Layton, the Society's first novice in America. That fall the boarding school opened, but it drew few girls whose families could afford the yearly tuition of sixty dollars. Within a few years enrollment leveled off at about a dozen boarders, perhaps because of the wretched condition of the Duquette house, about which Mother Mathevon wrote: "When a storm rages, we fear it will collapse on our heads. When it rains, the kitchen is always flooded." Future growth would be impossible without a new building.

Chapter 5
1830-50

Cemetery Expansion

Immigration to the St. Charles area picked up speed in the 1820s. During that decade, the population of Missouri more than doubled, and by 1840 it more than doubled again. St. Charles was the largest steamboat destination along the Missouri River and the origin of the Boone's Lick Trail, which led to the Santa Fe Trail and other paths west. Many of the newcomers were Germans, who began immigrating en masse to the St. Charles area in the 1830s. A sizeable number of Irish settlers arrived somewhat later. Membership in St. Charles Borromeo increased accordingly.

Probably one of the most crowded of the parish properties was the log church cemetery. During his visit in October of 1828, Bishop Rosati blessed a new burial ground for the parish, located much closer to the stone church than the old cemetery. Just up the hill on Block 122, the new burial ground was the parish's first use of the land upon which the present church building stands. Even before Rosati's dedication, the tract was used for burying—in an entry dated August 26, 1828, Father Smedts noted that the body of parishioner Emilie Laurain had been laid to rest "in the new

cemetery."

In light of this entry, it is puzzling that over two decades later Father Verhaegen, having returned to St. Charles, wrote in a detailed memo concerning the parish real estate that the Block 122 land had been used as a cemetery since 1831, the year that Father Smedts took out a 999-year lease on Block 122. Perhaps Verhaegen overlooked the burial entry of Emilie Laurain. The records do not indicate how many other burials occurred in the new ground between 1828 and 1831, but it is possible that between the two years the Jesuits found it necessary to document their right to use the land. If so, Smedts' lease served its purpose during his life, but after he died the question arose of who would succeed him as lessor of the land. This matter was finally resolved in 1869, when St. Louis University took title to Block 122.

Through the years, the burial registers have provided little information about the parish cemeteries, and records from other sources fall far short of filling in the gaps. To understand the transition from the old burial ground to the new cemetery, it is helpful to look at a similar transition in St. Louis.

Like St. Charles' earliest Catholics, those of St. Louis buried their dead in the yard of their log church (near the site of the Old Cathedral). Burial grounds of this era differed from modern cemeteries in several ways. Urban development, for one, continued just outside their boundaries and soon limited the graveyards to their own narrow confines. This sometimes led to double and even triple burials in a single plot. More recent burials, being shallower, were sometimes exposed after a heavy rain, making a sturdy fence around the graveyard necessary for sanitary as well as aesthetic reasons. In St. Louis's earliest churchyard, graves were dug wherever space was available, and family members were usually scattered throughout the tract unless their deaths occurred very close in time.

The 1815 document from the Jesuit Archives concerning the upkeep of Borromeo's log church cemetery fence suggests that at least one section was reserved: following the names of Joseph Cote and two others is the note "in the enclosure of the negress." Altogether, about eighty parishioners or their heirs shared the responsibility of maintaining this fence, but exactly where these people were buried is unknown. The opening of a new cemetery did not necessarily mean that no further burials occurred in the old; in St. Louis it was customary for people who had reserved spaces in an old burying ground to be interred in it, regardless of the existence of a new cemetery, until all such spaces were used or the ground condemned for new construction.

In 1823 the trustees of the City of St. Louis passed an ordinance forbidding further burials within the city's limits, and soon a new burying ground about a mile outside town came into use. Whether such legislation was passed across the river in St.

John Schoenmakers, S.J., was pastor between 1846 and 1847.

Richard L. Vinson

Charles is not known, but probably there was some concern in the town about the condition of the old graveyard. The parish had buried on Block 28 for nearly forty years; surely people must have realized that its space was running out. Some may also have wished to bury the victims of infectious diseases away from the town's residents, most of whom then lived well east of Fourth Street.

Tradition holds that in 1831 the old cemetery's burials were transferred to Block 122. If such a removal occurred, it did not move all the deceased. The 1981 excavation that uncovered human bones and the remains of a casket behind a store at 407 South Main Street raised the question of whether other burials were left behind, and the 1990 archaeological dig of the northeast corner of Block 28 left this question unanswered. Further information is lacking.

It is helpful to consider what happened in St. Louis when the first graveyard was closed in 1830 to make way for construction of the Old Cathedral. A St. Louis undertaker who assisted in the removal of the graves later wrote that friends and relatives of those buried at this site claimed the remains of their loved ones, and had them reinterred at a newer cemetery outside the city's limits. Those burials left unclaimed, he wrote, were placed in a pit where the cathedral was eventually built. This story was contradicted nearly a century later by a church historian, who claimed that all graves had been moved west to a newer cemetery.

In St. Charles all graves were clearly not moved off Block 28. No large construction, like that of the Old Cathedral, ever necessi-

tated removing all the burials from the old churchyard. During the 1830s and later, many St. Charlesans still lived in relative poverty, and the parish's rather sketchy records make no mention of an exhumation. Given the lack of documentation, it cannot be assumed without further proof that there was a concerted effort to move all graves, but it is likely that the families and friends of some deceased parishioners moved their loved ones from the old cemetery. This same question arises concerning whether the parish later removed all burials from Block 122 to the present cemetery on Randolph Street.

Cholera

No matter what eventually happened to the old burying ground, by leasing Block 122 Father Smedts inadvertently provided enough burying space to accommodate the many parishioners who were to die within the next few years. The burial register lists thirteen entries for 1829, fourteen for 1830, but about thirty each for 1831 and 1832. Burials more than doubled in 1833, totaling over seventy, and in a letter dated August 7 of that year Lucille Mathevon elaborated:

> The city of St. Charles has been well-hit. Lots of fathers and mothers of families of the best residents have been victims of this cruel illness, and we have been sick. There is only one left to tend to the sick. Madame Eulalie [Guillot, of Louisiana, who had joined the St. Charles nuns in 1831] was the most sick and has not regained [her strength]. . . .
>
> We have begun our school again that we called off for a month because of the sickness. We have lost several of

our children who have had the misfortune of losing their parents.

The "cruel illness" was cholera, a bacterial disease easily spread in unsanitary water. During the summer of 1833 it peaked in St. Charles, causing a record number of deaths. Many families lost more than one member; the Becketts (probably an Anglicized version of Becquet) and Bellands each lost four; the Pallardys, three; the Chauvins and Peyros (also spelled Perrault and Pereau), two apiece. The survivors of Antoine Janis (who had died in 1832) were hit especially hard: that summer his widow, one son, two daughters, and several grandchildren died. Although Borromeo's burial register did not routinely list causes of death, the sheer numbers of people buried in such a short time suggest that cholera devastated St. Charles in the summer of 1833, just as it did St. Louis and New Orleans. Burying so many people so soon after the opening of the new cemetery must have made Fathers Smedts and Verreydt wonder how long the new burial ground would serve the parish.

During the short intervals between burials, the priests were often baptizing. Fear of an untimely death seems to have inspired more than a few St. Charlesans to seek baptism for themselves, their children, and even their slaves, during July and August of 1833. In the baptism register one of Borromeo's priests commented on the popularity of the sacrament "during cholera."

The epidemic interfered with construction of a much-needed building on the grounds of the parish school for girls. In the spring of 1833, the Society of the Sacred Heart granted Lucille Mathevon permission to build a new convent at St. Charles, and put up enough funding to get the project started. But more money was needed, and Father Van Quickenborne asked Borromeo families for their help. Within a short time he had pledges totaling $1,500. Then the epidemic hit, shutting down classes and presumably other operations. For a while Mother Mathevon hesitated whether to proceed without further funding, but a loan from parishioner La Freniere Chauvin helped make up her mind. Trusting that the balance would trickle in just as it had for construction of the stone church, she authorized work to begin in September 1833.

Sacred Heart Expansion

The plans called for a three-story brick building, forty-two by thirty-six feet, located just south of the stone church. This new convent would house the boarding school and its students, and thus free the Duquette cabin (for a time) for the education of the parish girls. Funding did arrive from many sources, and by late 1835 the convent was habitable. The nuns and boarding students moved in early in January, 1836.

The completion of the brick convent caused a widening of the gap between the boarding school and the free school, which after 1835 became more parochial. A distance at least of social class had always been maintained between students who boarded and those who attended the free school for parish girls; now a physical distance separated the two institutions. Although a few Borromeo girls attended the boarding school (Caroline Chauvin, daughter of La Freniere, for one) many more attended the parish school. It is unfortunate that Borromeo's once intimate ties with the Sacred Heart Society began to loosen at this early date.

Despite its size, the brick convent lacked a cloister chapel. Visiting the stone church was frequently a trial for the nuns, especially during their frequent illnesses. Shortly after the convent was completed, Lucille Mathevon asked the Jesuits to allow the construction of an addition between the church and convent, so that the nuns could have their own private chapel overlooking the church's sanctuary. Father Verhaegen granted permission but apparently neglected the legalities of the matter; after all, a rather wide strip of yard surrounding the church had been reserved for the parish when Van Quickenborne gave part of the Duquette tract to Philippine Duchesne. Years later Verhaegen worried about this oversight until the execution of a deed settled the matter.

The convent chapel was dedicated in

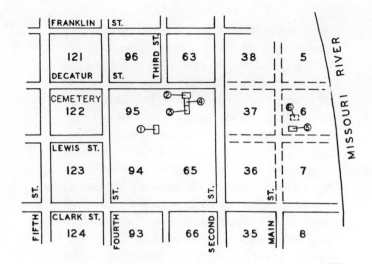

GROUNDS AND BUILDINGS USED BY THE PARISH AND RELIGIOUS OF THE SACRED HEART IN THE 1830s AND 1840s.

Legend

1. Duquette House, used as a school for the parish's girls, 1818-19, also 1828-40. Now the site of Regis Hall.
2. Stone church
3. 1835 convent and boarding school
4. 1840 addition - in a basememnt room measuring 20 feet by 35 feet. The parish's girls were taught, sometimes by St. Philippine Duchesne, between 1840 and 1858.
5. Frame rectory used from 1828 to circa 1850
6. Possible location of a wooden school for the parish's boys. It is said to have stood near the rectory.

1840. Shortly afterward, Mother Mathevon wrote about the gradual but steady progress the Society had been making in St. Charles since 1828:

> This section is being populated so quickly that our establishment should soon be in a flourishing condition, for education is more highly appreciated now, and religion is making great progress. Our first pupils, both boarding and day, are now good mothers of families, constant in the fulfillment of their duties, domestic and religious, and sending their children to school at the Sacred Heart.

Much of the Society's success in St. Charles had to do with the character of Lucille Mathevon. Born in 1793 to a French family that, like Mother Duchesne,

had harbored priests during the Revolution, Mother Mathevon was formed to religious life at the Grenoble convent by Philippine herself. She made her final vows in 1818 and four years later joined the Florissant community, where she cared for the Indian girls sent for schooling and tended to the sick. So impressed was Mother Duchesne with Lucille Mathevon that she sent her and Mary Ann O'Connor to St. Charles in 1828 to reinstitute the Society's foundation in that town.

After thirteen successful years in St. Charles, Mother Mathevon worked with the Potawatomi tribe at Sugar Creek, and later at St. Mary's, Kansas. When the mission was closed in 1868, she was gravely ill and returned to St. Charles, where she worked as a counselor and did various odd jobs. During this time the Indians, as well as the Jesuits and nuns, begged for her return, and so she moved back to Kansas in 1871. For five years she counseled, did various jobs, and spent hours on her knees. She died suddenly of pneumonia in 1876.

An account book kept for the Sacred Heart boarding school between 1840 and 1869 sheds some light on the civic development of the region. For example, the sizeable minority of the schools' non-Catholic girls from Missouri reflects the growing population of Protestants in the state. Some girls (both Catholic and Protestant) came to St. Charles from newer towns to the west (e.g., Franklin and Hermann), others came from St. Louis and Illinois, and a few came from far away (Texas, Louisiana, and the Upper Missouri territory). Annual fees for tuition and board totaled $80 in 1840; apparently few St. Charles families could afford this luxury for their daughters. Laundry service and music lessons cost even more. The few local girls named as boarders included various Chauvins, Jane Yosti, and Emilie Durocher of Portage des Sioux. True to its mission, in the 1840s the Society cared for

Peter De Smet, S.J., with an Indian delegation in Vancouver, 1859.

and educated, free of charge, an orphan named Josephine Myers.

Toward the end of that decade, other Germanic surnames (sometimes spelled phonetically) began appearing in the ledger—Snider, Schwendeman, Behrens, Eisman. A few St. Charles boarders of the late 1840s and early 1850s had English surnames, among them, Newbill and Potter. Although the St. Charles contingent in the boarding school never amounted to a majority, it varied, sometimes widely, from year to year.

Perhaps the most important change at the Sacred Heart convent was the return in 1842 of Mother Duchesne from the Potawatomi mission in Kansas. Allowed to work among her beloved Indians just one year because of her failing health, the old woman was sent back to St. Charles to run the parish school for girls and to recover her health. Probably Lucille Mathevon had planned for Mother Duchesne when she oversaw construction of the new convent addition in 1840—the building had a single bedroom on the first floor.

After returning from the Indian mission, Mother Duchesne for several years headed the parish school, which was located in a corner of the basement of the 1840 addition. In 1848, she was listed in a report as teaching Christian Doctrine. Throughout the 1840s she spent long hours praying, sewing, teaching French, and spending time with the children of the free school, some of whom threaded her needles because of her failing vision.

Two of the original Belgian Jesuits, Peter Verhaegen and Peter De Smet, shared the nun's zeal for the Indian missions. Verhaegen (then superior of the Missouri Jesuit Mission) had accompanied Mother Duchesne to the Potawatomi mission in 1841, one year after sending De Smet to the tribes of the Pacific Northwest, where he labored with unparalleled success. No matter where they were, both men kept in touch with their old friend. In the early 1850s, Verhaegen moved back to St. Charles Borromeo as pastor and spiritual director of the Sacred Heart convent and school.

In the 1830s French surnames began appearing in Borromeo's registers less often than before. At the same time Germanic surnames, occasionally tortured almost beyond recognition, began appearing. Various early entries for the Schwendeman (or Schwendemann) family list the surname as "Swendermonde" and "Schwenderman." Even the simple family name of Thro makes one appearance in the records as "Throh." Others appear in German characters—Tölle, Münd and Mügge. A few phonetic renderings, like the surname of Philomene "Weibloos" (Wappelhorst?) who was baptized in 1840, are almost impenetrable.

English usage began creeping into the parish registers in the late 1820s and early 1830s. By the 1840s a curious arrangement had evolved. Obviously the preferred language of most St. Charlesans, English was used in the entries concerning most parishioners with non-French surnames. French was generally used only in entries concerning the town's older French-speaking families. Although not all of Borromeo pastors required baptismal and matrimonial witnesses to sign the church's records, enough of such signatures appear now and then in the registers to make the cross-shaped mark, still used in the 1840s by some of the older French families, an obvious mark of illiteracy.

In 1839 Father Smedts began the annual recording of the names of first communicants. The following year he began a similar roster of those who were confirmed. These bare lists are perhaps the best evidence of population trends in the parish. In 1839 and 1840, French surnames persisted (among them Pallardie, Galernau, Dorlac, Martineau, Corbeille, Quenelle, Tayon, Janis and Soulard) but those of Irish and German extraction made up a large minority. In later years this minority grew as new immigrants settled in St. Charles and the French families died or moved away.

The same slim volume that contains these earliest records of first communions and confirmations also contains the names of Borromeo's members of three popular lay Confraternities—that of the Scapular, the Rosary, and the Sacred Heart. These lay sodalities offered parishioners of the middle nineteenth century a means of deepening their faith and of participating to a limited extent in church affairs. Father Van Quickenborne's successors, however, continued to run the parish; the era of a totally lay administration was over.

Annual reports to the bishop during this era prove that lay participation in the sacraments was indeed high. In the mid-1840s for example, the parish listed a steadily increasing membership, from 966 in 1843 to 1,145 in 1846. Baptisms for these years averaged over seventy, and Easter communions numbered consistently around 650. The number of weddings varied more widely during these years, but with no trend downward.

It seems that by 1850, St. Charles had indeed cast off its old reputation as an impious place. Attendance at Sunday Mass was high, the various schools of the Sacred

Heart nuns were growing in enrollment, and presumably so was the school on Block 6 for the parish boys. Since the 1820s the Jesuits had bought additional sections of this square, taking pains to establish clear title. By 1851 they owned the entire block.

A succession of pastors at St. Charles Borromeo carried on Father Van Quickenborne's reluctance to use the properties on Blocks 15 and 28 for anything other than rental income. Over the years, they leased parcels of Block 28 as follows: to Jacob Kibbler, for a hatter's shop; to James D. Earl, for a wheelwright or carriage makers shop; to Maximilian Janis and later to Samuel Pierce for a blacksmith shop. Parishioner Sir Walter Rice and a partner leased the northeast section of Block 15 for a stable, and others used the remaining sections for various commercial enterprises.

Evidence of slavery in St. Charles is much thinner than that of real estate title, but the parish records prove that the institution persisted in town until the end of the Civil War. The baptismal registers show that during the 1830s and 1840s, St. Charles' white inhabitants continued standing up for slaves and their children at baptism, just as they had during the Spanish regime. As before, these slaves usually lacked a surname, and were referred to instead by their given name followed by the name of their owner.

Several marriages between blacks occurred in the 1820s, although documentation in the records is generally sketchier than it is for marriages between whites. For example, sometime in 1827 a slave named Paul, of La Freniere Chauvin, married an unnamed woman of color. That same year, a slave named Cary was married to La Freniere Chauvin's Nelsey by Father Verhaegen. Two years later, Father Smedts

Judocus Van Assche, pastor 1835-36, leased a lot on Block 28 to Samuel Pierce for a blacksmith shop.

Jesuit Missouri Province Archives

baptized little Helene Anne Racine, noting in the register that she was the "legitimate" daughter of Sara and Pierre Racine, both "Negroes." These weddings and the others recorded illustrate that the Jesuits took their responsibility seriously to minister to all peoples, and probably encouraged slaveowners to allow their blacks to participate in the sacraments.

It cannot be overlooked, however, that the Jesuits brought slaves to Missouri in 1823, although they later refrained from splitting them up. Throughout the years before and during the Civil War, some leading Catholics (including Bishop Kenrick) kept slaves. Even Philippine Duchesne for a time owned a slave, who was presented as payment in lieu of tuition. Perhaps to make some people's dependence on forced labor appear more socially acceptable, writers of the parish records during these decades frequently substituted "servant" for the more forthright "slave." These blacks belonged both to old French families like the Baradas, Cotes, Papins, and Chauvins as well as to newer families with English surnames. Although references to slavery and race seem to dwindle over time in Borromeo's records, they persist nevertheless until slavery was abolished by law in 1865.

Sir Walter Rice and his wife, *Margarite McKay Rice:* Not a nobleman at all but a St. Charlesan named Sir, Rice operated a stable not far from the Missouri River on Main Street. During his lifetime he served as county surveyor, recorder, justice of the peace, postmaster, and trustee of St. Charles Borromeo church. Rice died in 1858. Upon the death of his widow several years later, she left to the priests of St. Charles Borromeo the munificent Mass stipend of $200.

Major James Morrison: A veteran of the War of 1812, Morrison and his brother Jesse moved to St. Charles from New Jersey in 1800, and later bought and operated the salt works at Boone's Lick in central Missouri. Morrison married into the Saucier family of Portage des Sioux and lived on Main Street.

Benjamin Emmons: an early immigrant to St. Charles, Emmons married a Chauvin and represented St. Charles County in the Territorial Legislature, as well as in the first state Constitutional Convention in 1820.

Louis Barada: son of an early inhabitant of St. Charles, Barada continued the family's tradition of involvement in parish affairs by helping build the stone church and serving as a trustee for many years. Barada supported his wife, Helene Gagnon, and eleven children by working as a butcher and a miller.

Francis Yosti: Son of an Italian businessman who emigrated to St. Louis in the late 1700s, Yosti married Emilie Adeline Morrison, daughter of Major James Morrison, and went into business with his father-in-law. The pair made several journeys to Santa Fe, New Mexico, where they sold mercantile goods from Missouri and points east. Yosti settled at last in St. Charles to pursue the mercantile business and sent daughters Emily Jane and Mary Margaret to the Sacred Heart boarding school.

The family of Laurent Beck: An immigrant from the Lorraine section of France, Beck sent his three daughters, Mary, Catherine, and Margaret to the Sacred Heart school for French classes only. To help pass the time the girls sewed and embroidered with Philippine Duchesne and assisted the old woman by threading her needles. All three later married in the stone church, Mary, to Bernard Rauch; Catherine, to William Ruf; and Margaret, to John Boschert.

The family of Joseph Pereau: An early French Canadian settler of St. Charles, Pereau married Marie Louise Savoye at the log church in 1807 and had nine children. Although Pereau died in the cholera epidemic of 1833, several of his children remained in the parish for many years.

Pastors and Other Priests

Charles Felix Van Quickenborne: Having come to America in order to work with native Americans, Van Quickenborne instead spent much of his priesthood attempting to revive the Catholic faith in Missouri. Although he opened the St. Regis Indian Seminary at Florissant and later traveled up the Missouri River to missionize the Kickapoo Indians, he met with disappointment in each venture. Among his successes were his far-sighted expansion of the St. Charles Borromeo church property and his efforts to develop the parish schools, as well as the sending of hardy, devoted priests like Peter Verhaegen, John B. Smedts, and Felix Verreydt to St. Charles. Van Quickenborne served as pastor for about two years in the early 1830s and made frequent visits to St. Charles until his death in 1837.

John B. Smedts: Borromeo's first resident pastor since the Spanish era, Smedts faced the unenviable task of ministering to a congregation noted for its indifference. He lived a quiet life in St. Charles, working hard to revivify Catholicism, and amply succeeded. In 1843 he became rector and master of novices at St. Stanislaus Seminary in Florissant. After his death in 1855, his colleague Peter De Smet wrote: "His whole life was irreproachable and exemplary. Shunning the world, simple in his manners and patient in suffering, he exhausted his strength in the service of the Lord."

Felix Verreydt: On and off for two decades, Verreydt rode out from his base at St.

Charles Borromeo to the surrounding missions of the Salt River District (from Troy to Palmyra) and the Missouri River (to Columbia and beyond). When other Jesuits were not available to teach the parish boys Verreydt filled in, although his natural bent lay in mission work. In 1835 he became pastor of Portage des Sioux. He ministered with varying degrees of success to different branches of the Potawatomi tribe. Although he suffered poor health during much of his life, Verreydt outlived the other Maryland Jesuits and died in 1883.

Judocus Van Assche: Pastor at St. Charles for only one year, Van Assche spent most of his career in Florissant as pastor of St. Ferdinand parish and briefly at the seminary as rector and master of novices. He returned to Borromeo as an associate and assisted Peter Verhaegen for several years in the 1850s.

Christian Hoecken: With an unusual flare for the languages of native Americans, Hoecken enjoyed more success as a missionary than did some of his colleagues. He assisted for two years at St. Charles Borromeo in the mid-1830s, then returned upriver to the Potawatomi missions of the Osage River and Sugar Creek, where he met and worked with Philippine Duchesne. In 1851 he contracted cholera aboard the steamboat *St. Ange* and died.

Cornelius Walters: Another Florissant recruit, Walters was assigned to St. Charles Borromeo, where he succeeded Verreydt

Henry Van Mierlo, S.J., Borromeo associate for more than twenty-five years

and Hoecken as traveling missionary. He served in this capacity two years, and died in the 1840s.

Henry Van Mierlo: As both missionary and parish priest, Van Mierlo assisted John B. Smedts and others at St. Charles Borromeo until about 1849, left for two decades, then returned for about fifteen years. He said the first Mass at the new Church of the Immaculate Conception in Augusta, and served as the last visiting Jesuit missionary to Portage des Sioux.

Peter De Smet: Though never formally assigned to St. Charles Borromeo, De Smet visited St. Charles in the early years of his priesthood to assist his fellow Jesuits. He founded the Council Bluffs Potawatomi mission in 1838 but discovered his true calling two years later when he traveled west to minister to the Flatheads and other tribes of the Rocky Mountains. So successful was De Smet in mission work that he helped negotiate with the United States on behalf of the Indians, many of whose descendants still venerate his memory.

Leonard Nota: A Jesuit from Naples, Nota arrived in St. Louis in 1841 and was promptly sent to teach at the novitiate. He was appointed Borromeo superior in February of 1845 to replace Peter Verhaegen and apparently served in this capacity until the arrival of Theodore De Theux later that year. Nota taught Latin and Greek but did not speak English well. After

having some difficulties with his superiors he was transferred to Maryland and spent his later years teaching philosophy. He died in 1870.

Theodore de Theux: Van Quickenborne's successor as superior of the Missouri Mission and master of novices, this Belgian nobleman also served the last year of his life as pastor of St. Charles Borromeo, where he died in February 1846.

John Schoenmakers: A native of Holland, Schoenmakers replaced de Theux as Borromeo pastor but left soon afterward to work among the Osage tribe in southern Kansas, where he stayed for the next thirty-six years, becoming the tribe's spiritual father and champion in dealings with the government.

Francis X. De Coen: Schoenmakers's successor as pastor at St. Charles, De Coen began his priesthood at the Sugar Creek mission in 1841, but five years later moved to the St. Louis diocese to teach and work as a parish priest. In 1861 he returned to Kansas, where he ministered to the Potawatomi until his death in 1864.

Joseph Aschwanden: Borromeo pastor during the formation of St. Peter's parish, Aschwanden was sent in 1850 to Cincinnati and two years later to Trinity Church in Washington, D.C. Shortly after the battle of Antietam, Union forces pressed Aschwanden's church into use as a hospital. He died in 1864.

Peter J. Verhaegen: Though a scholar, a missionary, and a friend of saints, Verhaegen also excelled as a small- town parish priest. For over fifteen years he successfully steered the parish, ensuring among other things that Borromeo had sufficient room to grow, but he never lost the common touch. Like many of the other Jesuits of his

Francis X. De Coen, S.J., pastor 1847-49 and 1850-51

Jesuit Missouri Province Archives

Peter Tschieder, S.J., who ran the parish from 1857 to 1858, during the absence of Father Verhaegen.

Jesuit Missouri Province Archives

time, he was buried at the Florissant novitiate.

Peter Tschieder: In the fall of 1857 Pastor Verhaegen left St. Charles to teach at St. Louis University, and Peter Tschieder was sent to Borromeo as his replacement.

Although Felix Verreydt, then a missionary to Portage des Sioux, may have served at the same time as superior of the house, Tschieder seems to have served as pastor until Verhaegen's return, in the fall of 1858.

Chapter 6
1850-69

Results of German Immigration

By the middle of the nineteenth century further expansions had become necessary. Cholera returned to the Mississippi valley in 1849 and caused Borromeo's recorded burials that year to soar. Only two decades had passed since Block 122's first interment, but two cholera epidemics and probably other outbreaks of fatal illnesses had gone a long way toward filling up the cemetery.

The parish buildings also were under increasing pressure. During these decades the stone church became too small for its large congregation, the school buildings for the parish boys and girls needed expansion or replacement, and even the rectory, which had housed the original trio of two priests and one lay brother, strained to accommodate the six Jesuits necessary to the parish in 1850. Partial relief from all of these pressures came in the form of a new parish.

Since the 1830s many German Catholics had settled in the St. Charles area, but some had grown discouraged by the unavailability of religious services in their own language. Borromeo's priests already preached and held separate liturgies in French and English; adding German services to the regular schedule was simply too much. In 1848 jeweler Louis Meyer met with other influential German immigrants in his Main Street store. The group drew up a petition asking Bishop Peter Kenrick for permission to organize a new parish, and Kenrick readily agreed. Construction began, and by 1850 a building which housed both a church and school was far enough along to be dedicated, under the protection of St. Peter the Apostle. Not long afterward, the new parish bought land just outside the city limits for a cemetery. Although many families with Germanic surnames remained Borromeo members, many others joined St. Peter's.

A more difficult problem which accompanied the German influx to the area was the spread of militant anti-Catholic sentiments, by German immigrants, as well as by Protestant settlers from the eastern United States. Foreign-born settlers, whose attitudes had been shaped in Europe, frequently confused Catholicism, and the Jesuits in particular, with international intrigue. This attitude blended with an understandable abhorrence of slavery, especially among German and Irish new-comers. In time the combination produced a volatile political movement. One anti-Catholic mouthpiece, the *St. Louis Tract Society*, regularly warned the public about the "Roman beast" and the "Popish system."

St. Louis Catholics responded by publishing the weekly *Shepherd of the Valley*. Written in part by the Jesuits, the paper gave frequent contributor Peter Verhaegen, who was then president of St. Louis University, valuable experience in countering the charges made against Catholicism by members of this movement, which later evolved into the Know-Nothing party. The matter came to a head when the party bought the *Shepherd* weekly and transformed it into the *True Shepherd of the Valley and St. Louis Know-Nothing*. Not long afterward, a riot broke out in the Irish section of St. Louis and spread to different parts of the city, including the St. Louis University neighborhood.

Comments made in *Historia Domus,* a multi-volume account of the Borromeo parish during most of its Jesuit years, reveal that Know-Nothing sentiments took hold for a time in St. Charles. One Jesuit author wrote at length on the matter in 1852 or 1853, under the heading "Points for the Annual Letters," in a manuscript now in the collection of the Jesuit Archives:

> But I must say that our congregation would be much more flourishing and pious, were [it] not for a multitude of German radicals and infidels that came to reside in St. Charles, where they established an infidel and radical association called the freemen's society, with a library and reading room for the dissemination of their principles. It is not, however, that they do harm by their learning or talents, because they have no extraordinary man among them; but they have good, strong, capacious lungs, they can talk aloud and boldly, laugh and ridicule every kind of religion, teach a doctrine apparently easier than ours, and by demoralizing people they are far more injurious than all the sophisms of Rousseau, Kant and many other[s] of the same gang.

The author then detailed the parish response:

> To check and counteract in some manner the evil effects of these missionaries of Satan, Fr. Verhaegen does not spare them from the pulpit, and if [he] cannot convert any of them, because I think they are confirmed in the highest degree of rascality, at least he prevents many from joining them. Besides as the most solid good is to be expected from the rising generation, we established a sodality of boys under the invocation of the Immaculate Conception, called the Sodality of the Children of Mary, whose constitutions are especially to practice boldly their holy Religion, to frequent the sacraments, and to avoid with the greatest care all suspicious company.

Verhaegen summed up the matter in *Historia Domus* in 1853:

> The town of St. Charles has a population approaching 2,000 souls. And for so small a town it has a large share of bigoted infidels and apostates. These people have succeeded in exciting prejudice against the Church. With such enemies we must deal prudently but strenuously. And we fight them with every weapon in our spiritual armory, so that they cannot boast of new triumphs over the Catholics. "Let God triumph, and his enemies be scattered."

In 1851 Peter Verhaegen returned to Borromeo, his favorite residence. Except for a brief interval between 1857 and 1858 when he left to resume teaching at St. Louis University, the aging priest served as pastor until his death in 1868. *Historia Domus* entries detail how Verhaegen and his several assistants divided the sometimes overwhelming duties of running the parish.

For example, in 1853 there were six Jesuits at Borromeo: Fathers Verhaegen, Charles Messea and Felix Verreydt, as well as Brothers George Miles (the gardener), Jerome Van Hutton (the cook) and Samuel O'Connell (the teacher at the boys' school). Verhaegen, "on account of his age and heaviness" could not travel out of the neighborhood to minister to the sick; most sick calls in town fell to Messea. Although some of the missionary stations once served by Borromeo's Jesuits had recently been taken over by diocesan priests, enough responsibilities remained outside St. Charles to keep Messea and Verreydt very busy. In 1853 the latter had charge of St. Francis of Assisi parish in Portage des Sioux, as well as a far-flung colony of German Catholics in Calhoun County, Illinois. Messea had charge of another station called St. Mary's, about twenty miles from town. Verhaegen served as chaplain to the nuns and students of the Sacred Heart.

In this capacity he administered the last sacraments to his dear friend, Philippine Duchesne, on the day of her death. Usually a restrained writer, Verhaegen eulogized the saintly woman at length in his burial register entry:

> On the 20th of November, 1852, I, the undersigned, buried the mortal remains of Madame Philippine Duchesne, professed religious of the Society of the Sacred Heart, aged 83 years.
>
> Madame Duchesne was a native of France, and came to the United States of America with a small number of religious of the Society of the Sacred Heart in 1818. She may be considered the foundress of all the houses of the Sacred Heart in the United States. Eminent in all virtues of religious life, but especially in humility, she sweetly and calmly departed this life in the odor of sanctity on the 18th day of November, 1852.
>
> P. J. Verhaegen, S.J.

Verhaegen buried Philippine in a cemetery on the Sacred Heart grounds. Records kept by the Society suggest that hers was the first burial on the grounds; nuns previously deceased had been buried in the old Common Cemetery of St. Charles. In 1855 Philippine's remains were exhumed and found to be intact. They were then placed in a new wooden coffin and reburied beneath the floor of an octagonal shrine, the cornerstone of which was blessed by Peter De Smet. Judocus Van Assche, then an associate at Borromeo, presided at the reburial.

Considering Philippine's devotion to the poor children of St. Charles, it is fitting that three years after her reinterment the parish built a schoolhouse close to her resting place. The two-room building was constructed of brick over a stone foundation,

On the twentieth day of November, 1852, I the undersigned buried the mortal remains of Madam Philipina Duchesne, profest Religious of the Society of the Sacred Heart, aged 83 years. Madam Du Chesne was a native of France & came to the United States of America with a small number of Ladies & sisters of the Society of the S. Heart, in 1818. She may be considered as Foundress of all the Houses of the S. Heart in the United States. Eminent in all the Virtues of a Religious life, but especially, in humility, She sweetly & calmly departed this life in the odour of Sanctity, on the 18th of Nov., 1852. R.I.P.   P. I. Verhaegen, S.J.

Verhaegen's obituary of Mother Philippine Duchesne, from the burial register

and opened directly onto Second Street in order to admit local children. An anonymous parishioner elaborated, in a letter to Jesuit historian Gilbert J. Garraghan early in the twentieth century:

> These were damp, dingy, ill-lighted rooms with windows on but two sides, the south and east. In contradistinction to the Academy, this was called the Poor school. The pupils were rigidly excluded from the grounds of the Academy, which was for day scholars and boarders and strict lines of separation were drawn between the pupils of the Poor school and the Academy.

This building served Borromeo until late in the nineteenth century. During the same year that this brick schoolhouse was built (1858), the Duquette house was at last torn down.

An archaeological dig by the University of Missouri-St. Louis in the summer of 1990 uncovered the foundation of the brick schoolhouse, estimated to measure approximately forty-five feet long by twenty-one feet wide. During the week-long excavation various common items, some of them school-related, were uncovered—an ink quill, graphite, pen nibs, bone buttons, and knitting needles. At the end of the week the site was filled in, but was marked to facilitate any future excavation. The University conducted another dig in 1991, with similar results.

Enrollment at both the boarding school and the day school increased in the 1850s. To meet this need, a wing was added on the south side of the 1835 building. This new space was used for classrooms as well as for the children's refectory and dormitory.

The 1850 Federal Census for St. Charles lists both the residents of the convent and those of the boarding school. Over a dozen choir religious and coadjutrix sisters lived

Missouri Historical Society

Above: This is the only known photograph of the 1858 parish school for girls. It is the small brick building in front of the Sacred Heart Academy and chapel. Right: UMSL students in 1990 unearth the outline of the old school. Below: After 1871 the second Borromeo rectory served as an office building for the St. Charles Car Company. It was demolished in 1910.

Jo Ann Brown

Richard L. Vinson

in the convent, and many of them came from Ireland. Most students in the 1850s and 1860s still hailed from Missouri, but a small group came from the West. The records kept by the school reveal the interesting origins or family connections of some. "Maria Culverson," for example, was probably Marie Culbertson, daughter of mountain man Alexander Culbertson and his Sioux wife. Sisters Josephine and Marie Champagne were Blackfeet Indians. Another pair of sisters, Helen and Frances Younger of Liberty, Missouri, were first cousins of the future James gang outlaw, Coleman Younger.

St. Charles surnames occur sporadically throughout the boarding school account book. Mary Dorlaque attended between 1854 and 1857. Florida McElhiney entered in 1856. In all probability Laura Krekel attended classes with the daughters of slave-owners, who may well have objected had they been able to foresee that a few years later Laura's father, Arnold Krekel, would command Union forces in Missouri, lead his battalion in several skirmishes, and offer asylum to runaway slaves.

James Bridger and St. Charles

One of the West's most famous mountain men, James Bridger, sent at least two of his children to St. Charles for a Catholic education in the early 1850s. Bridger was then a sort of folk hero, having guided numerous western expeditions, and was probably the first white to see the Great Salt Lake. He was also a friend and admirer of Peter De Smet.

Bridger's first two wives had died young, leaving him with at least four children to raise. In 1850 he married for a third time, to a Shoshoni woman who had several children of her own. Not long afterward, Bridger asked Father De Smet to oversee the education of a son named Francis Felix and a daughter named Elizabeth. The boy, then about eight years old, was enrolled in the Borromeo school for boys and lived in the Barada household. His seven-year old sister attended the Sacred Heart boarding school. In 1853, De Smet wrote Bridger of the two: "Felix frequents our school and is making progress. His sister lives in the Academy and under the immediate care of the Ladies of that well-conducted establishment, who have every regard for her that good Mothers could have for their own children. Both have been somewhat sickly during the winter, but are now doing well."

Other Bridger children apparently spent time in St. Charles. A "half-breed Indian girl, aged about 7 years" was baptized Mary Josephine Bridger by Pastor Verhaegen in 1853. In 1854, Father De Smet baptized four year-old John Bridger and six year-old Virginia Bridger. A letter from De Smet to Verhaegen that March suggests that Bridger planned to return to the mountains with Francis Felix and Elizabeth. Whether he did is not clear, but Borromeo's burial records prove that four year-old John Bridger never returned: Father Van Assche buried him in Borromeo's cemetery in August of 1854. Mary Josephine may also have stayed, because she joined John in the parish cemetery in September of 1857.

The Rectory and Boys' School

Borromeo's boys also moved to a new school building during the 1850s. For over twenty years Jesuit brothers had taught classes in a wooden building erected on Block 6 from material salvaged from the log church. In 1851, just after the Jesuits acquired title from the city of St. Charles to the northernmost strip of the block, they built on it a brick structure of two stories. Here the boys' school building remained until long after the industrial development of the area forced the parish to move classes up the hill to Third Street.

Just before this construction, however, the two-story frame rectory on the same block was replaced with another two-story house made of brick, built over a basement and capped with a mansard roof. From the back porch a wide view of the countryside opened to the north and south, and of the nearby river to the east. Once again the Jesuits set about landscaping the surroundings, planting hedges and gardening. By now they owned all of Block 6, but their enjoyment of the property did not last long.

Within a few years a flood washed away a considerable portion of the eastern section of the square. Why the Jesuits in the 1850s invested so much money and effort in Block 6 is not clear; within their recent memory (1844) the Missouri River had risen to a level unmatched by later floods until 1951. In any event, the parish continued using what was left of the block, but soon faced a new problem in the guise of the North Missouri Railroad. Father Verhaegen complained:

Another nuisance is caused by the proximity of the railroad, which runs along the street in front of our house. The puffing and smoke of the freight engines coming and going and backing up and the creaking noise of the cars day and night disturb our rest; and we fear a depreciation in the value of our property. In equity, compensation is due for damages; but though we hope for justice, no steps towards it have been taken.

Verhaegen did not remain passive for long. Within a few years the situation had become so obnoxious that he brought suit for damages against the railroad, retaining the local law firm of Alexander and Lackland. In the meantime, the railroad tried repeatedly to eject the Jesuits. At last Verhaegen deemed it wiser to negotiate than to continue resisting, and so he accepted a settlement of $17,000 for the entire block:

In the beginning the site of our residence was very pleasant. But for the last 8 years, owing to the offices and shops built in the neighborhood, the thick volumes of smoke belch forth from the chimneys and the noise of the shops and continual racket of the cars, night & day, made life disagreeable. Besides, the danger of fire from sparks of passing engines falling on our frame buildings gave us constant alarm. And to go [to] the church, we had to walk some distance up the hill. Hence a change of residence became desirable.

Verhaegen took the settlement and through St. Louis University (a corporation

The second rectory (1) and brick school for boys (2), circa 1887. Note railroad facilities in front of rectory.

then owned by the Jesuits) bought near the corner of Third and Franklin Streets the northern half of Block 96, which included:

a spacious House, a garden and other buildings. The site of our new Pastoral Residence combines health with beauty, and it is only 200 yards from the church. The front is embellished with a double porch, and from the higher one the view extends for 5 miles over the fields and the river; and even the woods on the left bank of the Mississippi River appear on the horizon. Considering that we were forced to sell to the railroad, it is certain we are gaining in the change, since our new residence is in every respect superior.

At about the same time, the Jesuits bought the tract just to the west of this property. Along with this land came a large frame house fronting on Fourth Street. For some reason, the Jesuits called this building the "Texas" house.

During the summer of 1864, Verhaegen purchased (again, through St. Louis University) land on the opposite side of Third Street between Decatur and Franklin for the boys' school. In roughly the center of the tract (the western section of Block 63) the parish built a brick schoolhouse of three rooms, and used the remaining land for a playground. Later this building was sold to the city and reopened as the Franklin School.

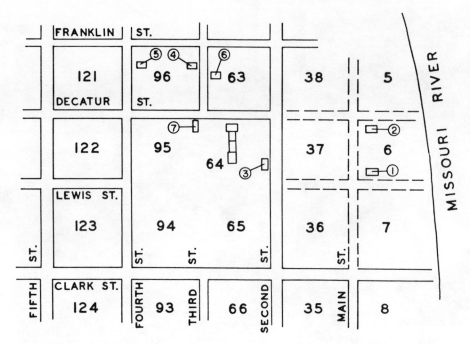

"BORROMEO BUILDINGS" EAST OF FOURTH STREET FROM 1850 TO 1892.

Legend

1. Brick rectory completed circa 1850.
2. Brick school for boys built in 1851.
3. The parish school for girls 1858 to the 1890s.
4. Two-story brick building used as a rectory from 1863 to circa 1873.
5. "Texas House," possibly used as a rental property.
6. Brick school for the parish boys from 1864 to 1870. Later known as the Franklin School.
7. Two-story brick school built in 1892 for the parish girls, although it was never used as such.

Map of parish building east of Fourth Street   Dave M. Arnold

The third pastoral residence, now 723 North Third Street.

Gene Buehrle

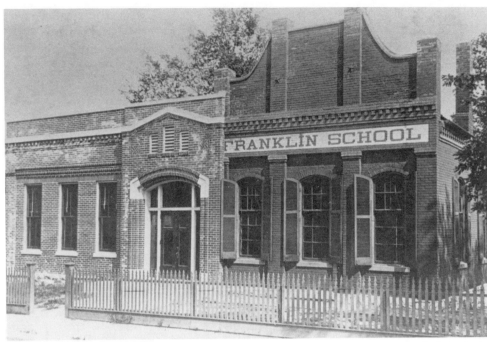

Franklin School, originally Borromeo's school for boys (on right).

Richard L. Vinson

Borromeo's Rural Cemetery

Unfortunately, Father Verhaegen's legacy of buildings did not last long. All traces of his residence and schools on Block 6 were eventually buried under the American Car and Foundry. The stone church that he labored so hard to build was torn down shortly after his death. Later occupants of the buildings he purchased or built on Blocks 96 and 63 greatly modified the original structures. Though not a building, his only contribution in the nature of real estate that remains more or less intact is the present cemetery on Randolph Street.

In 1853 Father Verhaegen bought, in his own name, eleven acres along a road that led out of town to the Marais Croche. The next year he deeded the land to St. Louis University to ensure perpetual use for the parish. Sellers Sir Walter and Margarite Rice warranted the title to this land back to a Spanish land grant made in the previous century to Antoine Janis. In purchasing this large rural tract for a burying ground, Ver-

haegen was not only making possible the future development of the present parish block; he was following a popular trend of that era in favor of rural cemeteries.

Bellefontaine Cemetery was the first true rural cemetery in the St. Louis area, being founded in 1849. Based on a concept originating with Boston's Mount Auburn Cemetery, the rural cemetery was an attractive alternative to the crowded, depressing churchyard, and was located far from the noise and grittiness of the city. These cemeteries were more than mere graveyards; they were carefully designed and landscaped pleasure grounds, with natural plantings and paths wide enough to admit a carriage out for a Sunday drive. They soon became popular as picnic spots as well as tourist attractions. By the Civil War nearly every large American city had one. In time, the success of the rural cemetery movement inspired another movement toward the conservation of rural lands as public parks.

Within a year of the purchase, the sale of family lots had generated enough revenue to repay Father Verhaegen the entire purchase price of $350. The parish records have little else to say about the cemetery, except that a sexton lived in a house on the acreage. Various burial records during this period contribute little beyond the bare recitals of interments, but they do suggest that occasionally Protestants were buried in the cemetery. Causes of death were not routinely noted until the 1870s, but sometimes the priests added a few comments of their own. Following the November 10, 1855, burial of thirty year-old Emilian Yosti, for example, Verhaegen noted that the death had been caused by "the breaking of the bridge over the Gasconade River, on the Pacific Railroad. . . ." The previous February Father Van Assche felt it necessary to record the alias of deceased Michael Concannon: "he deserted from the American Army and was since called Michael Coyne."

No entry from 1853 or later gives a clue as to when the Randolph Street cemetery was inaugurated, but tradition holds that it received its first burial in 1854. Whether the parish attempted to move all graves from the Block 122 graveyard is simply not provable. In 1915 workmen digging the foundation of the present church brought up a bushel basket full of human bones and various tombstones dated 1820 and thereabouts. One such tombstone bore the name Schmidt and the date of death of 1834. Clearly all graves on the site were not moved, just as all graves were not moved from the Block 28 cemetery. It seems likely that surviving relatives moved some loved ones to the present cemetery, as a few markers there indicate deaths occurring before 1854. The parish records are silent as to what happened to unclaimed graves.

The "Mystery" of Rebecca Younger

One of the oldest tombstones in the Randolph Street cemetery reads: "In memory of my beloved wife Rebecca Younger, wife of Coleman Younger, of Liberty, Missouri. Born March 20, 1826. Died at Memphis, November 28, 1850." Over the years, this Rebecca has been fancifully described as the wife of the outlaw Coleman Younger, as well as the sister of Frank and Jesse James.

In reality, she was born in Liberty as Rebecca Smith. Her husband, Coleman Purcell Younger, was the uncle and namesake of the outlaw, as well as a native of St. Charles. After his first wife died, leaving him with four children (two of whom attended the Sacred Heart boarding school in 1850), he married Rebecca. The couple lived in Liberty. In 1847 she bore him a son but died three years later, allegedly from another childbirth. In 1851, Coleman married for a third time and later moved to California, where he became a wealthy cattleman.

Despite the cemetery marker, the "mystery" of Rebecca Younger is where she is buried. By 1850, the Jesuits at Borromeo had been keeping careful burial records for over a decade, but there is no entry in the parish archives for her burial or for the placing of her tombstone. It is not known whether her remains, or at least her tombstone, started out at the older cemetery on Block 122, which was probably used up until Verhaegen's 1853 purchase of the Randolph Street property. The archdiocese, which administers the present cemetery, has no evidence that she was buried here.

According to a tradition in Liberty, a wife and child of Coleman Purcell Younger were buried together on the family farm around 1850. If this is true, that wife and child may well have been Rebecca and her infant. Even so, it is still not clear why the Protestant Younger would see fit to memorialize his second wife, a Protestant with little direct connection to St. Charles, with a marker in the Borromeo cemetery.

Historia Domus

In the early 1850s priests from the St. Louis Archdiocese took over some of the mission stations served previously by Borromeo's clergy. The demand for priests from far-flung Catholics, however, did not diminish. Many times during the day and night urgent sick calls came in, often from Irish immigrants. One of the writers of *Historia Domus* praised the faith of these newest Catholics to the area:

> A railroad was under construction which was to lead from St. Louis to Hannibal, a town on the Mississippi River, there to connect with a road leading to St. Joseph. Many Irish laborers were employed on this work; and exposed as they were to the hot sun, lodging in miserable huts and destitute of wholesome food, the cholera broke out among them. In consequence, the Fathers of this House were called on, day and night, to attend the dying. These navvies [unskilled laborers], whose work takes them from place to place with the rare opportunity of hearing Mass, are usually negligent in their religious duties, although they hold on to the faith. Many of these Catholics in the pains of the cholera longed to confess to a priest; and when he came they were overjoyed to receive the Sacraments of the Church, [of] which they had been deprived for ten or as long as 15 years. To afford them the opportunity of being reconciled to God, one of the Fathers used to go of evenings to one of the big tents in the vicinity of the crowd of laborers, and used to hear confessions all hours of the night & often into the morning; then he would say Mass and administer Holy Communion. As the progress of the railroad took them far beyond St. Charles, they still would send for the priest; and they were seldom refused. In this way many were brought back to their religious duties; and, what was more consoling, some of them who were married, settled their home in St. Charles, where they are now leading Christian lives among our parishioners.

The same Jesuit Archives manuscript that details the Know-Nothing movement in St. Charles recounts a memorable visit by Father Messea to another group of Irish Catholics:

> F. Messea in one of his excursions twenty miles far from St. Charles found about fifty Irish Catholics that for some years never had a chance to see a priest. F. Messea went there to see an old Irish woman nearly seventy years of age for whom he was called in a great

Tombstone of Rebecca Younger

Jo Ann Brown

hurry because they thought she would soon die. But I think the poor creature was more frightened lest she should die without seeing a priest than really sick; in fact about three quarters of an hour after having received the sacraments with that devotion which is peculiar to the Irish people, she got up from her bed to go at the door of the room to meet the Father, and thank his Reverence and shortly after she could smoke her pipe.

Afterward Messea paid regular visits to this colony. When an old man among them died, Father Verhaegen was so impressed that the dead man's children brought the corpse to St. Charles Borromeo for burial in the cemetery that he wrote, "Indeed these poor people will rise on the last judgment against so many who neglect their religion near a church having the opportunity of practicing it."

Sometimes Catholics were able to attend missions, special revival-like services that usually led up to certain feast days. To celebrate the canonization of the Japanese Martyrs, a mission of eight days was held in St. Charles, and a triduum (lasting three days) was held in Portage des Sioux. According to *Historia Domus,* the triduum "brought 200 to Holy Communion, among them some backsliders of 7 to 10 years. In the miserable condition of the country roads, it was edifying to see the farmers coming from a distance, and where the horses broke down, they walked the rest of

the way." Results were no less noteworthy in St. Charles:

A lady living with an infidel husband got prejudiced against Catholics and had apostatized, so much so that she had her daughter grown up unbaptized and on the point of becoming a presbyterian. This inclination of the daughter made her mother reflect about joining some church. And she began to visit Protestant churches, but was not satisfied with their preaching. She came back to the Catholic church, and was under instruction for 4 months, when the mission came on, and she was finally converted and found peace with God. She told her happiness to her daughter, who also came for instruction and was baptized. And these 2 ladies continue to attend the services of the church with edification to all.

Conversions occurred with some frequency during this period. Statistical reports sent annually to the bishop show an average of about five conversions per year in the 1840s. Verhaegen estimated that about ten per year occurred in the 1850s.

In the 1860s, the parish instituted a free lending-library, for the purpose of "spreading good books among non- Catholics and for guarding Catholics against bad books," a reference perhaps to the German radicals' library. Within a few years, the parish collection contained over a thousand volumes.

The Civil War Years

Although Pastor Verhaegen was old and in poor health by the early 1860s he continued ministering to the parish when able, and occasionally wrote in the registers in his small, meticulous hand. His treatment

of the War between the States is brief but impassioned:

The Civil War, which began in 1861 and raged in the State of Missouri nearly all that year, thanks be to God! did not disturb St. Charles with the strife of battle and destruction of property; nevertheless, its blighting effects have been felt by all, the rich as well as the poor man. And we still feel the hard times. It is a Scourge of God. May it soon stop! and may sweet Peace, so dearly bought and so earnestly longed for, be restored to us!

Because Missouri was not one of the rebellious states at the start of the war, the Emancipation Proclamation did not apply within its boundaries, and slavery was legal until 1865. This heated relations between residents of Missouri and those of its neighboring states. Although most Missourians favored neutrality, a powerful group of farmers from along the Missouri River agitated for states' rights and won the support of Missouri's militia. In St. Louis, a large coalition representing the city's railroads, industries, and immigrant workers favored the Union.

During most of the war, Unionist forces (which were made up of many non-Missourians) controlled St. Louis and guarded railroad lines through outlying towns like St. Charles. The Confederacy, which became more popular after the Unionist forces arrived, engaged in scattered guerilla actions but never managed to establish a permanent base in Missouri.

St. Charles was a microcosm of the divisions in the state. As a Missouri River town it had plenty of contact with the pro-Southern growers upstream. It also had its own extensive history of slavery, as well as many family connections with the southern states of Kentucky, Tennessee, and Virginia. On the other hand, for the previous three decades the town had been populated with many Germans, and recently had become an important railhead. Both Union and Confederate forces attracted a large number of sympathizers from St. Charles, and these sympathies usually split along ethnic lines.

Young men from both factions tended to join local para-military organizations. For the Union, Captain Henry B. Denker commanded dozens of St. Charles men with Germanic surnames, including the following from the Borromeo records: Becker, Schreiber, Thro, Weber, and Elmendorf. For the Confederacy, Dr. C.M. Johnson of St. Charles commanded many local men in a battle at Mount Zion, Missouri, among them: William Dugan, Daniel and Wesley Dyer, and Warner Briscoe. Perhaps the most famous St. Charlesan involved in the war was Arnold Krekel, whose various pro-Union fighters were the scourge of Confederate forces in the area and in outstate Missouri as well.

With so much military preparation on both sides, hostilities often spilled over onto the local people. From Cottleville in 1861, D. K. Pittman urged the provisional governor to disarm the Union Home Guards, who "seem to go at will about the village, drinking and insulting with pleasure all that cross their path." Whether Krekel's forces in St. Charles caused the same objections is not known, but over the years the war engendered so much fear and suspicion that it led to sporadic acts of violence around St. Charles.

How members of St. Charles Borromeo responded to these acts of violence is not known, but some of them continued owning slaves until the end of the Civil War. On October 12, 1863, Father Messea baptized an adult woman named Mary Judith who belonged to Mr. Cribbin. That same week, a daughter of Mr. Powell's Adeline received baptism, with a slave of Mr. Yosti serving as godmother. Apparently Mr. Yosti retained his slaves right up to the January 11, 1865, emancipation act passed by the pro-Union state government: just three days earlier, a black man named Jack Lincoln married "Ann, a servant of Mr. Yosti's," presumably at the stone church.

Peter Verhaegen survived the Civil War by three years. After his death on July 21, 1868, he was eulogized with a lengthy entry in the burial register:

> The Reverend Peter J. Verhaegen was born in Belgium June 1, 1800 and came to White Marsh, Maryland in 1821, and to St. Louis in 1823 in one of the little bands of Jesuit missionaries whom the venerable Bishop Dubourg had succeeded in obtaining for his diocese. Shortly after his ordination when he had completed a church in St. Charles he was appointed (the first) Resident of St. Louis University (1829) and Superior of the Western Missions (1836-1843); he was next appointed Vicar General of St. Louis. He was also appointed to govern the Jesuits of Maryland, and after that he became (the first) President of St. Joseph's College of Bardstown, Kentucky in 1848. The last years of his life (1851-1868) were spent at St. Charles, Missouri (the place he seemed to love most dearly) where he labored with great zeal for the people committed to his charge.
>
> Father Verhaegen was a man of superior mind, of profound knowledge and of a most genial manner. He was the friend of all who knew him, was cheerful and had a kind word for all who came near him. During a long career of usefulness in high positions which he successfully filled, as Rector of Colleges, as Superior of the Missions, as Provincial of 2 provinces of his Order, as Administrator of the Diocese of St. Louis, he gained, what he did not seek, a great name and extreme popularity;

Peter J. Verhaegen, S.J.

Jesuit Missouri Province Archives

and he promoted, what was the sole object of his ambition, the good of religion & education, and the Greater Glory of God. His remains were taken to Florissant at the Novitiate for interment, and were accompanied by many of his weeping parishioners.

From start to finish, the era of the stone church was the era of Peter Verhaegen. Without him, the log church might never have been replaced, and the school for boys might not have prospered as it did on Block 6, and later on Block 63. The educational efforts of the Ladies of the Sacred Heart might well have suffered without Verhaegen's staunch support. The Block 122 cemetery would have continued filling up, leaving the parish no room to expand at its present site. Without Verhaegen, it is difficult to imagine the Jesuits establishing a strong or lasting foundation in St. Charles.

Part 3
The Brick Church Era

Chapter 7
1869-85

Building the Brick Church

Late in the pastorate of Peter Verhaegen several improvements were made to the stone church. A low tower was added to the front of the structure, and the roof of wooden laths was restored. Inside, the church's windows were veiled with curtains and the organ was overhauled.

These improvements only delayed the inevitable. The stone church was simply too small for its congregation, and had been since great waves of foreign immigrants had settled in the St. Charles area. The creation of St. Peter's parish had merely slowed Borromeo's growth. In addition, by 1869 there was little empty ground left around the stone church, which had stood nearly alone when built in the 1820s. Shortly after Verhaegen's death, the parish began preparing to move liturgical services up the hill to Block 122, part of which had once served as the parish cemetery.

Who made this decision to move is not clear from the parish records, but it is very likely that Father John Roes, who had been stationed at Borromeo since 1867 and had succeeded Peter Verhaegen as pastor, was the driving force. Although the parish lacked comprehensive funding for the con-

struction of a new, larger church, on May 9, 1869, Archbishop Kenrick laid the cornerstone for a new structure.

This cornerstone would be little more than a footnote had the brick church not been destroyed by a windstorm in 1915. During the demolition of the remaining building the cornerstone was discovered and opened, revealing a tin box that contained: one ten-cent currency paper dated March of 1863; one five-cent nickel from 1868, one three-cent nickel from 1865, one two-cent copper from 1865, two one-cent pieces, one from 1845 and the other from 1855; a copy of the *Western Watchman* of May 8, 1869, which contained an invitation to the laying of the cornerstone on the next day; a copy of the *Missouri Republican* of May 8, 1869; a copy of the local *Cosmos and Sentinel* of May 6, 1869; an explanatory note written in Latin; and a long list of subscribers and contributors to the construction project.

No fewer than nineteen levels of contributions were listed, ranging between five hundred dollars and two dollars. Heading the list were Henry Beck, Henry Beckman, Clement Boyse, Lawrence Cribben, Francis

The unfinished brick church, circa 1871. Four large clock faces were added in 1893.

Richard L. Vinson

Dorlaque, St. Louis University, and Francis Yosti, all of whom contributed $500. In the $250 category were Laurent Beck, Charles Hug, Jane Kirkpatrick, William Kirkpatrick, William Schaefer, and Emily Vick. John Hilbert, Edward Kelleher, and Henry Kemper put forth $150, and over twenty parishioners contributed $100. The five dollar and ten dollar categories were the largest, comprising an interesting cross-section of the parish membership.

Contributions continued trickling in, so that by the end of 1870 the brick church was roofed in. Funding then slowed for a while, and so did construction. An entry in *Historia Domus* states for 1871: "This year the church tower is nearly built up; but for want of money, the church remains in the same state, because superiors have decided it is better to delay work on it than to be loaded with a debt."

The following year the still-incomplete structure was consecrated. On October 13, 1872, the archbishop's coadjutor, Patrick J. Ryan, dedicated the church under the protection of St. Charles Borromeo. Visiting

Jesuit John de Blieck preached in English, and Peter Tschieder (who had replaced Father Verhaegen at Borromeo from 1857 to 1858) preached in German. Singing the High Mass was Judocus Van Assche, former pastor and one of the last of the original Belgian Jesuits.

The brick church closely resembled three St. Charles churches standing today which were also designed in the 1860s by John Henry Stumberg—St. Peter's, Immanuel Lutheran, and St. John United Church of Christ. At least one of the builders of the brick church, Henry Kister, had worked on some of the other Stumberg structures. Like many other St. Charlesans of the time, Kister was an immigrant from Alsace. After working his way across the United States, he settled in St. Charles, where he took part in many large construction projects in the late 1800s, as well as in civic affairs.

Stumberg had designed the new church on a scale that must have seemed immense to Borromeo's parishioners: measuring 145 by 66 feet, the structure covered nearly three times the area covered by the stone

For many years this portrait of St. Charles Borromeo was a focal decoration of the brick church.

church. When the steeple was at last added, the building towered over others in the vicinity.

The elderly Borromeo parishioner who detailed his recollections of the parish and its buildings for Jesuit historian Gilbert Garraghan wrote that various properties (on Blocks 15, 28, and 96) were still owned by the parish when the brick church was built. "In consideration of the fact that these properties, when sold, would yield more than sufficient to defray the church debt, the Bishop was induced to consecrate the Church." Accordingly, the parish sold a great deal of "the ground previously owned by the Spanish King" in 1873.

A sizeable debt still remained on the brick church, perhaps in part because the Ladies of the Sacred Heart were unable to purchase the stone church, which they had been using as a chapel. Later they paid

$2,000 for the building's site, and built upon it their own convent chapel made of brick. This structure still stands, but is now connected to other parts of the complex.

The parish had the old church demolished but saved the stones, timbers, and other materials for use in a new rectory. After the demolition, the relics of St. Dieudonne were discovered under the main altar, and were temporarily held by the Religious of the Sacred Heart until the brick church was far enough along to house them. At last, on August 10, 1873, the relics were ceremoniously placed under the main altar of the new church.

Many furnishings from the old church were transferred to the new building, including the organ, pulpit, a side altar, statues, and the stations of the cross. The main altar from the stone church found a home in the basement chapel beneath the brick church.

One new decoration to grace the brick church was a life-size copy of an original oil painting in Milan, depicting Charles Borromeo. This copy had been made-to-order at the request of the family of John Roes. Before it arrived in St. Charles, it was displayed in New York and then in St. Louis. For around twenty years it hung over the brick church's main altar. Afterward it was moved to the basement chapel of the church, then to a storeroom of the coal cellar. Later it was kept behind a door in the Jesuit's rectory on Block 122. After being discarded in 1963, it was salvaged by Edna McElhiney Olson, who donated it to the St. Charles County Historical Society. The painting was later displayed in city hall.

Work on the church's interior progressed over the winter of 1872-1873, so that the building was ready for services in the spring. On March 30, 1873, the brick church was at last opened to the people "by the exercises of a mission, which was preached by two of our Fathers, morning & evening with great success."

The New Rectory and School

During the construction of the church, the parish embarked upon two other major building projects on Block 122. On July 31, 1873, the feast day of St. Ignatius Loyola (founder of the Jesuit order), the cornerstone for a large brick residence was laid near the corner of Fourth and Lewis streets. An entry in *Historia Domus* from about the same time explains that the Jesuits desired to have a new residence next to the church because of the unpleasantness in walking through snow and rain from the rectory on Third Street.

Father Roes envisioned the new rectory as more than just a residence for Borromeo's priests and brothers; he wanted a building large enough to accommodate visiting missionaries, writers, and administrative officers of the Jesuits' Missouri province. The stones from the old church made a high foundation upon which two stories of brick were laid. It seems that Roes had wanted a building with three brick stories and had ordered a great deal of millwork for the third floor, but only two brick stories were completed above the foundation. Accordingly, fifteen window frames, sashes, shutters, and door frames, all made-to-order for the third story, were never used in the rectory. After being stored many years in the church's steeple, they were used in the 1890s in the construction of a new convent at the corner of Decatur and Fifth streets.

The unsigned letter to Father Garraghan suggests that Father Roes halted construction of the rectory before the third floor, perhaps because of the controversy created by the size of the building:

> Seeing such a substantial residence, one individual who never contributed anything to the church or priest[s] and moreover had neglected his religious duties for many years asked Father Roes if the parish was expected to provide for a community of eight or ten priests. Such a question was resented by the entire congregation. Father Roes explained that the parish was expected to furnish the usual salary for the pastor and one assistant. While the pastor was at perfect liberty to invite as many priests to come and live with him as he desired even to the extent of keeping a small seminary. As he would defray all such expenses from his own salary, it was a matter which did not in any way concern the congregation.
>
> Father Roes in disgust stopped the building of the residence but erected a stable and built several out houses, leveled and beautified and also enclosed the grounds with a fence.

Even without a third brick story the residence was ample, and over the years provided lodging and hospitality to a constant stream of visitors. When it was completed, one of its occupants described it in *Historia Domus:* "Our new house cost $8500. It stands 70 ft. by 48 ft. front . . . and it commands a wide view of the city and the river, the grounds of the Madames [of the Sacred Heart] across 4th St.—and the American Car Works with their smoke stacks rising on Main St. in the background."

In 1875, shortly after the Jesuits had moved in, the coadjutor brothers cleared a large tract of land for a garden measuring 125 feet long by 100 feet wide, between the new rectory and the church. They soon made an unwelcome discovery. The writer of *Historia Domus* elaborated:

> This year also (1875) the coadjutor brothers planted a garden near the house and church. Since twenty years ago this ground was possibly still a burial place, and the bodies buried there may have only partly been moved to the new cemetery and may have partly returned to dust; however many bones are still found are deposited under the church.

In 1870, the parish sold the three-room school building on Franklin Street to the city of St. Charles for $3,500. The building was later used for many years for "Negro education." Father Roes used the proceeds from the sale to construct a new brick school behind the church. This structure, costing a total of $4,000, was much larger than the old one on Franklin Street, according to *Historia Domus*:

Richard L. Vinson

The fourth pastoral residence stood at the corner of Fourth and Lewis. The brick church is to the far right.

Below: Several blank report cards from the 1870s remain from the boys' school.

A. M. D. G.

SAINT CHARLES CATHOLIC DAY SCHOOL,
FOR BOYS.
ON FIFTH STREET, BETWEEN DECATUR AND LEWIS STREETS.

MONTHLY REPORT,

Showing the attendance, deportment and progress in Studies of Master .... during school month ending 187

N. B. The standard of perfection in attendance, deportment and scholarship, is one hundred merits. Hence, parents may estimate the progress and deportment of their children by their approximation to one hundred in each department.

Parents should see that their children bring home their books and prepare lessons for next day.

Number of half days absent
Number of times tardy
Attendance (expressed in per cent.)
Deportment.
Scholarship
Average standing.

Teacher.

Parents or Guardians will please sign this slip and return it to the teacher.

Parent or Guardian.

To this school we added a second story, to afford a hall for school exhibitions, and to give a reading room and place of meeting for members of the Library Association and for the young men who spend evenings at saloons and theatres, because they have no better place or higher amusement.

This second story was financed by members of the parish, especially William Kirkpatrick, Joseph Maher, Bernard Rauch, and Clem Boyse. Known as the St. Charles Borromeo Library and Hall, it served the parish for many years.

Classes were held in rooms on the first story of the new school building. *Historia Domus* suggests that for several years there were not many students:

Many parents are careless in sending children to school, and some use the Public Schools because they are free of tuition. We hired a second schoolmaster for 2 years; but the number of boys did not justify the expense, which was beyond our means; so now we get along with one teacher who is a Brother of the Society.

For a year or two in the mid-1870s, an unnamed "Catholic lady" managed the school, probably because the parish temporarily lacked a teaching Jesuit brother.

Parish Records

Borromeo's priests methodically recorded baptisms, marriages, and burials throughout the era of the brick church, but they did not always make frequent comments in *Historia Domus,* especially during the 1870s and 1880s. For this reason it is difficult to appreciate the human dimension of parish life or the personalities of the people involved.

Father Roes is one of the few priests who revealed a little of his personality in the records. In 1867 he began writing detailed entries in a new and large burial register, the pages of which were divided under the following headings: Date, Name of Person Interred, Age, Disease, Cemetery, Priest, Remarks. For several years Roes performed a majority of the parish burials, and sometimes filled the Remarks column with interesting information and comments.

A large number of these remarks reflect on Roes as well as on the religious sentiments of the day: "W. [a young man who died of consumption] died a very edifying death, he was sick over 8 months & bore his sickness with great patience." "Her mother [of a young girl] took her last year from the parish school to the public school. God has, I am afraid, rewarded her.

. . . "; "He [an old man from the parish] was a negligent Christian, died as he lived, without the sacraments." "Hers was a sad one. She [a young mother] leaves a natural child by a man . . . and 4 orphans. She offered her life to God as a punishment for her folly"; and "He [a toddler who died of spotted fever] was partially paralyzed; happy for him to have gone to heaven."

Roes was also the first priest who routinely recorded causes of death. He noted the following killers with some frequency: pneumonia, measles, lockjaw, meningitis, old age, paralysis, croup, premature birth, dropsy, pleurisy, typhoid, cholera, dysentery, flux, malaria, childbirth, and consumption. In addition, he carefully recorded the age of the deceased and the cemetery of burial—nearly always Borromeo's, although a few of the deceased were buried elsewhere. Following the convention of the day, sometimes those who lived less than pious lives and died unrepentant were not accorded Catholic burials.

Certain descriptive notes made by Roes and others on the first pages of the large burial register refer to the deceased's involvement in the parish, as well as resi-

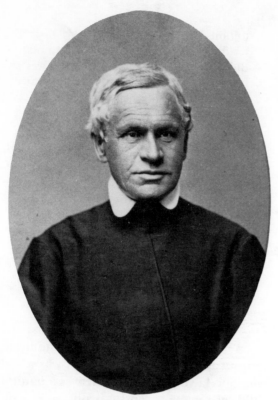

John Roes, pastor 1868-79

dence and type of funeral: "convert," "sodalist," "not brought to church," "died in the poorhouse [or the insane asylum]," "simple service," "High Mass," and "not buried from the church."

In 1870 Roes listed a schedule of the various costs of funerals and burials. Starting with the most expensive service, a "First Class Funeral with Mass and the altar draped in mourning," (which included a "solemn High Mass with Deacon and Subdeacon and the Priest accompanying body to the graveyard in Cope with acolytes"), for $25, the schedule descends in ceremony and cost to a "Second Class Funeral for Children," for two dollars. Though higher and more detailed, these rates correspond somewhat to those of the Tariff of Havana from the previous century.

Catholic weddings occurred with frequency during the brick-church era, and Borromeo's priests recorded them by means of simple recitations in the marriage registers. Most entries lack the signatures of the bridal couples; probably most priests did not even request them. When they did, however, most couples signed, but a few still could not: the cross-shaped mark occasionally substituted for a signature, especially among those with French names, until the late 1800s.

The baptism register best reflects the demographic make-up of the parish (and the town). African ancestry, then noted as "colored," was still marked in the book's margins. The only other group so noted were converts. Most parishioners were of German, French, English, or Irish ancestry. A page from 1869 typifies this ethnic mix with the following list of surnames: Kemper, Edelen, Bryers, Plough, Brown, Thro, Graham, Fulkerson, Woods, Harraghan, Laughlin, Conly, Tebaut, Pallardie, Dorlacque, Bordeau, Berthe, McAuliff, and Walsh.

A brief financial abstract from the year July 1, 1876 to July 1, 1877, now on file in the Jesuit Archives of St. Louis, shows that pew rentals, ordinary and special collections, and ceremonial fees provided a large part of the parish revenues for these years. Beyond the ordinary expenses of living and running the parish were one-time expenses for plastering an unnamed building, as well as for buying a side altar and a statue of St. Joseph.

Historia Domus

For some reason Father Roes and the parish's other priests did not write much in *Historia Domus* for over a decade after the death of Peter Verhaegen. Between 1882 and 1886, however, regular additions were again made to the journal. The first of these entries were written entirely in Latin, but English phrases and usage gradually crept in. By 1886, the language of *Historia Domus* was English. Highlights from these pages include:

Summer, 1882: Victor Van der Putten succeeds Joseph Zealand as pastor. A Jesuit named P. A. Lambert gives a lecture in the church on spirituality, to benefit the Library Association. The cost of admission was .50, and the parish netted $91.75.

Fall, 1882: Father Van der Putten becomes sick. Dr. Johnson, later assisted by Dr. Mudd, diagnoses typhoid fever, which lingers over a month. A Jesuit named Matthew Smith comes from the novitiate to help, then an Alexian named Brother Pius. Father Van der Putten receives the last sacraments but later recovers. Brother Pius leaves.

Winter 1882-1883: Students from the Sacred Heart Academy give an "entertainment" in the school hall. Many attend; the admission of .25 yields $50, part of which is paid to the parish Library Association. At last Father Van der Putten is well enough to say Mass. Father Adrian Hoecken [brother of Christian Hoecken and formerly a missionary to native Americans as well as to black residents of Cincinnati] begins instructions for First Communion.

Spring 1883: Officials of the Library As-sociation are elected: William Kirkpatrick, P. Dolan, J. Holmes, and M. Cleary. During Holy Week the church is dusted and a visiting Jesuit gives a sermon on the Passion to a large crowd. Confirmation instructions and Marian devotions begin. A drama called "The Good-natured Man" is given by young people in the school hall.

Summer 1883: Sixteen Sacred Heart boarders, three from this parish, are confirmed. A procession in honor of the Sacred Heart is held, S. Garneau is Grand Marshall, assisted by L. Brucker, John Mittelberger, and W. Kirkpatrick. Others processing include acolytes, members of the Men's and Women's Sodalities, and children carrying flowers, lanterns, and banners. A "school pic-nic" is held in Reed's Grove, where "soda-water" is sold for .05 per bottle. Later, a strawberry festival is held at Mittelberger's Opera House.

Fall 1883: A Requiem Mass is sung for former pastor John Roes. Two new sodalities are begun, one for boys and the other for girls, and each soon has nineteen members. An oyster supper is given at Mittelberger's Opera House for the benefit of the church, but poor weather keeps the attendance slim, and the parish nets only $139.15. The author of the *Historia Domus* entry noted, "Dances after[ward] till 2 A.M.: only square dancing. Nothing objectionable."

Winter 1883-1884: As is the custom, the parish celebrates Christmas around December 28, distributing $14 worth of candies, also religious pictures and objects, to the altar boys and choir girls.

The parish schoolchildren, assisted by day students from the Academy and adults, give a "literary, musical, and dramatic entertainment" in the Library Hall to pay for the new organ. "Very well executed."

Although many entries note the regularly occurring celebrations in the liturgical calendar as well as the comings and goings of the Jesuits, occasionally they note rare events, like the 300-year anniversary of St. Charles Borromeo, on November 9, 1884. Twelve priests assisted at the solemn High Mass offered by visiting Jesuit P. J. Hoeffer. On December 8 of that year, Father Van der Putten celebrated a well-attended Mass in honor of the 300-year anniversary of the Sodality of the Blessed Virgin Mary.

Many entries in *Historia Domus* concern the health of the Jesuits stationed at, or visiting, St. Charles Borromeo. 1885 was a hard year on the parish priests and brothers: in January, the aged Father Van Mierlo developed a fatal case of pneumonia just one day before Brother George Miles died of a long illness. After Miles' burial, Van Mierlo received the last sacraments and died. Both Jesuits were buried at the Florissant novitiate. Various Jesuits visited and helped out for the next several months.

People

Dr. James R. Mudd: Born in 1844, Mudd served as County Coroner and superintendent of the St. Charles Asylum for the Poor. He lived at 701 North Third Street (at the northwest corner of Third and Decatur) and served the parish Jesuits for many years as house physician. Upon his death in 1913, a solemn funeral Mass was celebrated in the brick church by three Jesuits.

John C. Mittelberger: Elected mayor of St. Charles in 1872, Mittelberger for many years operated a dry goods store at 311 North Main Street. The second story of this building was known as Mittelberger's Opera House, and it hosted numerous Borromeo functions over the years. Mittelberger's son, John N., continued the family business and lived in an elegant brick house at the corner of Benton and Clark Streets.

Father F. X. Willmes: Not a parishioner at all but the long-time pastor of St. Peter's, the "German church," Willmes maintained close ties with Borromeo. *Historia Domus* enumerates the many ways he cooperated with the parish priests: giving missions in St. Charles and elsewhere, assisting at special Masses at the brick church, helping escort the bishops who came to St. Charles, and taking an active role in the various lay groups of the two parishes.

William Kirkpatrick: Son of Wallace and Jane F. Mudd Kirkpatrick, William was born in 1837 and grew up on a farm near St. Charles. He married Sacred Heart student Ursula Kestler and became a large landowner as well as a successful farmer and businessman. For many years Kirkpatrick served the parish as an active member of the Catholic Knights of America and Knights of Columbus.

William Dugan: One of the parish Confederate sympathizers during the Civil War, Dugan died in 1874 after being kicked by a mule. According to his widow, the incident occurred while Dugan was under the influence of alcohol. She memorialized her husband by having a depiction of the fatal

Joseph Zealand, S. J., who served as pastor from 1879 to 1882.

Victor Van der Putten, pastor 1882-85

accident carved on his tombstone, located at the present Borromeo cemetery.

Henry F. Pieper: A young man when the brick church was built, Pieper had previously worked on the family farm and as a carpenter. During the Civil War he served as a home guard for the Union. Afterward, Pieper went into the mercantile business, selling at various times groceries, grain, and farm implements. For six years he served as city treasurer and for another six as county treasurer. He married Caroline Boschert in 1868.

Frank Oberkoetter: A native of Hanover, Oberkoetter worked as a shoemaker before immigrating in 1842 to St. Charles, where he eventually opened a successful shoe and boot store. He became involved in numerous business and civic causes, serving as president of St. Charles' gas company as well as of the Union Savings Bank, and spent several years as city councilman. He contributed $75 to the construction of the brick church.

Etienne (Frank) LaBarge: A Missouri riverboat captain from the middle 1830s until 1868, LaBarge sold his imposing two-story residence on Third Street to the Jesuits in 1863. A good friend of Peter Verhaegen, LaBarge remained a generous supporter of the parish after Verhaegen's death, and

contributed $100 toward the construction of the brick church. During his career he piloted many Jesuits on their way to or from the Indian missions along the Missouri River.

Louis Brucker: Born in St. Louis in 1847, Brucker made trunks for a living, then became a clerk. In 1875 he and his brother John B. Brucker opened a used furniture store in St. Charles, then later began selling new items. Louis Brucker married Josephine Hodapp in 1874. He belonged to the Catholic Knights of America, the Men's Sodality, and the St. Charles Benevolent Society.

The "kicked by a mule" tombstone of William Dugan.

Chapter 8
1885-99

The Centennial Celebration

There is another long gap in *Historia Domus* entries, between April 1886 and August 1895. A few documents from this period, mostly brief annual reports made by Borromeo's pastors to their superiors, are kept at the Jesuit Archives in St. Louis. The parish registers prove that the sacraments were administered as usual during these years, but little other material sheds light on this very eventful period in Borromeo's history.

Joseph Rosswinkel became pastor in late 1889, and he soon interested the parish in a unique idea: celebrating the upcoming 100-year anniversary of Borromeo's history along with the 400-year anniversary of Columbus's discovery of America. Charles Charroppin, Rosswinkel's colorful, multi-talented assistant, was intrigued, as were several key laymen, especially Dr. Mudd and James Lawler, who a few years later became district manager of the St. Charles plant of the American Car and Foundry. Soon preparations were underway.

Several copies of a fifty-six-page commemorative program of the celebration survive. In the florid language of the day, author James J. Conway, S. J., described the events:

Saturday, the 15th of October, the festivities were inaugurated by a torch-light procession from the Wabash R. R. depot to the pastoral residence, as a reception to Monsignor Ryan, Bishop of Alton, who was the guest of the parish during the festival and the celebrant of the Centennial Pontifical Mass. Sunday, the 16th, the centennial day, dawned most propitious, and there were none who failed to turn out in honor of the occasion. At the early Mass, celebrated by the centennial pastor, Rev. R. Rosswinkel, S. J., the sodalities, societies, conferences and clubs attached to the Church assisted in regalia and wearing their centennial device, a medal commemorating the event, hung from a purple badge fastened to a steel clasp. Numbers, either with their organizations or individually, approached the sacred table in thanksgiving. The children's choir at this Mass was a devotional accompaniment to the sacred services, a tribute to the taste and piety of the pastors and an exceptionally beautiful feature of the centennial celebration.

Joseph Rosswinkel, paster 1889-95

After naming the many priests and dignitaries in attendance, Conway detailed several particularly memorable features of the celebration:

> The music at this Mass, under the conduct of Prof. E. H. Wolf, of the Lindenwood Seminary, was extremely choice in taste and execution. The professor himself presided at the organ, and it is due to him alone that the music and the choir proved so eminently satisfactory. There were some exquisite solos, and the chorus filled the church with a perfection of devout and very appropriate sentiment. Besides the officiating clergy, the sanctuary was well filled with acolytes in red, white and dark soutanes, surplice-waists and sashes. Their pious and recollected attitude, easy and reverent evolutions, contributed largely to the solemnity of the services, and afforded a large number of the families of the parish the happiness of thus participating in a more intimate manner in the commemorative Mass.
>
> The quadricentennial feature of the Mass was the Columbian Oration by the Rev. Thos. E. Sherman, S. J. [son of the famous Civil War general, and then on his way to becoming a leading public orator among the Catholic clergy]. The occasion, the large audience, the superb theme itself, and the eloquence of the speaker, all contributed to render the sermon a most glowing eulogy of the great navigator. In an exhaustive review of over an hour, the Rev. Father retraced in passages of rare animation,

An accomplished photographer, Charles Charroppin, S.J., may have taken this portrait of himself in the early 1890s, during his first residence in St. Charles.

> and rising at intervals to the heights of the loftiest expression and sentiment, the varying fortunes of the Genoese admiral. The sermon was full of keen appreciation of the inner meaning of the life of Columbus—the glory of God and the interests of the Church. It dealt briefly, but unsparingly, with the leading calumnies against Columbus, and exhibited with much skill and force the lasting claim which his life and great discovery have upon the gratitude of those who, through his providential mission, enjoy all the blessings of religious and civil freedom.

That afternoon, Bishop Ryan confirmed one of the Sacred Heart classes, while many parishioners attended rehearsals, society reunions, entertainments, and religious classes. The day's closing services

The commemorative centennial medal

Gene Buehrle

began at 7:30 with a hymn, then Father Conway delivered a long, ornate lecture on the history of the parish. Benediction followed, and a band concert concluded the day's events.

Monday, October 18, was the "grand reunion day," when out-of-towners visited the church and "were pleasantly entertained by the ladies of the congregation." Children played on the grounds, and some engaged in various games and competitions. A bazaar, music, speeches, and "a number of rare intellectual treats . . . contributed to render the second day of the festivities immensely enjoyable to the congregation and its visitors."

Tuesday, October 19, dawned cold and damp. Rain began falling by midmorning, turning the streets to mud. Nevertheless, people from town and the surrounding area began arriving for the most vivid event of the celebration—a "grand centennial parade." The commemorative program elaborates:

There were upwards of two thousand men in line, many of them from the remotest corners of the county. The congregations taking part observed the following order: At the head of the column was a numerous detachment from the congregation of St. Charles Bor-

romeo. They were followed by a splendid body of men from St. Peter's parish. . . . Following . . . were the men from All Saint's parish, St. Peter's, Mo. After these marched the societies from St. Paul's Church, St. Paul, Mo., the parishioners of the Immaculate Conception parish, Dardenne, Mo., and the various conferences of St. Francis' Church, Portage [des Sioux], Mo..

After naming the many parading clergymen (who stayed clean by riding in carriages) the program continued:

Captain H. B. Denker, with an active body of aides from the neighboring parishes, was in charge of the parade. Forming at the church, the column, headed by Grand Marshal Denker and his staff, traversed the principal streets of the city, accompanied by music furnished by a number of local and visiting bands. Returning to the parish grounds, the little army was addressed in English by Hon. O'Neil Ryan [a prominent Catholic lawyer who later became a judge of the circuit court as well as dean of the St. Louis University School of Law] and in German by Hon. Henry Spaunhorst [a German-born Missouri state senator who supported Catholic causes throughout his public life]. Notwithstanding the inclemency of weather, both speakers were very happy in their allusions to the twofold celebrity, and did not lose this opportunity of mingling politics—the elections were just impending—with religion, tracing the true source of our freedom in both to the genius of the immortal Christopher Columbus.

In all, the festivities were a big success, and earned the parish an unexpected windfall—enough money to buy a huge four-faced clock designed to ring every fifteen minutes—for the brick church's steeple. The clock was installed around Pentecost the following year.

Loretto Nuns

Father Conway's lecture on the history of St. Charles Borromeo paid lengthy homage to the contributions made by Philippine Duchesne and the other members of the Society of the Sacred Heart to the parish. That same year—1892— construction was completed on the Sacred Heart grounds (at the corner of Decatur and Third streets) on a two-story brick school building for the parish girls. Seemingly, the bonds between the parish and the Society were as strong as ever.

Between 1892 and 1893, however, several events occurred which led rather abruptly to the Sisters of Loretto taking over the education of Borromeo's boys and girls. Unfortunately, *Historia Domus* is silent for these years, and little pertinent information on the matter exists in the Archives of the Society of the Sacred Heart.

Traditionally, Jesuit brothers taught the parish boys, managed the rectory and garden, and served around the church as bellringers and sacristans. The number of Borromeo's Jesuit brothers (and priests as well) shrank in the 1880s. In 1890, there were only two priests and one brother stationed at Borromeo. In 1891, another priest arrived but not another brother. It seems likely that by 1892 the parish was sorely in need of another brother, possibly to teach in the school.

Perhaps to fill this gap, around 1893 a representative of the parish (almost surely Father Rosswinkel) asked one of the religious in charge at the Sacred Heart community that her nuns take on the teaching of the parish boys. What happened next is not clear, but within a short time, the women of the Sacred Heart were teaching neither the parish boys nor its girls. The new school building on the Academy grounds was never used for education, and was instead pressed into service as a laundry building.

A combination of several possible factors seems to have produced this result. First, in the late 1800s, there was a trend in Catholic education toward parochial schooling; that is, toward a system of education organized under a diocesan bishop and controlled to a great extent by pastors of the diocese's parishes, rather than by members of the various religious orders teaching in the schools. At about the same time, many parishes in the United States were deciding that educating boys and girls in separate schools was an extravagance.

Within the Society of the Sacred Heart and other orders as well, rules of cloister had become stricter throughout the 1800s. Overall, the Church expected more monastic practices from its orders during this time, even from active congregations like the Jesuits. It is likely that just crossing Fourth Street to teach school or to attend Mass would have provoked criticism of the St. Charles Sacred Heart community.

The original Loretto convent, a two-story building until 1909. The stone over the front door says, "Parochial Academy."

At the same time, there was a widespread sentiment against religious women having contact with men and adolescent boys. During the Civil War, much controversy had resulted when certain religious orders allowed their women to nurse wounded soldiers. During the 1890s, a related controversy raged over the higher education of women, and whether women's colleges should be located near men's colleges. These questions were addressed by the Vatican in a "Roman Rule" around the turn of the century, and remained controversial for a long time.

It is not known which Sacred Heart nun was responsible for the refusal to educate Borromeo's boys. The superior then in charge was Louise Du Mont, and the principal was Mary Fancette. The Society's *Lettres Annuelles* for St. Charles, 1892-1893, do not elaborate; they state simply that circumstances at that time deprived the order of the joy of having a parish school. It seems likely, however, that whoever made the ultimate decision made it hastily, without consulting the Mother General.

In September 1893 the Sisters of Loretto at the Foot of the Cross took charge of the St. Charles Borromeo School. At about the same time, the parish began construction of a two-story brick convent at the corner of Decatur and Fifth streets. Until the convent was completed, the sisters lived in the

Mudd residence at the northwest corner of Third and Decatur Streets. Their superior was Sister M. Donata Sullivan. Teaching the boys were Sisters Joseph Ann King and Henrietta Mudd. Sisters M. Stella Williamson and M. Bernardine Bersterman taught the parish girls in impromptu classrooms located at Fourth and Decatur in the Alexander house, later used as the parish rectory. Sister Syra Ripple kept house.

Unlike the religious of the Sacred Heart, the Loretto nuns belonged to an order founded in America. Though also dedicated to teaching, they were somewhat less restricted in movement than the Sacred Heart nuns. Founded in Kentucky in 1812, their order was operating fifty-nine foundations by 1890. The blossoming of the parochial school movement during this time increased the demand for their services and drew numerous young women to their order.

For many years after the change of orders, the religious of the Sacred Heart desired to resume their work with the parish children. In 1899 Superior General Mabel Digby visited St. Charles. A note she penned during this time expresses her regret over the loss of the parish school, as well as her hope that the Society could someday resume teaching the parish children.

In 1906 the parish and the Sacred Heart nuns explored this possibility. Both the Loretto order and the parish were struggling financially. Documents from that year in the archives of the Society of the Sacred Heart indicate that Borromeo's Jesuits asked the Sacred Heart nuns to teach all eight grades of the parish 220 boys and girls, in the school building on Block 122. Up to three different grades were taught in each of the school's four classrooms, and some of those grades included boys of up to fifteen years of age. Again the problems of cloister and coeducation arose. For a

106 † St. Charles Borromeo

while there was some discussion of splitting up the Sacred Heart community, so that several of its nuns could live in separate quarters on Block 122. The project was eventually deemed too expensive, and the Sisters of Loretto remained in charge of the parish school until 1932.

Liturgical Events

A great deal of the information recorded in *Historia Domus* has to do with services and celebrations related to the Church's liturgical calendar. Many of these events have changed little over the years while some have changed greatly, and some have nearly disappeared. The following excerpts are from 1896:

Feb. 16— Today the 3-day Adoration of the Most Blessed Sacrament was begun. Very few people came to adore.

Feb. 18— The adorers were few yet, but not so few as yesterday. The adoration was closed today according to the "Instructio Clementiae", but without a procession.

Feb. 19— Ash Wednesday. Tonight Fr. Meuffels began the lenten sermons. Subject to night "Memento homo, quia pulvis es et en pulverem reverteris." [Remember man, you are dust and into dust you shall return.]

Feb. 21— Tonight the Way of the Cross and Benediction of the Bl. Sacrament and this will be on every Friday night in Lent.

Feb. 26— Tonight Fr. Wolters took up the lenten sermons, taking for his subject the history of the Passion, which he will treat until the end of Lent.

Mar. 14— Fr. Rogers came to give a triduum to the pupils at the convent.

Today he helps us in the confessional.

Apr. 2— [Holy Thursday] Tonight Passion Sermon.

Apr. 3— [Good Friday] Tonight Stations.

Apr. 5— [Easter Sunday] Solemn High Mass with Orchestral Music. Celebrant Fr. Wolters, Deacon & preacher Fr. Meuffels, Subdeacon Mr. Germing. Master of Ceremonies Mr. Smith. [Germing and Smith were visiting Jesuits.]

Apr. 22— Fr. Wolters went to Dardenne Mo. to preach at the laying of the corner-stone of the new church, and returned same day.

Apr. 26— Patronage of St. Joseph. Solemn High Mass.

May 1— Beginning tonight there will be May Devotion every day at 7:30 p.m.

May 10— Today there was first Communion in the Convent.

May 11— Our own garden and that of the Convent were blessed today it being the first of the Rogation Days.

May 21— Today Fr. Sebastian [from the novitiate] began a triduum for our first Communicants.

May 24— This morning 56 children made their first Communion in the 7:30 (Low) Mass. At 10 a.m. there was a High Mass without sermon. At 3 p.m. the first communicants were enrolled in the Scapular.

May 30— Fr. Conway preached in the High Mass and at night services. At the latter the new officers of the 6 Sodalities were installed, a procession in honor of the B.V.M. was held, an act of Consecration to the B.V.M. read and Benediction with the Bl. Sacrament given.

Jun. 12— High Mass at 5 a.m. sung by Fr. Meuffels, at 8 a.m. Low Mass by Fr. Klocker. This morning again there were very many Communions. After the Low Mass the Bl. Sacrament was exposed for an all-day adoration. At 7:30 p.m. procession with a statue of the Sacred Heart and the Bl. Sacrament around the square, reading of the act of reparation and Benediction.

Jul. 1— 10 a.m. Fr. Meuffels went to give a retreat to the Sisters of the Good Shepherd in St. Louis.

Jul. 16— 10 a.m. Fr. Wolters went to Milwaukee to give 2 retreats.

Sep. 7— Today the Mass of the Holy Ghost was said in the Convent (this year only a Low Mass).

Oct. 1— Today October devotions were begun . . . both in the Church and in the Convent.

Oct. 30— Feast of St. Alph. Rodriguez, Bro[ther]. – S.J. – Both our Brothers went to the Novitiate for the celebration of their feast and returned in the evening.

Nov. 8— Solemnity of St. Charles Borromeo 10 a.m. Solemn High Mass with panegyric.

Dec. 6— Tonight there was a supper at the house of Mr. James Short for the singers of our choir in honor of St. Cecilia.

Entries from other years between 1885 and 1900 describe how certain holy days were celebrated. Christmas, for example,

Joseph Meuffels, pastor 1895-97

Jesuit Missouri Province Archives

was observed with a Midnight Mass and a 7 a.m. Low Mass at the Sacred Heart convent. Up the hill at the brick church, parishioners had their choice of a 5 a.m. solemn High Mass, an 8 a.m. Low Mass or a 10 a.m. Solemn High Mass, followed by Benediction. Every year in late December, the parish gave the children a party around a Christmas tree in the school hall. In 1898 popcorn, peanuts, and green apples were given out, courtesy of James Lawler, James Short, and B. Dixon. Later that night, the church's ushers were honored with a supper. On the next day, the Feast of the Holy Innocents, the parish choir girls and altar boys were thanked for their services with a meal in the refectory.

During the tenure of the Loretto nuns, the school children were usually given a free day from classes during Passion week, in honor of Our Lady of Sorrows, patron of the Loretto order. For Borromeo children of the late 1800s, Thanksgiving Day was a school day on which awards were distributed.

A schedule of only two Sunday Masses, called the "winter order," began in late November, probably for the purpose of keeping down the parish heating costs. During June the "summer order" began— 7:00 Mass on weekdays, and a 9:30 a.m. Low Mass with a sermon on Sunday. Because of the high cost of gas lighting in 1897, services usually held at night were held instead during the afternoon.

Missions and triduums were special devotional occasions which sometimes led up to certain feast days. The Jubilee of St. Joseph as patron of the Universal Church, the Feast of the Sacred Heart, and the Feast of St. Ignatius of Loyola (founder of the Society of Jesus) were often preceded by such devotions.

Historia Domus

Occasionally the Jesuits of the late 1800s wrote about the political trends of their day, just as Father Verhaegen and earlier Jesuits had written about German radicals and the Know-Nothing movement of the 1850s. Borromeo's priests shared the concern of their fellow citizens over "big business," agrarian reform, and inflation. During the 1896 presidential race, Democratic candidate William Jennings Bryan accused Wall Street and the railroads of being enemies of the common man, while Republican candidate William McKinley supported monopolies, but promised Americans "a full dinner pail."

Chautauquas—educational entertainment presented outdoors in large tents—came to St. Charles during the brick church era, and at least one of them featured Bryan as a speaker. *Historia Domus* notes that the parish priests attended chautauquas and suggests that they occasionally got caught up in political issues. On Election Day, November 3, 1896, one of the Jesuits wrote: "Fr. Wolters was very much pressed to vote and he did vote in the afternoon. (Dem[ocratic] ticket)." But enough other Americans voted for a full dinner pail to put McKinley, not Bryan, in the White House.

The parish also took notice of international events, especially an ongoing conflict in Italy between the secular government and the Vatican. An entry dated September 18, 1895, reads: "According to the desire of his Grace, our Most Rev. Archb., a protest meeting of all our parish societies was held in the school hall,

and resolutions setting forth the condemnation of the Italian government were drawn up and forwarded to his Grace." Two days later, the author wrote, "A 25th anniversary of the taking of Rome [by the Italian government], all the faithful were invited to visit the church in order to pray for the Holy Father. . . . "

Shortly after Constantine Lagae took over as Borromeo pastor in January 1897 for Joseph Meuffels, he began working to involve the laity to a greater extent in parish affairs. During the first weeks of his pastorate, he signed up nine parishioners to serve on the newly created Sanctuary Society. In February 1897 he chaired the first meeting of the Altar Society, which numbered twelve members. Lagae had less success with the already-formed Cemetery Committee, which for several years rarely turned out in force for meetings.

Other parish groups were the Catholic Knights of America, Married Men's and Married Women's Sodalities, Young Men's and Young Ladies' Sodalities, Boys' and Girls' Sodalities, the League of the Sacred Heart, and until 1896, a Philaletic (debate) Society. A Young Men's Social Club began in November 1896, as one of the Jesuits wrote, "to give them [the young men of the parish] a chance to look for enjoyment away from saloons and other such resorts."

Like other Americans before the age of electronics, Borromeo's parishioners created their own amusements. *Historia Domus* speaks frequently of picnics at Cribben's Grove for the children, and of dramatic performances given by the school at Mittleberger's Opera House. Commencement exercises and school "exhibitions" were also gala affairs, and frequently were held at the Opera House. In 1897 the St. Charles County Fair was a sort of parish event as well—the church sponsored the Prize and Eating Table.

Very often Borromeo's women managed to socialize and raise much-needed money for the parish at the same time. A favorite fund-raising event was a type of card party called a euchre. On January 20, 1897, the writer of *Historia Domus* observed, "The Young Ladies Sodality had a progressive euchre for the benefit of the Sodality in the Kemper building. It was very well attended." During February of that year, the Married Ladies' Sodality put on another euchre, paying off the parish coal bill with part of the proceeds and saving the remainder "for putting electric lights into the church." In June 1897, the parish held an evening "lawn-festival" in the schoolyard, and earned $330 to help pay the interest on the building debt. That November, the Married Ladies' Sodality held another euchre, this time to benefit the Sisters of Loretto.

The whole parish pitched in on a bazaar in August of 1899. On the first day, despite the "booths gaily decorated, principally with bunting of red, white, and blue," attendance was light. Larger crowds turned out on the second and third days, but the bazaar was held over a fourth day, mainly "for the purpose of raffling off things." After one last band concert and cake walk, the parish cleared about $100.

People

James C. Holmes: Born one of eight children in 1851, only Holmes and one brother lived to adulthood. After receiving a measure of higher education at Christian Brothers College in St. Louis, he became the editor and proprietor of the *St. Charles News.* In October 1909, to mark the centennial of incorporation of St. Charles, Holmes compiled a lengthy historical treatment of the city, paying special attention to St. Charles Borromeo's role in civic development.

Antoine Dorlaque: A descendant of one of the earlier French Canadian families to the area, Dorlaque became a prosperous farmer and a dealer of livestock. He owned a large farm in the county, as well as a 300-acre tract on one of the islands in the Mississippi River. He and his wife, Edna Ford of Kentucky, had a large family, some of whom later moved to town.

Caspar Ehrhard: Nephew of John B. Thro, Ehrhard left Alsace for St. Charles in 1863, where he clerked for his uncle's dry goods business and later for Thro's clothing store. In 1871 he bought out his uncle. In 1877 he took his cousin, John B. Thro, Jr., into the business. Ehrhard served as financial secretary for the Catholic Knights of America.

Henry Angert: Born in St. Charles in 1845 of German immigrants, Angert attended little school but managed to educate himself enough to be employed as a clerk, then opened his own business selling groceries and dry goods. He prospered to the point of becoming a vice president of St. Charles' First National Bank and county treasurer. In 1869 Angert married Josephine Thro. After her death he married Adie Brooker, the widow of his late partner in business, August Brooker. Angert and his family were benefactors of the parish.

Albert Deemar: A German immigrant who learned the hotel and tavern business before moving to St. Charles, Deemar worked in this capacity until 1878, when he became warden of the St. Charles County Asylum. In 1859 Deemar married Mary A. Trendley. The couple had three sons, Henry, George, and Herbert. Deemar belonged to the Catholic Knights of America.

Augustus A. Meyer: Although his father, Ludwig Meyer, helped organize St. Peter's parish, Augustus worked over fifteen years as Borromeo's organist. Despite his gift for music he followed his father into the jewelry trade. In 1854 Meyer married Lizzie Steinbruegge, and the couple had five children.

James Short: An Irish immigrant to New York in 1862, Short migrated to Chicago, then to St. Charles. He soon prospered as a masonry contractor and later as a paving (then called macadamizing) and grading contractor. Short married Anna Boil and the couple had eight children. A document found in the cornerstone of the brick church states that Short contributed $100 to that building's construction.

Religious of the Sacred Heart in Charge of the Parish School, 1828–1892

The following religious worked at St. Charles between 1828 and 1840, but it is not clear who ran the free school for the parish's girls. A good possibility is Mary Ann O'Connor, who had done similar work in Florissant:

1828–1831	Lucille Mathevon, Mary Ann O'Connor, Sister Ann Haggerty
1832–1838	Lucille Mathevon, Mary Ann O'Connor, Sister Ann Haggerty, Suzanne McKay, Eulalie Guillot
1839–1840	Lucille Mathevon, Mary Ann O'Connor, Sister Ann Haggerty, Suzanne McKay, Sister Adele Verret

In 1841 Lucille Mathevon left for the Potawatomi mission and Regis Hamilton became superior at St. Charles. Suzanne McKay and Sister Ann Haggerty remained, Sister Adele Verret left, and two new choir religious and one new coadjutrix sister arrived. After this year, the Society published a catalog listing each religious and her employment.

1842–1844	Regis Hamilton was in charge of the parish school, assisted by Mary Duffy and Sister Eliza Lynch.
1845-1847	Philippine Duchesne was in charge of the parish school, assisted by Mary Duffy, Marcella McMahon, and coadjutrix novice Mary Myers.
1848–1849	Philippine Duchesne was listed as teaching Christian doctrine in the parish school; who else taught was not recorded.
1850	Bridget O'Neil was in charge of the parish school; Mother Duchesne was too feeble to teach but occasionally helped with difficult children.

Following is a list of only the heads of the school:

1851–1858	Suzanne McKay
1859–1865	Rose Ann McDonough
1866–1870	Ann Daly
1871–1873	Catherine Guidery
1874	Ann Daly
1875–1878	Catherine Guidery
1879	Margaret Bourke
1880–1882	Catherine Guidery
1883–1888	Rose Ann McDonough
1889	Ellen Bulger
1890	Susanne Lalor
1891	Ann McCoy
1892	Mary Fancette

Chapter 9
1899-1915

The School Addition

The new convent for the Sisters of Loretto was completed in 1894. Located at Fifth and Decatur Streets, it originally stood two stories tall. For several years it served not only as a residence for the nuns but also as a school for Borromeo's girls, who were taught separately from the parish boys. Because this segregation led to added expense—nearly a double teaching staff was needed—it was soon dropped, and the girls joined the boys in the brick school. But crowding resulted, so for many years portions of the convent building were kept in use for classes.

This did not totally solve the problem of crowding; some sort of school building expansion was necessary. In response, the parish elected a building committee consisting of James Lawler, Julius Rauch, and James Farmer.

On May 10, 1899, work began on the construction of a school building addition. Contractor John Heckmann of St. Charles was the lowest bidder, promising to do the work and furnish the materials for $3,148. The parish records do not specify much about the new building, except that it added two additional classrooms to the school and enlarged the meeting hall.

On May 15, while digging the cellar of the new building, Heckmann's workmen discovered several skeletons, presumably left over from the old burial ground. *Historia Domus* states that the bones were moved to the present cemetery.

Afterward, the foundation work progressed so that the cornerstone was placed on June 11, 1899. To mark the event, a procession of school children and the various sodalities and societies of the church marched around the block. A commemorative document was read to the crowd in attendance, then the document was ceremoniously placed inside the stone. After a blessing by Father Lagae, visiting Jesuit Father Thomas Brown delivered a lecture on the importance of a Christian education. Lagae closed the ceremony, "urging the people to be generous in their contributions towards paying the expenses of the new building."

The addition was not ready when classes resumed on September 4. All 124 students were taught that day and the next in the older section or in the convent, but classes were cancelled for the next several days due to hot weather. Still, parents continued to register their children, pushing the school's enrollment to 137 by September 11.

On September 13 the Jesuits hired two "tramp artists" who had been recommended by James Lawler and Julius Rauch to paint and to install drop curtains and scenery for a new stage. The next day, Father Lagae went to St. Louis and bought a piano for the new hall. Although work on the classrooms ended around September 25, work in the hall dragged on, much to the chagrin of the Jesuits and the building committee. At last, on September 30, the "tramp painters" finished the stage work,

although not everyone was satisfied with their efforts.

In late September the Loretto nuns staked out the newly completed classroom space: Sister Henrietta took the room on the south; Sister Bernardine took the room on the north; and Sister Superior Jane Frances moved her class from the convent to the library room. At last, on October 8, 1899, the school hall was opened with a ceremony that featured a lecture entitled "The Courage of Conviction" and vocal selections by the church choir. The next month, the ladies of the parish staged the new hall's first play, *Placer Gold,* and drew a crowd of about 300.

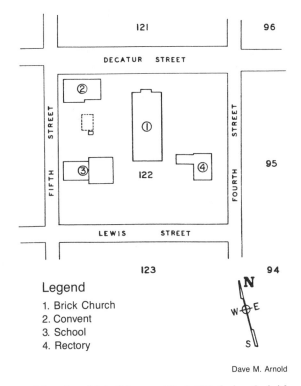

Map of parish buildings on Block 122 during the brick church era.

Above right: Behind the original brick school fronting on Fifth Street, a square two-story addition was built in 1899.

Right: Room 3 of the brick school in 1907. Boys and girls sat on opposite sides of the classroom.

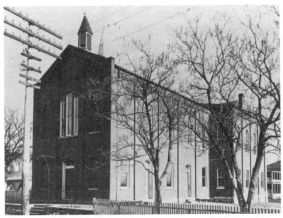

In the early 1870s, when the brick church, rectory, and school had been built, indoor plumbing was nearly unknown. Outhouses, chicken coops, gardens, and stables dotted the backyards of St. Charles. Most of the water used in town came straight from the river or from private wells and cisterns. Electric lighting had not yet been invented. Although "gas" heat (produced by the large-scale combustion of coal) was in its infancy, most townspeople still relied on their fireplaces for warmth.

Conveniences like tungsten lights, sewer service, sidewalks, and steam heat were available by 1900. St. Charles Borromeo took full advantage of these new technologies by embarking on a long campaign of modernization. To record the parish progress toward this goal, Father Lagae began keeping a special register of the improvements made to the brick church, rectory, school, and convent.

The first such improvement noted was the laying in 1900 of a modernistic surface called granitoid pavement in front of the church, from Fourth to Fifth streets, "with the Plaza in front of the church and all its new steps. . . . " for $1,225. Father Lagae wasted no time in making this upgrade; St. Charles did not commence installing granitoid sidewalks, gutters, or curbs throughout much of town until 1907.

The next year, Borromeo entered the age of steam heat. Previously, *Historia Domus* entries had noted the annual lighting of the heating stoves in the school and rectory. Starting in August of 1901, work began on excavating a boiler room and installing a steam "apparatus" for the school, church, and rectory. In November the system was tested: "For the first time steam was turned into the pipes and radiators in the residence, school, and church, to test the pipes and radiators. Several of them were found wanting and had to be replaced. . . . On the whole, the new heating apparatus promises to give great satisfaction and to be in perfect working order in a few days." The job was finished by early December.

In 1902 underground sewers on Second Street were connected "with all the ramifications of pipes in all directions. . . . " with the buildings on the Sacred Heart grounds, and also with newly constructed water closets in the priests' house. Nevertheless, the parish outdoor privies remained near Lewis Street to the south of church for many years.

In 1903 the brick church received a slate roof, and its steeple was topped by a new copper cross 17½ feet high, covered with gold leaf. The six turrets of the building were covered with copper. The total cost for the work on the roof amounted to just over $3,100.

The next year a Chicagoan named Louis Rusca frescoed the interior walls of the church. Rusca set up scaffolding in early June, and completed the job "to the satisfaction of everybody" on October 1, 1904. After the scaffolding was carefully removed, "the church was washed by about half a dozen German women, who had offered themselves spontaneously, and they had to work like heroines to finish the job before darkness set in."

Interior of St. Charles Borromeo Church before the tornado. Note the frescoes, sounding board over the pulpit, and electric lights.

The projects for 1905 were the laying of more granitoid pavement for a sidewalk along Fifth Street (between Lewis and Decatur) and the construction of a handsome, double staircase in front of the priests' house. Probably because a fire of unknown origin had burned a hole in the roof of the priests' house in 1896, this building also received a new slate roof and copper gutters.

The granitoid paving of the sidewalks, curbs, and gutters on Block 122 continued in 1906. Stations of the cross were installed inside the church in December, 1906. Father Lagae's special register commemorates the parishioners whose families who donated $125 apiece for each station: Mary E. Hebling, Mrs. C. Ruf, Mrs. Cecilia Meyer, Dr. J. Mudd, James G. Lawler, Bernard Feuerstein, Dan Cavanaugh, Henry Etling, Henry Ehrhard, Mrs. Charles Rechtern, Henry Angert, Frank Bernhoester, the late Wm. Yosti and D. Shore, and M. Dixon.

Other improvements made to the interior of the church within the next few years included: the addition of two white marble holy water fonts donated in 1907 by the Altar Society; the addition of a statue of our Lady of Victory, donated by Frank Tainter and blessed by Father Lagae on Ascension Day, 1907; the installation of a sounding board over the pulpit and of a communion railing with a marble slab, both in 1908; the installation of an electric motor into the church's organ, in 1909.

The long-awaited electric illumination of the church, at Christmas 1908, caused much excitement. On December 24, the Jesuits were nervously anticipating the effect of electric lighting on the congregation at Midnight Mass: "Electric lamps all hung and enough bulbs placed for the illumination. But supply not complete. Mr. Antony the Contractor appears and is satisfied with the arrangement and design of lights, beyond expectation."

The effect that night was indeed gratifying:

> At the Gloria, lights on the Altar produced a magic effect. Arches of light

around the 3 statues, red around the Tabernacle and red around the Cardinal St. Charles, over the Tabernacle; a circle of white above that, and the cross overtopping all in red lights. The good people were amazed and gazed in delight. Lights turned off on the altar after the Gloria.

Father Lagae wished all the blessings of Xmas, explained how the electric lighting was the fruit of the bazaar. . . .

At the Credo, lights were turned on, at side altars a lamp over each and an arch around the statues. Before the Elevation, the illumination was complete and the people were in raptures of admiration.

In 1909 the convent building was topped with a third story containing four classrooms, only one of which had electricity and heat. *Historia Domus* relates that a dispute erupted between the Jesuits and the Sisters of Loretto over the use of this addition, and that each side appealed to its superior. Exactly how the matter was resolved is not explained, but in 1910 the parish opened a high school on the third floor of the convent.

Entertainment and Special Events

Technological breakthroughs made new pastimes and forms of entertainment available to people in St. Charles during the early twentieth century. The various writers of *Historia Domus* frequently mention how Borromeo's priests and parishioners took advantage of these new opportunities.

One of the earliest such entries is from April 30, 1900: "This evening, a magic lantern show [an early slide show, typically with glass slides] was given by Fr. Spalding to the school children." Father Spalding, a visiting Jesuit, had given an illustrated lecture the night before on Father Jacques Marquette.

The World's Fair of 1904 introduced many local people to the wonders of technology. Even before the fair began, its promoters visited towns like St. Charles in order to arouse interest. In February of 1903, one such promoter visited the parish and gave a stereopticon slide show (in which two slides, shown at once, seemed to dissolve into each other) of Jerusalem. Interest in the fair ran high; its opening on April 30, 1904, is noted in *Historia Domus*. August 26, 1904, was St. Charles Day at the fair, so Father Lagae and his assistant, Father Aloysius Averbeck, dutifully attended. Probably many parishioners did as well.

On June 14, 1904, a sample of the fair came to St. Charles Borromeo. *Historia Domus* relates the sensational event: "Grand Strawberry & Ice Cream Festival for the benefit of the Church: A wild Philipino Moro chief is on exhibition from 1 p.m. till 10 p.m. It took a few shoe black boxes to fix him. Great success—till midnight the grounds & hall are full of people."

During the same era, similar forms of entertainment persisted in St. Charles, especially the minstrel show. *Historia Domus* writers wrote about the men of the parish who blackened their faces and regaled parishioners. During a parish bazaar in 1908, the program included acrobatic and gymnastic exhibitions, a violin recital, a band concert, a recitation by the school children, and "comic negro recitations."

People of the parish attended lectures in the school hall on such topics as the exploration of the North Pole and "Wonderful Japan." National pride ran high, and so did a sense of civic responsibility. In 1901, when a cornerstone was laid for the new St. Charles County Courthouse, about 100 children from the parish turned out to march in a big parade.

On October 18, 1908, the men of the parish participated in another parade, this time in St. Louis. The occasion was the blessing of the cornerstone for the new cathedral on Lindell Boulevard. Three chartered rail cars picked up the marchers at the foot of Clark Street and took them to the Wabash depot, where the men connected with the St. Louis line. At 2 p.m. the parade started. Seventy-seven parishes from St. Louis participated, as did fourteen country parishes, forty-one brass bands, three bugle corps, and several fife and drum bands. Fathers Lagae, O'Meara, and Averbeck, accompanied by about 150 parishioners, marched behind the banner of St. Charles Borromeo parish.

Another gala celebration took place in July of 1910, when Borromeo associate Aloysius Averbeck celebrated his golden jubilee as a Jesuit. Over a dozen other priests assisted at the celebration of a Solemn High Mass on July 17, after which the parishioners gave a reception in the school hall. The church choir (composed of Edward L. Meyer, Chauvin Emmons, Mrs. Fred Meyer, Edith Rauch, Clementine Kaemmerlen, and Maurice Thro) sang "Ecce Sacerdos," "Ave Maria," and "Holy Mother, Guide his Footsteps."

Historia Domus describes the remainder of the reception:

Adolph Thro read an address of congratulations to Rev. A. Averbeck, and offered him a purse of $50.00 in the name of the Married Men's Sodality. Mrs. James Audrain, in the name of the Married Ladies' Sodality, offered him congratulations with an offering of a full set of priestly vestments valued at $300.00. The Young Men's Sodality,

Kathleen Netsch

An end-of-the-school-year pageant, circa 1911, featured (from left, back row) Kathleen Lawler, Leona Bernhoester, Mazie Feuerstein, Urilla Eberius, Madeline Thro; (from left, front row) Ivy Mills, Kay O'Grady, Helen Koeller.

having Joseph White as the spokesman, offered him a purse of $6.55. Joseph Lackland, in the name of the Borromeo Clubs, congratulated him and offered him a five dollar gold piece. The Young Ladies' Sodality, through Mrs. Mary Holmes, offered him a gold ciborium valued at $80.00. The Borromeo parochial school's Miss Mazie Feuerstein offered a beautiful handmade lace surplice. Then the parishioners came up to Rev. Father Averbeck to shake hands and to wish him many more years of life.

Several weeks later, Averback entered St. Joseph's Hospital with symptoms of typhoid. Shortly after his release he suffered a paralyzing stroke and returned to St. Joseph's, where he died a month later of a strep infection.

Borromeo assistant Aloysius Averback, pastor Constantine Lagae, and Bro. James McNeive

A Renaissance Priest

Twice during the era of the brick church, Charles Charroppin—one of the Jesuits' most brilliant, congenial, and eccentric priests—served as associate pastor of St. Charles Borromeo. For three years between 1891 and 1893, Charroppin assisted Pastor Joseph Rosswinkel. Nearly two decades later he returned to the parish to live out the rest of his life as assistant to Pastor Joseph Rielag.

What people best remember about the bearded, portly priest was his thick, Caribbean accent, his telescope, and his seemingly far-fetched talk about the future. Margaret Thro Nunes, whose parents' house Charroppin frequently visited, recalls that often the priest amazed her family with information about the heavens and predictions of such things as the coming of air travel. Madeline Wilmes remembers that on certain Sunday evenings Charroppin gazed at the stars through his telescope, which he had set up in the front yard of her neighbors, the Schreiber family.

Charles Marie Charroppin was born in 1840 on the island of Guadeloupe in the West Indies. In 1863 he entered the Jesuit seminary in Florissant, where he soon developed a passion for science and the new technology of photography. During the 1870s and 1880s he roamed the grounds of the institution with his camera, documenting the daily life of the priests, brothers, and seminarians. After his ordination, Charroppin taught rhetoric, mathematics, chemistry, and astronomy at St. Louis University. He pioneered the use of the photographic stereopticon and became an expert on magic lantern slides.

Charroppin studied and photographed the heavens, even during a four-year stint as a missionary in Central America. He returned to the St. Louis area in 1898, and spent the next twelve years giving missions and lecturing about outer space and life in the tropics. During these years he made several visits to St. Charles Borromeo.

Around 1912 the aging Charroppin was named assistant to Father Joseph Rielag and chaplain of the Sacred Heart convent. Although he seems to have succeeded in the former capacity, he failed in the latter. "Fr. Charroppin made some new difficulty for the religious of the S. Heart," wrote one of his colleagues in *Historia Domus* in

November 1914. The next morning, "again another difficulty." In March 1915, another priest took over as the nuns' chaplain, and Charroppin received new orders to say daily Mass in the priest's private chapel. By this time, Charroppin was weakened by intermittent malarial fevers and other problems. He died later that year.

During his last years, the contributors to *Historia Domus* wrote frequently about the various types of slide shows put on by the Jesuits and the parish. The subjects of these shows were frequently religious, such as the life of Christ and "Eucharistic Views." Others concerned travelogue subjects like the Colorado Rockies, Glacier Park, and the Austrian Tyrol. Because of the great interest in photography, one of the Jesuit brothers built a darkroom in the rectory.

At about the same time, many parishioners watched early motion pictures projected through a device called a kinetoscope. The priests complained in *Historia Domus* about the difficulties of keeping their kinetoscope in repair. When it was operational, they offered weekly "sacred picture shows" in the school hall and did a brisk business ordering and returning films rented from a distributor in New Jersey.

Parish Demographics

Two curious records dated 1899 survive in the parish archives. Although comprehensive records were kept that year on baptisms, marriages, burials, and improvements to the church, as well as the day-to-day entries in *Historia Domus,* these two documents are unique. One contains the oldest surviving list of parish members, their addresses, annual pew rents and Easter contributions, as well as enough advertising to open a window onto life in St. Charles at the turn of the century. The other is a resolution to build the two-story addition to the brick school.

The first document is a crumbling booklet of twenty-eight pages entitled "Semi-Annual Bulletin" and dated April, 1899. Following a page of advertisements is a schedule for High and Low Masses, vespers, benediction, confessions, Sunday School instruction, and Sacred Heart devotions. Next comes a page of rules regarding pews and pew rentals, then a listing of sodalities and lay associations, their meetings and spiritual directors. After this page comes a large directory of parish families, with corresponding addresses and pew rents.

Just over 260 families are represented, with at least eighteen of them (nearly seven percent) living outside the city limits at such places as Harvester, Portage Township, Boschertown, Cul de Sac, and Black Walnut. Joseph Ruenzi, Sr., is noted as living at a "County Farm," John Leclaire (sexton) at the parish cemetery, and John Thompson at "Becker's Place." The Galt House and the Hoffman House are also listed as residences. Many parishioners lived on Benton Street, then known as "5 1/2 Street."

Subsequent bulletins offer more information on the demographics of the parish. In 1904, for example, the number of listed pew renters had risen to 277, of whom twenty lived outside the city limits. But in 1910 the number of pew renters had dropped to 165, of whom only eleven had rural addresses. Despite this drop in rentals, the 1910 bulletin is thicker than

Charles M. Charroppin, S.J., astronomer and character

previous editions. Increased advertising accounts for a few more pages, but a series of anonymous articles on religious themes takes up over fifty pages. Some titles include "The Infallible Authority of the Church," "Is One Religion Not as Good as Another?" "Witnesses for Nuns," "I Felt Two Feet High When I Left the Pope," and "The Truth about Mixed Marriages."

In the 1899 edition, a diagram of the church's interior and a schedule of pew rents follows the roster of pew renters. Rents were based on the location of the pews. Those closest to the altar in the central part of the church fetched nine dollars for the entire pew, or two dollars per sitting space. Side pews nearest the altar went for eight dollars, or $1.75 for each space. Sitting in the central section cost more than sitting to the left or right, even at the back of church—-the rearmost central row of pews cost six dollars in the aggregate or

$1.25 per space, while the rearmost side rows cost five dollars and one dollar, respectively. Flanking the side pews nearest the altar at both the left and right were several narrow "free" pews.

A list of parishioners and "their" pews and spaces comes next, then a record of who gave how much money for the 1899 Easter collection. Most members contributed about a dollar, although many gave less. Over twenty gave more.

The advertisements are perhaps the most interesting feature of the 1899 booklet. Not only parishioners took advantage of the chance to publicize their trades; a few local businesses not owned by Borromeo members advertised as well. So did the Sisters of Loretto. Their full-page ad for the "Parochial School" reads "Preparatory and Academic Courses, Music, Instrumental, and Vocal, Bookkeeping, Ellis System; German, and Needlework Taught. If Desired, in Private Lessons. *Punctuality and Neatness Especially Required.*"

In the same vein, an ad for the St. Charles Savings Bank boasts a capital of $50,000 and a surplus of $41,000. Not to be outdone, the First National Bank claims a $50,000 capital and a $50,000 surplus. Both the Charles E. Meyer Drugstore and the H. D. Meyer & Son Pharmacy notify readers of their services, as does Theodore H. Hackmann, Druggist.

A Thro's Clothiers advertisement appears in the front section and an ad for its competitor, the Palace Clothing Company, appears inside the back cover. Charles Rechtern's Red Store for Men advises the reader "Try us the next time you need anything in these lines." Henry C. Dallmeyer advertises an unusual business combination—"all kinds of furniture" and "a general undertaking business." E. H. Steinert, Bakery & Confectionery claims "foreign fruits a specialty." The booklet also contains ads for "base ball goods" at Fulkerson Brothers' store, P. F. Pallardy's stoves and tinware, George Ruenzi's tobacco products, and Mary C. Hebling's butcher shop.

In short, by the turn of the century many Borromeo parishioners were operators of small businesses. Some of these entrepreneurs were descendants of Creole families, but many were of German descent or birth. Certainly many other parishioners were farmers or worked for large employers such as the American Car and Foundry, but the existence of so many merchants and craftsmen was one sign of a growing middle class in St. Charles. By most accounts life was still difficult, but new opportunities for advancement existed, at least for those with a certain amount of drive and good luck. The standard of living of many members of St. Charles Borromeo was slowly rising.

With this material improvement came a great deal of concern for civic matters. The 1899 document concerning the school addition reveals a mixture of parochial and civic pride. The first page of the resolution sets forth the reasons for building a school addition, then lists in great detail the various lay associations and sodalities, their members and directors. On the second page is an exhaustive list of all national, state, and local politicians, from President William McKinley and his cabinet, to Missouri governor Lon V. Stephens and the state's officers, down to various county and city politicians, including Mayor Edward Paule and the city's councilmen. (Paule was the last nineteenth century mayor of town from the parish; others included John Hilbert, John C. Mittelberger, and Charles Hug.)

In language reminiscent of a chamber of commerce brochure, the importance of the American Car and Foundry to the economy of St. Charles is set out in detail. Then follows a paragraph on "a movement . . . to build a wagon and motor bridge across the Missouri River at this point, and also to a street car line between this city and the city of St. Louis." Parishioner Julius F. Rauch is named as treasurer of this "bridge company." Below his name is a roster of the city's three banks and their officers, many of whom were members of the congregation.

Last of all is a list of contributors to the school addition and their donations. Topping the list are Mrs. Bardo Weinert of St. Peters and James Short, both of whom paid $100. At the bottom of the list are the unnamed "colored ladies and gentlemen of the congregation," who donated a total of $4.75. Many parishioners donated $6.50, the value of a thousand bricks.

Pastors and Other Priests

John Roes: Apparently a persuasive, ambitious manager of the parish as well as a meticulous record keeper, Roes suffered in health during part of his pastorate. Around 1871 his flock presented him with "a very fine carriage . . . for the reason that his advanced age made horseback exercise too severe." Before coming to St. Charles, Roes spent several years at St. Louis University.

Borromeo was one of the pastor's last assignments; he was replaced in 1879 and died four years later in Chicago.

Joseph Zealand: A native of Holland, Zealand came to America in 1853 as a Jesuit novice recruited by Peter De Smet. After his ordination he served as dean, then president, of St. Louis University, as

Adrian Sweere, S.J., pastor 1885-88.

Jesuit Missouri Province Archives

Henry Baselmans, S.J., pastor 1888-89.

Jesuit Missouri Province Archives

well as president of Creighton College and St. Ignatius College of Chicago. Between 1879 and 1882 he served as Borromeo's first pastor after John Roes. For five years Zealand traveled the southern and eastern United States preaching missions, then returned to teaching. He died in 1904.

Victor Van der Putten: Born in the Netherlands in 1845, Van der Putten came to the Florissant novitiate in 1868. After his ordination as a Jesuit he taught at St. Ignatius College in Chicago, then traveled the country giving missions. Later he took charge of a black parish in Cincinnati and taught at that city's St. Xavier College. Not long after losing two of his assistants—Brother George Miles and Father Henry Van Mierlo, Van der Putten was transferred to Milwaukee to serve at Marquette College.

Adrian Sweere: With only one priest and two coadjutor brothers to assist him, Sweere for three years managed the parish with only two thirds the normal complement of Jesuits. Perhaps for this reason the recording of information into *Historia Domus* stopped early in his pastorate. It did not resume for another decade.

Henry Baselmans: Another Dutch recruit, Baselmans began his career in the United States by teaching at St. Louis University and ministering to the city's blacks. He later spent many years in Cincinnati as an assistant pastor and hospital chaplain. After

serving as pastor of St. Charles Borromeo, Baselmans moved to Chicago and spent the last years of his life as chaplain of Cook County's institutions for the less fortunate. He died in 1907.

Joseph Rosswinkel: A child immigrant to the United States from Germany, Rosswinkel entered the Jesuit novitiate at Florissant in 1871. After his ordination eleven years later, he worked at Marquette College in Milwaukee, served as superior of the Osage Mission in Kansas, and pastored St. Charles Borromeo for six years. He spent most of the remaining twenty-six years of his life as a traveling pulpit orator, giving parish missions and clerical retreats. He settled in 1920 at St. Mary's, Kansas, and died in 1922.

Joseph Meuffels: Historia Domus states that when word of this priest's departure from Borromeo in January of 1897 reached his parishioners, "they were moved to tears." Shortly afterward, Meuffels was sent to British Honduras, where he spent the remaining thirty-three years of his life. Known there as "El Padrecito" (the little father), Meuffels worked as a missionary and as a college chaplain in Belize. He died in 1931.

Constantine Lagae: A Belgian recruit of Father De Smet, Lagae came to the United States in 1870. He was ordained in 1875. Between 1880 and 1885 he traveled around the country giving missions. In 1885 he was assigned to a Chicago parish. During his years of service there he directed the Married Ladies' Sodality, which eventually numbered nearly 3,000. His next assignment was the pastorate of St. Charles Borromeo, where he served until 1911. He returned to his former Chicago parish, where he celebrated his golden jubilee in 1914 and his diamond jubilee in 1924. He died in 1925.

Joseph Rielag: A talented musician with a taste for jazz, Rielag began his priesthood as a teacher, but had trouble keeping order in the classroom. Afterward he served in various capacities until he became pastor of St. Charles Borromeo, where he seems to have succeeded very well. He died ten years after he left St. Charles, and a single newspaper notice of the Requiem Mass to be sung at Borromeo the day after he died drew enough mourners to pack the church.

Jesuit Missouri Province Archives

"Padrecito" Joseph Meuffels (at far right), missionary to British Honduras after his pastorate at Borromeo

Florentine Boudreaux

Jesuit Missouri Province Archives

Florentine Boudreaux: Like Charles Charroppin, Boudreaux was one of Borromeo's most brilliant and multi-talented Jesuits of this era. One of nine orphaned children from Louisiana, Boudreaux left the Florissant novitiate as a teenager because of his poor grades. After spending several years doing manual labor, Boudreaux reappeared at Florissant and this time took his studies by storm. He mastered Latin in a few months and developed a lifelong interest in chemistry. For some years after his ordination he taught college. Although Boudreaux preached in English, French, and Spanish, he reached a wider audience with his popular books, *The Happiness of Heaven* and *God Our Father.* He died in 1894.

Francis X. Kuppens: Another of Peter De Smet's Belgian recruits, Kuppens served as Borromeo associate in 1880 and again between 1901 and 1903. A young priest in the 1860s, he spent several years in the Montana territory ministering to native Americans and miners, then was assigned to St. Mary's Potawatomi mission in Kansas. He arrived too late at the steamboat landing to join De Smet on the trip to St. Mary's, so Kuppens built his own raft and floated downstream several hundred miles until he caught up with the other Jesuit. Later in his career Kuppens lived among the Sioux and Arapahoe tribes. After his second stint at Borromeo, he spent his remaining years at Florissant.

Part 4
The Present Church: Jesuit Era

Chapter 10
1915-26

Destruction and Aftermath

At 8:30 in the morning of Wednesday, July 7, 1915, former pastor Constantine Lagae, who had returned to the parish to witness the wedding of Marie Alexander and Joseph Neubeiser, celebrated the marriage in grand style in the brick church. Afterward, the couple and their families and friends left the building. The structure was deserted by the afternoon.

Sometime around 3:30 P.M., St. Charlesan Albert W. Heck took a walk across the Missouri River bridge, where he noticed the approach of a fierce windstorm. His description of the spectacle was later paraphrased in the *St. Charles Cosmos-Monitor*: " . . . there was an angry looking cloud of various colors approaching from the southwest and another equally as frightful coming from the northwest." When the two clouds came together, Heck said, they changed in color from greenish-gray to almost white. He heard a boom of thunder and felt a rush of wind, and observed that the mass of clouds, drawing nearer to St. Charles, began to bob up and down.

The storm first touched down in Wentzville, where it flattened several houses, killing one resident and blowing her two year-old daughter sixty feet through the air until she landed, uninjured, against a fence. A short distance to the east, the wind crushed more than a dozen buildings and killed another county resident. An O'Fallon man tried to outrace the threatening clouds while riding in a buggy with his wife and daughter, but was knocked unconscious by a flying object. When he came to, his team and buggy were gone and his wife and child dead. The winds raced on to St. Peters, collapsing houses and gravely injuring several people, but

Charles M. Charroppin, S.J.

Fr. Joseph Rielag's wrecked Metz "Runabout"

Margaret Thro Nunes

The destroyed nave and vestibule by S.G. Redden

avoided All Saints Church, rectory, and school.

St. Charles Borromeo was not as lucky. Sometime after 4:00 P.M., the storm blew into St. Charles and cut a path near the center of town. Eyewitness Sister M. Flaget of the Loretto community described what happened when the winds reached the parish buildings: "We lighted a blessed Candle, began prayers, when all at once we heard glass falling, saw trees breaking and in an instant such a crash."

The noise was the sound of the brick church being blown apart. In a few seconds the wind leveled the east and west walls of the structure, but it left portions of the front and rear walls standing. The roof was suddenly peeled off, opening the interior to the elements. Statues of St. Ignatius Loyola and St. Charles Borromeo fell to

the floor, but other statues remained unharmed on their pedestals. The Blessed Sacrament and several items from the destroyed sanctuary were swept into the air and fell through a hole torn in the rectory.

Outside, the hands of the south face of the huge steeple clock stopped at 4:12, but the hands of the east face continued moving until they came to rest at the 4:30 position. Even after the hands stopped moving, the clock continued to chime the hours. The steeple above the clock was swept off.

Father Joseph Rielag immediately ran over to the convent where he found the nuns frightened but uninjured. Closer to the rectory, he discovered that the Jesuits' newly purchased Metz roadster had been crushed by fallen debris. An unbroken piece of slate from the church's roof was later found, driven deep into a board, near the home of Arthur Mudd.

Within an hour of the storm, people began arriving to view the wreckage. So many turned out on July 8 that Father Henry Wolters, then the keeper of *Historia Domus*, complained: " . . . our premises are surrounded with sightseers from everywhere, especially from St. Louis. They come in all sorts of vehicles & motors till late in the night." Perhaps hoping someday to rebuild the Metz roadster, Brother Frank Murphy took the vehicle apart and stored the parts.

Archbishop John Glennon joined the visiting throngs the following day, offering his sympathy and a donation of $500. On July 10, two confessionals were set up in a classroom. That same day the girls of the parish began selling ice cream and soda at the ruins, and soon the married ladies added sandwiches and coffee. Two boxes for donations were set up on the site. Gradually, money began trickling in.

On Sunday, July 11, over a hundred parishioners met in the school hall to make plans for the construction of a church of "at least the same proportions and beauty as the old church." Elected to oversee the effort was a general building committee consisting of twenty-three of the parish men. An oral pledge campaign then commenced, and soon about $8,000 was promised. Several parishioners also promised to donate labor. Afterward, those on the General Committee elected Julius Rauch as chairman and J. T. Kaemmerlen as secretary, then divided themselves into subcommittees: one for debris removal, another for finances, and a third for building a new church or rebuilding the old one, if possible. The debris removal team went to work the next day.

On July 13 Montrose W. Hayes, district forecaster for the U. S. Weather Bureau, filed a report based on his investigation into the nature of the storm. Hayes had visited St. Charles on July 8 and had measured the path of destruction at about four-fifths of a mile long and 1,000 feet wide, with the greatest damage being done "over a stretch about 2,500 feet long and 150 feet wide," and ending at Borromeo Church. Hayes' report noted that the structure's side walls and roof had fallen to the east, leaving little debris to the west. Finding no evidence of an explosion, he surmised that a good deal of the damage may have been due to poor construction, because "between most of the bricks and mortar of the west wall there was no bond; the mortar was of lime and sand." Hayes then ruled, based on this and other evidence (such as the direction in which trees near the path had fallen) that a tornado had not occurred. His conclusion is still debated, especially by those who witnessed the storm.

Insurance adjusters visited the site on the same day that Hayes ruled out the possibility of a tornado. They returned for the last time on July 14. "We won't know the result for some time. . . , " wrote Father Wolters in *Historia Domus*. "Anyhow, we can now remove all debris without let or hindrance."

But before the wreckage was disturbed, photographers from all over captured the scene on film. Shots taken by S. G. Redden of St. Charles soon became picture postcards. Charles B. Bromschwig of St. Louis mounted his views on thick cardboard frames and perhaps sold a few at the site. Still professionally active, eighty-year-old Rudolph Goebel photographed the wrecked interior. Even Father Charles Charroppin, who died a few weeks later of a perforated gall bladder, set up his camera in the sanctuary and recorded the main altar partially buried under splintered lumber.

For the next few months the school building, St. Peter's Church, the Sacred Heart convent, and various other locations were pressed into service for Masses, confessions, funerals, baptisms, weddings, and other activities. As debris removal got underway, a crowd of architects, builders, contractors, and agents of all sorts began calling on the Jesuits.

Preparing to Rebuild

Throughout July, volunteers and paid laborers continued to clear the site and visitors continued to arrive. The Married Ladies Sodality swept and dusted the school hall, the temporary place of worship, but because no musical instrument had been procured only low Masses could be offered. Father Rielag went to St. Louis on July 19 to look at some new churches, and that evening the Lyric Airdome held a benefit for the church by showing a well-patronized film (with "no objectionable features," according to Father Wolters).

Father Rielag and the Building Committee returned to St. Louis two days later. A power outage did not prevent the group from meeting in the Jesuits' parlor that evening; by candlelight the men talked over plans for construction of the new church. One of the architects they discussed was the German-born Louis Wessbecher, who, since immigrating to St. Louis in the early 1880s, had designed many religious buildings in the St. Louis area, including the churches of St. Engelbert, Holy Ghost, St. Hedwig, and Sacred Heart of Florissant, as well as the new buildings at St. Stanislaus Seminary in Florissant and the convent of the Sisters of the Precious Blood in Ruma, Illinois. His firm was called Wessbecher and Hillebrand, and his office was located in downtown St. Louis.

On July 22 the parish engaged Wessbecher to draw up plans and specifications. Salvage operations were already well underway; parishioners and paid help combed the ruins for copper and kindling, both of which were sold. Additional funds arrived that week from lawn socials given by the families of Joseph Lackland and Julius Rauch. The Finance Committee circulated a letter to brother Knights of Columbus throughout the land with this grandiloquent appeal: ". . . believing that you are actuated by the noble spirit and lofty aspirations which induced the Knights of old to sacrifice fortune and even life in an endeavor to rescue from desecration the resting place of the Saviour, to aid us in the rebuilding [of] the church we loved so well. . . . " Contributions from councils as far away as New York, Texas, Louisiana, and California began arriving, along with many donations from the midwestern councils.

On July 28 the General Committee met in the school hall. First came the news that the foundation of the brick church was unsuitable for new construction. Then the committee announced the employment of Louis Wessbecher, based on his estimate of $52,000 for a new Romanesque structure, "allowing all the old material left from the old church suitable for use to be taken." The group voted unanimously to endorse Wessbecher as architect and to carry out his plans. The Finance Committee reported that pledges amounted to $11,584 and that cash donations totaled $3,156. Tornado insurance on the wrecked church amounted to $6,000.

The Jesuits looked outside the city limits for help. On July 30 Henry Rauch drove Father Wolters to St. Peters, O'Fallon, and St. Paul, where Wolters "secured the good will of the pastors to solicit among their parishioners." That evening he added in *Historia Domus* that he had been "received

Louis Wessbecher

Architect,

Office:

Rooms 46 and 47 Koken Bldg

715 Locust Street,

ST. LOUIS.

―――――――

Kirchenarchitektur Specialität.

One of architect Louis Wessbecher's professional advertisements, in English and German.

very kindly by all." The next week, Henry Rauch's brother Julius drove Wolters to Portage des Sioux, where the pastor of St. Francis Assisi parish donated five dollars and announced the need for additional funds at Sunday Mass.

During the second week of August, representatives of wrecking companies submitted bids on demolishing the remaining structure. A clockmaker removed the dials from the steeple clock on August 9. Soon afterward, the parish retained the St. Louis wrecking firm of Schweitzer & Lynch Company. Demolition began August 12. The work proceeded so smoothly the first week that all the brickwork at the rear of the church was cleared. Schweizer's crew then got busy removing the foundation of the east wall and taking the bells down from the steeple.

Inclement weather occasionally caused delays, but labor unrest soon resulted in work stoppages that recurred on and off until the church was finished. Father Wolters first wrote about these problems on August 23: ". . . the city teamsters made [a] difficulty and stopped the other teams." Exactly what happened is unknown, but at about this time labor organizations in many sections of the United States were struggling to become established. Tension must have resulted on August 28, when Schweitzer & Lynch's wreckers refused to continue working after 5 P.M., and at noon on September 6 when they left the job in honor of Labor Day (a national holiday for certain workers since 1894).

Excavation on the south end of the church began August 24. Although *Historia Domus* did not mention the discovery of skeletons, the *St. Charles Cosmos-Monitor* did:

Workmen excavating for the new Borromeo Church are making some

John F. Ueberle, owner of the Ueberle and Son Construction Company

Carl J. Ueberle

grewsome [sic] finds in the old church yard which was for many years used as a cemetery. . . . They are finding skeletons and tomb stones under the ground. The bones are being carefully preserved and will be buried in the cemetery of the church.

The wreckers collapsed the steeple on August 26, cleared the resulting debris, then excavated the north side. By the middle of September the excavation was deep enough for the building committee to take bids on a basement for the new church. Ueberle and Son, a St. Charles contractor, submitted the lowest bid and was unanimously awarded the job.

Schweitzer and Lynch's men discovered the cornerstone of the brick church on September 23. With little work remaining, their force split up two days later. Several men, four teams of draft animals, and three wagons returned to St. Louis. Those men left behind annoyed the Jesuits by taking another week to finish the job. *"Deo Gratias"* ("Thanks be to God") wrote Wolters in *Historia Domus* when the excavation was all over.

Ueberle and Son got to work almost immediately. Gravel was delivered on October 7, and the next day concrete mixers began pouring. Within a week, stone masons were laying the foundation and steamfitters were making connections with the boiler room. As work progressed, the Building Committee held frequent meetings to consider bids on the different types

of work to be done, such as steel erecting, plumbing, and wiring. Cold weather slowed construction, but other activities continued. Late in October, Father Rielag bought another vehicle, an "auto runabout," and with Brother Murphy set about learning how to drive. The two men put their new skills to work by motoring out to the country on November 9 "to collect among the farmers."

Steel erection got underway in November, prompting the Building Committee to consider bids on the upper structure. At this point the parish had still not decided whether to build the new church of brick or stone. At a General Committee meeting on January 16, 1916, Julius Rauch reported that "the difference in the cost of the brick under that of the Bedford stone was not more than about $6,000." All in attendance voted for a stone church, provided that the Archbishop approve the plan and additional financing be arranged.

On January 21, Ueberle and Son won the contract to build the rest of the church. Snow, sleet, and cold temperatures slowed construction until the spring. Workers

Steel erection went on throughout the winter of 1915-16.

So many gathered for the April 16, 1916, laying of the cornerstone that Archbishop Glennon was unable to process around the block.

Irene Knoblach

poured a concrete floor on March 9 and the steps on March 11. On March 21, Father Rielag met with Archbishop Glennon to make arrangements for the laying of the cornerstone. Palm Sunday (April 16) was the date chosen. Father Henry Kister, formerly of St. Charles, agreed to speak at the event but later declined due to poor health. In his place Father Rielag secured Father Michael Stritch, S.J., a St. Louis University professor of philosophy and a noted orator.

On March 23 the first carload of Bedford stone arrived. The next day a steam engine for the derrick was put up. Steel erection progressed when the weather allowed but labor problems sometimes interfered. One day after the unionized steelworkers dropped and bent the first truss, Louis Wessbecher showed up at the site and ordered the men to perform their jobs well. Work then proceeded slowly for a few days. On April 10 Father Wolters wrote in *Historia Domus:* "Steelworkers did not come in spite of their promises and most favorable weather." But a few days later, when a mishap involving the same men occurred, he wrote " . . . thank God, but little damage resulted."

Three weeks before Palm Sunday, the General Committee decided "that the cornerstone laying of the new church should be celebrated with all the possible ceremonies." The group resolved to invite neighboring parishes, to process to the construction site in a parade with at least one marching band and to sell souvenir buttons and badges. The Finance Committee than moved to issue bonds to help pay for the construction. The group approved, and also voted to raise additional money with a special monthly collection.

April 16 was a threatening, cloudy day. Archbishop Glennon arrived in St. Charles around 4:00 but was unable to process around the block because about 5,000 people had gathered on the property. According to *Historia Domus,* the archbishop then "made the rounds and [blessed] the walls on the floor of the church. Fr. Stritch preached a fine sermon and His Grace followed him with a few most appropriate remarks." The *St. Charles Cosmos-Monitor* noted that priests from fifteen nearby parishes attended.

Into the new cornerstone went the contents of the brick church's cornerstone; photographs of the inside and outside of the brick church and of its ruins; photographs of the current construction and an artist's conception of the finished church; a newspaper from July 8, 1915, featuring a description of the destructive storm; issues dated April 15, 1916, of the *Cosmos-Monitor* and *Banner News;* the April 16 issue of the St. Louis German daily, *Amerika;* a long list of contributors; a document signed by Louis Wessbecher, John Ueberle, and the Building Committee; and a special memorial written in Latin, in the elegant script of the Sacred Heart nuns.

Construction and Dedication

Structural work on the church progressed during the spring of 1916. Parish fund-raising continued. On April 24 the school children held a benefit bazaar in two of the classrooms. The priests distributed special envelopes at all the Masses on April 30, instructing parishioners to return them "with a day's wages in them."

As the weather improved, construction picked up speed, but labor problems were never far away. Father Wolters wrote in *Historia Domus* on April 24, 1916, that "union officials came out and made some trouble on account of non-union laborers." On May 11 he noted that "a couple of union men from St. Louis came this morning and made some difficulty among our laborers." Unrest may have resulted; by May 15 only Fred Ueberle, son of the contractor, was working as a stonemason. "It is a sheer impossibility for him to keep ahead of the brick masons," noted Wolters. Two days later, another man went to work helping Ueberle set stones. Entries in *Historia Domus* indicate that the Jesuits expected more stonemasons to report for work, but that none did.

However slowly, the walls rose. On June 16 the masons struggled to position a keystone over one of the front doors. Later that month the workers began lifting the blocks with a steam hoist, and work continued to progress. On June 26 an "... agent for the Dubuque, Ia., Church Furniture Co. was here with a sample seat and 3 samples of ends for seats." The next day, representatives of glass firms called on the Building Committee. The Young Ladies Sodality presented altar linens for the new church on June 29. The next day Father Wolters wrote: "Brick masons could work only part of the day, because the stone setters could not keep enough ahead."

Although nearly every entry made in *Historia Domus* during 1916 concerns work on the new church, a few entries reveal how national events influenced the people of the parish. News of Pancho Villa's daring raid on Columbus, New Mexico, coincided with a lawn social given on June 20 and 21 by Mr. and Mrs. John Kelly, and probably helped boost attendance. Two weeks later, Dr. Frank Tainter came by the rectory to say farewell. He was being mustered out to staff a hospital on the Texas front, as General John J. "Blackjack" Pershing was assembling forces along the border to chase Villa back into Mexico.

By July 1916 the walls were high enough for sanctuary windows to be installed. Fred Ueberle and the one other stonemason finished the west wall on July 29. Perhaps because no other laborers had reported to work, "some negroes hauled stone as long as necessary" that day. The next shipment of stone arrived in mid-August. On the

24th of that month, steelworkers began to raise the supports over the sanctuary. On August 29 someone left unnamed in *Historia Domus* "tried to palm off some second-hand bricks on us but did not succeed." Louis Wessbecher responded by returning to St. Charles and criticizing some of the work. Progress slowed for the next few days.

Although a clear connection cannot always be drawn between labor problems and progress on the church, it seems that bad feelings between union and non-union workers probably led to certain delays. Again, on September 11 a crew of tinners disputed a point in their contract, and four days later stopped work because of a conflict involving the copper hangers. Wessbecher returned. A crew of slaters began roofing in September. Plasterers got to work on the interior walls that month; the brickwork and most of the stonework were finished. Laborers dismantled the steam hoist, moved it, and put it back together for work on the steeple. The spire of the short steeple went up October 3, the same day that a stone cross over the central front door was set in place. On October 4 the hoist began lifting rocks and mortar to the steeple.

The following morning a crate of dynamite fell off a railroad car near an explosives plant at Grafton, Illinois. The resulting blast killed three men and injured many others, tore trees out of the ground, knocked a panel off a passing steamboat, and rattled buildings in St. Charles. That afternoon, nine workmen at the church safely rode the hoist to the steeple, perhaps to make sure that the newly-placed louvres held tight. Also, according to Father Wolters, a slater "had some trouble with the union."

On the morning of October 6, with about two days' work left to do, thirty-five year-old Fred Ueberle and three carpenters boarded the hoist for the steeple landing, though the hoist was normally used only for freight. As the men neared their destination the cable broke. All four plummeted

C. Fred Ueberle not long before his fatal accident.

Carl J. Ueberle

nearly fifty feet to the ground and were rushed to the hospital. The three carpenters recovered slowly, but Ueberle, whose back and feet had been crushed, developed complications and died on October 13. His funeral three days later drew a large crowd of people to St. Peter's Church.

Ueberle's family believed that all but two strands of the cable had been cut. Labor problems had dogged his company throughout the job: on several mornings his men had arrived to find broken glass and cinders in their concrete mixers. They believed that union workers had planted the material in order to intimidate non-union workers. Similarly, they believed that whoever sabotaged the cable could not have known that men, not freight, would go up in the lift that morning. Witnesses agreed that the hoist had safely carried several loads of rocks and mortar before the accident, and that the cable was relatively new. A neighbor claimed to have seen a man running from the construction site early the morning of the accident, but nothing was ever proven.

Eleven days after Ueberle's death Father Rielag met with union officials, but no record remains of their discussion. The three surviving carpenters brought suit against the Ueberle Company and won, collecting so much in damages that John F. Ueberle went out of business. He tried to reestablish his business in St. Louis but had

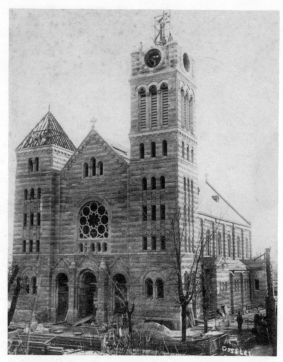

The nearly completed church, with elevator hoist inside the west tower

little success. The widow of Fred Ueberle went to work to support the couple's four children and never remarried.

One day after the funeral, James Lawler, Julius Rauch, and the family of Henry F. Pieper offered to donate the sanctuary windows. Soon afterward, the glass began to arrive. Just before Thanksgiving, the parish held a large bazaar in the newly finished basement. The usual games and booths did well, but the most successful novelty of the fair was the parcel post booth, in which patrons bought "mystery" items donated and shipped via parcel post by out-of-town friends. Shortly after the bazaar, the basement was furnished with benches and confessionals. Masses were then held under the church, freeing the school hall.

Much of the inside work progressed rapidly over the winter, but cold temperatures slowed work outdoors. Still, progress was made. On December 22 all three bells were

ready for use. The next week, slaters installed a lightning rod over the short steeple. Carpenters built stairs inside the steeple tower in January. On February 10, the main steeple cross was mounted. "A splendid sight," commented Father Wolters.

In March craftsmen applied scagliola, an ornamental marble-like finish, to the concrete pillars and flat pilasters. That same month a Chicago glazier finished installing stained glass windows. In April a laborer named Max Neumeyer erected the three altars from the brick church. A terrazzo floor was laid in the baptistry and vestibule, and a lapidolith finish was applied to the concrete floors.

In May workers installed pews and the communion railing and volunteers helped clean the building. The new church was ready to be blessed by the Archbishop on May 27, 1917. The *Cosmos-Monitor* described the happy occasion:

> The ceremonies carried out in the blessing of the new St. Charles Borromeo Church were imposing and a large crowd was present notwithstanding the threatening weather. The exterior of the church was first blessed, then the interior. At the blessing of the interior the litany of All Saints together with a special invocation in honor of St. Charles Borromeo was added to ask heaven's blessing on the church and city.
>
> The blessing of the church was followed by a solemn High Mass with Rev. Joseph Rielag as celebrant and Rev. Henry Wolters and Rev. Arnold Acker as deacon and subdeacon. Besides the Archbishop, John J. Glennon, there were present the following priests: Bernard Otting, Michael O'Connor, F. X. Willmes, Patrick Ryan, John Foley, Florentine Bechtel, Michael Garraghan, Henry Kister, Andrew Ganss, Constantine Lagae, and James O'Meara.

After the dedication Father Rielag bought cloth for confessional curtains.

Mrs. Theodore Schlueter gave a lawn social on June 18 to raise money for a new organ. The following week, clockmaker George Hoffmann began to install the four clock faces from the brick church steeple into the tower of the new church.

World War I

Life gradually returned to normal after the dedication. Although the major construction was finished, the church was not yet truly completed. Embellishments such as frescoing for the walls and stained glass for the upper windows were not added until years later. Statues arrived one by one for a long time—two adoring angels for the main altar, and Saints Ignatius Loyola, Aloysius Gonzaga, and Charles Borromeo for other prominent locations. Work on the church's heating system lasted well into the winter of 1917-1918, so that many Masses and other services during those months were held in the church basement.

For perhaps the first time in over two years, Father Wolters wrote about the Jesuits' kinetoscope in a *Historia Domus* entry dated September 4, 1917. Other entries mention euchres, benefit card parties, chautauquas, and similar diversions frequently noted in the journal before the destruction of the brick church. But time had not stood still; on November 12, 1917, Brother Frank Murphy reported to the Navy recruiter in St. Louis for a physical examination. Three days later he left for a naval base in Chicago. The "Great War" had reached St. Charles.

War-related activities affected life for a long time. In December 1917, Father Rielag delivered a speech at a Red Cross meeting in Portage des Sioux. The following February, Father Wolters referred to a national emergency measure when he wrote in *Historia Domus,* "The euchre this evening was well-attended, despite the very cold weather. A few minutes past 10 P.M. we could turn out all the lights, hence the civil order was practically not transgressed." Daylight Savings Time went into effect for the first time in the nation on March 30, Holy Saturday, "Before retiring, our clock was advanced 1 hour and until October services will take place in accordance with that time." Wolters later wrote that he was not accustomed to "clock time."

Father Rielag attended several Liberty Loan meetings in April 1917. Fearing that May devotions would conflict with "Red Cross doings," the priest rescheduled them to the daytime. Wearing his Navy uniform, Brother Murphy visited the parish one last time before shipping out. Spanish influenza, which afflicted one of the Loretto Sisters in May, swept through the parish in October. "By order of an ordinance we had to suspend the school and church services until further notice and the church is to remain closed," wrote Father Wolters. The order was rescinded on November 1.

The parish celebrated the end of World War I twice within one week, on November 7 and 11, 1918:

> About noon [on November 7], the whistles blew and the bells were rung to announce that Germany had signed up for an armistice. In the afternoon the noise was repeated and there was marching headed by a band, and after all that [the] news turned out to be a veritable "hoax."
>
> At 6:30 a.m. [on November 11] the news came that now there is really an armistice and immediately the people repeated the celebration.

The cast of At the End of the Rainbow

Borromeo held its own celebration in the form of a "Victory Bazaar" on the next day.

Everyday life settled back to normal, and parish life assumed a pace similar to that enjoyed during the last years of the brick church. Borromeo's young men and women gave a popular play, "At the End of the Rainbow" on May 20 and 21, 1919. Missions, triduums, retreats, and devotions resumed as before. A major change was in store, however, in the person of a new pastor. On August 21, 1919, Borromeo's first Irish-American pastor, Father Stephen McNamara, arrived.

Because much of Joseph Rielag's pastorate had been taken up with unpleasant matters—rebuilding the church, soliciting funds, negotiating with builders, and seeing the parish through the war, among others—Father McNamara probably had an advantage over his predecessor in winning the parishioners' cooperation. By all accounts he amply succeeded: Father "Mack" is remembered by many as a pastor who won the peoples' hearts as well.

Father Wolters recorded the parish return to normalcy until he became ill in September 1921. His entries in *Historia Domus* note that on September 22, 1919, classes were dismissed "on account of the circus." Shortly after McNamara arrived, the rectory, convent, and school all received a new coat of paint. The parish young people put on a comedy in November, and movies resumed on a regular schedule in the school hall. On January 30, 1920, the parish purchased an electric player piano from the Pup Saloon for the school hall. The next month, Borromeo's young men and women held a Valentine party in the school hall (and no doubt put the saloon piano to use). The stereopticon got a workout on March 18 of that year, as McNamara gave the school children an illustrated presentation about his travels in Glacier Park. The next month, magician Karl Kringsberg entertained a large crowd in the school.

On July 6, 1920, the parish showed motion pictures to an "immense" crowd on the school lawn and served ice cream and cake afterward. During the summer Father McNamara cooled off at Weber Lake and went fishing. The following winter, Borromeo's basketball team took on the St. Louis University basketball team and several other teams. An acting troupe from St. Peters, Missouri, put on "For the Love of Johnny" before a large audience at the school. The parish's own players staged a comedy called "The Districk Skule" in the spring of 1921, netting $433.50.

Popular dancing seems to have returned during the pastorate of Father McNamara: Father Wolters recorded that on the night of July 21, 1920, a dance was given in the school hall. Wolters, who was much older than McNamara, had apparent reservations about such frivolity. On May 13, 1920, after Father McNamara had brought his own teenaged nephew to St. Charles for an overnight break from prep school, Wolters suggested in *Historia Domus* what may have transpired: "Tonight there was a tacky party in the school hall."

After Father Wolters stopped writing in *Historia Domus,* the journal was neglected until 1926, when McNamara was replaced as pastor. But the parish kept other records during those years, among them a book of minutes from Mothers Club meetings concerning the parish school. These minutes cover the years from 1922 to 1928 and reveal a good deal about the issues concerning Borromeo's parents during that era.

The Mothers Club discussed buying desks for the seventh and eighth grade students at their first meeting in 1922. Various members donated up to five dollars each, and Mrs. Edith Emmons and Mrs. Adolph Thro agreed to negotiate for the desks with the board of education. At the next meeting, Mrs. Emmons reported that enough desks for the whole school had been purchased, at $2.00 and $2.50 each, but that $300 was still unpaid. Father McNamara then loaned the club $300.

At the next meetings, McNamara and the mothers deliberated about the condition of the boys' toilet (deciding to let the men

of the parish handle the matter), the need for an additional teacher (postponing a decision until the next year) and various means of raising money to repay the $300 loan (holding a bake sale, a "picture show benefit," and an apron sale). The women put on all three fund raisers and eventually paid the debt.

Next they raised money to buy small desks, tables, and chairs for the primary room. "We are to send all of our old desks to a mission school in Mexico," noted the secretary. At further meetings, the women discussed purchasing a drinking fountain and two lavatory wash stands. Father McNamara changed his mind about letting go of the old desks, advising the club that "he had a plan for reconstructing them into seats for the basement of the church." A hot lunch program was deemed impracticable in 1923, as was a movement to start a free school based on voluntary pledges.

The club decided to give a school picnic on June 20, 1923: "Each child to bring 25 cents to the Sisters and in return to be given a ticket for which they could get their dinner, two ice cream cones and a bottle of soda, each ticket to be punched four times." The women raised enough money to have the windows washed and the screens covered with new screening, but a paper drive went awry when they col-

Father McNamara and the Men's Choir. From left, Oliver ("Sam") Denker, Edward Schreiber, Chester Boschert, Stephen McNamara, S.J., Edward L. Meyer, Ed McGinnis, and Joseph Marheineke

The cast of The Districk Skule

lected more old papers than they could store. A benefit dance on May 16, 1924, featuring a five-piece orchestra, was "a social as well as a financial success, netting us the sum of $132.70." Through the years the club funded the school picnic, the children's Christmas party, various improvements inside the school building, and the periodic oiling of the school's yard.

Although he was stationed in St. Charles only seven years, Father McNamara is remembered with deep affection. He organized and refereed football games, which were played at times on the Sacred Heart grounds. He made impromptu appearances on stage during school plays to steal the scene and tell a few jokes. Children of the 1920s recall that the fun-loving priest enjoyed riding around town with his Ford

full of schoolchildren. Billye Wentker Williams remembers his explanation of how he got along without a functioning speedometer: "At the first ten miles the fenders rattle, at the second ten miles the whole car rattles, and at the third ten miles your bones rattle." Father "Mack" had a temper, however; one parishioner remembers that when the priest found an older boy fighting a boy from the first grade, he quickly settled the matter with a punch to the older boy's nose.

McNamara had a knack for getting along with his adult parishioners. *Historia Domus* mentions his hunting and fishing trips with some of Borromeo's men and his visits to parishioners outside the city limits, but he called on close neighbors as well. Some remember that Father "Mack" occasionally asked them on short notice to serve as altar boys, choir girls, or occasionally as matrimonial witnesses. Like the other priests of his era, he responded at all hours to sick calls and to confession calls made by means of an electric bell hooked up to the church's confessionals.

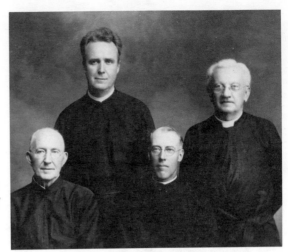

Borromeo's Jesuits, 1921. Front row: Brother Edward McGuire and Father Stephen McNamara. Back row: Father John Foley and Father Henry Wolters.

Pastors and Associates

Stephen McNamara: Before coming to St. Charles in 1919, Father McNamara worked five years in Wyoming on the Wind River Indian Reservation. Unable to reach all his far-flung mission stations by horse, McNamara was given a new Ford by his many friends—parishioners of all ages as well as Protestants. Always a "people priest," McNamara spent his six years at Borromeo administering the sacraments and devotional services, visiting the sick, entertaining the children, and maintaining good relations with the adults. During his pastorate he organized many ice cream socials, movies, and dances. In 1926 he traded places with Father Henry Ehrhard—Ehrhard became pastor of Borromeo and McNamara took over for Ehrhard at St. Francis Xavier church in Kansas City. McNamara later returned to mission work on the Pine Ridge Indian Reservation.

Henry Wolters: A Dutch recruit to the Florissant novitiate, Wolters taught philosophy for several years at St. Louis University. He began parish work in rural Missouri,

then did mission work in British Honduras. After returning to the United States, he served at Jesuit parishes in Kansas City and Chicago before coming to St. Charles as an associate pastor in 1911. Besides saying Mass, Wolters heard confessions, taught catechism, moderated several lay associations, and made daily entries in *Historia Domus*. He died in 1922 at the age of sixty-eight.

John Foley: Born in Massachusetts to Irish immigrants, Foley dropped out of school after the eighth grade and went to work in a textile mill. Discovering that steel mills paid more, he joined the steelworkers union and worked his way across the eastern United States. At the age of twenty-two, he met St. Louis University's Father Francis Finn, who interested him in becoming a Jesuit. Foley attended night classes at the University and worked during the day in a foundry, then completed his education at St. Mary's College in Kansas, where he also became a famous football player. Because he was older than most of his classmates,

IN MEMORY OF
Rev. Joseph M. Haas, S. J.

Born August 30, 1868
Entered the Society of Jesus
September 1, 1891
Died October 26, 1943

MAY HE REST IN PEACE

Jesuit Missouri Province Archives

Memorial card of Joseph Haas, S.J.

many called him "Dad." He was ordained in 1908. Six years later, Foley was appointed pastor of St. Ignatius church in Chicago, where he developed nervous problems. He was transferred the following year to St. Charles as an associate pastor. While at Borromeo, Foley led missions and devotions, organized sports events, and illustrated his sermons with stories from his years as a laborer. He later served in Detroit and Milwaukee, then retired to St. Mary's, Kansas. He died in 1944.

John Otten: A bronze plaque that hung for more than three decades in the vestibule of Borromeo church erroneously listed Otten as pastor from 1925 to 1926, but during that time McNamara served as pastor and Otten served as superior of the house. After Henry Ehrhard took over both functions in 1926, Otten worked as chaplain of the Sacred Heart community until 1928. As a young man, Otten came to America to escape German military service and to acquire an education. He studied at St. Mary's College and at St. Louis University. After his ordination he pastored the St. Joseph parish of St. Louis and the Sacred Heart parish of Florissant, and traveled the mission circuit of German communities. Around 1913 Otten developed diabetes, from which he never fully recovered. His worsening condition forced him in 1928 to return to Florissant, where he died in 1930.

Joseph Haas: Born in the state of New York in 1868, Haas entered the Prairie du Chien novitiate in his early twenties. He was ordained in 1901, spent time in Holland, then went to work teaching. He performed pastoral service at Mankato, Minnesota, and later in Cleveland. He lived in St. Charles from 1922 to 1926, during which time he excelled in service to local poor people. He lived afterward at St. Mary's in Kansas and died in 1943.

Brother Edward McGuire: A native of Ireland, McGuire came to the United States at the age of nineteen. Three years later he entered the Florissant novitiate, where he studied and worked in the kitchen. For forty-six years after entering the Society of Jesus he cooked his way through parishes in Florissant, Normandy, St. Charles, Omaha, Kansas City, and again at St. Charles. McGuire retired from Borromeo's rectory kitchen in 1924 and went to work in the sacristy. He celebrated his diamond jubilee in 1937; a clerestory window in church memorializes the occasion. After his death the following year, the School Sisters of Notre Dame took charge of the sacristy.

People

Alton and *Anna Dryden:* Two of Borromeo's black parishioners, the Drydens moved to St. Charles from Silex, Missouri, before 1900 in order to have their many children educated. Because Borromeo School was not yet integrated, their children attended Franklin School. In church the Drydens sat in the rear rows set aside for blacks. Their long membership in the parish was not mentioned in the surviving annual bulletins from that era. Alton Dryden worked for the St. Charles Ice and Coal Company. He and his wife are buried in the parish cemetery.

Bernard Dyer: A native of St. Paul, Dyer attended Valparaiso University in Indiana and the Chicago Law School before moving to St. Charles. For move than fifty years he practiced law in St. Charles and also served briefly as a circuit judge. Dyer acted as the first chairman of the parishioners interested in rebuilding the destroyed church and later served the parish in many other capacities. He died in 1954.

James Lawler: One of Borromeo's most influential parishioners from this era, Lawler headed the church rebuilding effort. He believed that the parish would soon outgrow a church the same size as the old one, so he insisted that the new structure be larger. A native of Indiana, Lawler came to St. Charles in 1879 seeking work as a blacksmith, and found it at the St. Charles Car Company. He soon made foreman, and rose through the ranks until becoming superintendent of the entire plant.

Lawler adopted St. Charles Borromeo parish with gusto. He helped organize the St. Charles Council of the Knights of Columbus and served as the group's first Grand Knight. He also belonged to the Catholic Knights of America and many civic organizations. His wife, Elizabeth, involved herself in various lay groups and took a leading role in putting on the parish bazaars. The couple had seven children. The Lawler residence still stands at 305 Morgan Street.

Charles Mudd: A son of the Jesuits' doctor, Mudd grew up in the family home at Third and Decatur Streets. He influenced parish affairs as a banker and a community leader and served in various ways during the rebuilding effort. Shortly after the present church was completed, Mudd helped lead a campaign to build a new public high school.

Henry G. Rauch: With his brother Julius, Rauch organized the St. Charles Electric Express Company to haul freight over the Highway Bridge (now Route 115, or the "old" bridge) between St. Louis and St. Charles. In later years he organized both Rauch Lumber Company and Rauch Truck Lines. After the brick church was destroyed, he joined the General and Finance committees, and drove the Jesuits around St. Charles county as they begged for funds. He and his family lived at 515 North Benton. Rauch died in 1953.

Julius Rauch: Born in Evansville, Illinois, Rauch moved as a child to St. Charles. In

Henry G. Rauch

Henry and Elizabeth Rauch

James G. Lawler

St. Charles County Historical Society

1885 he married Aggie Machens in the brick church and remained a very active parishioner all his life. Rauch worked as a bank cashier and later became an executive of the First Union Bank. He and his family lived in an elegant brick house at the corner of Jefferson and Fifth Streets. He died in 1946.

Katie Shore: One of St. Charles' most philanthropic women, Miss Shore converted to Catholicism from the Episcopalian faith. For many years she lived in her parents' Second Empire mansion at 535 North Benton. She donated thousands of dollars to Borromeo parish and in later years funded Father William Sommerhauser's ill-fated

effort to write the history of the parish. Miss Shore was active in the choir. She died in 1942.

Henry Wilmes: A native of Josephville, Missouri, Wilmes married Bernadine Kersting and eventually moved his young family from St. Louis to St. Charles, where he opened the St. Charles Ice and Coal Company. The father of five children, Wilmes belonged to the Married Men's Sodality and joined the committees to finance and rebuild the new church. His family later donated one of its stained glass windows. A successful businessman until the Depression, Wilmes died in 1931.

Chapter 11
1926-42

Father Henry Ehrhard

Father McNamara had problems as an administrator despite his success with people. From September 1925 until August 1926 he was relieved of his position as superior of the house, an office almost always held by a pastor. Unfortunately, the records do not tell why. The new superior was the ailing Father John Otten, a man few parishioners remember. McNamara continued as pastor until replaced in August 1926 by Father Henry Ehrhard. Shortly thereafter McNamara and Otten departed, leaving Ehrhard to serve as both pastor and superior of the house.

Henry Ehrhard was Borromeo's first "hometown" pastor. Born in 1877 to Robert and Elizabeth Borgmeyer Ehrhard, he attended St. Peter's school and St. Mary's College in Kansas. In 1898 Ehrhard entered the St. Stanislaus Seminary in Florissant and later studied theology at St. Louis University. He was ordained at the age of thirty-five. After teaching at Rockhurst College and serving as assistant pastor of St. Francis Xavier parish in Kansas City, Missouri, he was assigned pastor of St. Charles Borromeo.

Ehrhard promptly explained the situation he had inherited in looseleaf addi-

tions to *Historia Domus:*

> Fr. McNamara left on the 11:30 Wabash. . . . Frs. Ehrhard and De La Grange [Justin De La Grange, an associate pastor] and quite a number of the parishioners saw him off. Before Fr. McNamara left, Fr. Superior [Ehrhard] in the presence of Fr. De La Grange had reports from him regarding Mass Intentions etc. over which there seemed to be some difficulty. Fr. Mc[Namara] insisted that he met all obligations, sent a check for some $235 to Fr. Wallace, the Procurator of the Province.
>
> As Superior, I signed all documents from August 27 [1926], as things are rather discouraging, mixed up, and I will not take the responsibility of my predecessor's carelessness.

Part of the reason for the confusion may have been the lack of helpers during much of McNamara's pastorate. Father John Foley, Borromeo associate for about six years, was transferred to Cleveland in 1921. Henry Wolters was stricken with paralysis in September of that year and died in February 1922. His replacement, Father Valentine Hormes, soon fell ill and was

*Henry Ehrhard, S.J.,
in Mankato, Minnesota*

Kathleen Netsch

hospitalized in St. Louis. Several priests helped out temporarily, among them Fathers Herman Pickert and John Grollig. Eventually Father Joseph Haas arrived and stayed until 1926, but for several years Father McNamara got along with fewer assistants and Jesuit brothers than previous pastors had.

Ehrhard described in his looseleaf additions to *Historia Domus* how he broke with several traditions of his predecessor. On September 4, 1926, he reinstituted the old practice of ringing the church bells at 7:00 on Saturday nights. Two days later he met with Julius Rauch and Charles Mudd to go over the parish insurance coverage on the church, rectory, school, convent, and sexton's house. Ehrhard wrote, "It was deemed advisable to raise the tornado insurance on the church to $40,000. An insurance for fire was put on the sexton's place."

Afterward, Ehrhard called a meeting of the Church Committee, "first one for a long time." Julius Rauch, John B. Thro, August Boschert, John W. Kelly, and Charles B. Mudd made up the group. On September 8, Ehrhard presided at the first meeting of the Ushers Club. With Andrew Eberius,

Michael Kelly, Phil Smith, and others, the priest decided to have five ushers at each Mass, two at the main door and one at each of the side doors. The group also decided to revise the list of pew holders.

After deciding to equip the church basement once again as a chapel, Ehrhard had Joseph Bottani improve the entrance to the cemetery. Knowing that many parishioners visited the graves of their loved ones on the Sunday after All Souls Day and on Decoration Day, Ehrhard directed a crew of workers to tidy the grounds before each celebration. In October Ehrhard revised the seating arrangement of the school's children at daily Mass. Instead of having the children sit in the center aisle, he directed that they spread out over the width of the church, so that more could see the altar.

Ehrhard wrote little in *Historia Domus* about the school, but years later he described the sorry condition of the building during the summer of 1926:

> I called on Frank Feuerstein, Fire Chief, and Joseph Lackland, Mayor—regarding the condemned and locked School. Plans had been made, I was informed from reliable sources, that the school building could not be used in the condition it was. Mr. Feuerstein, Mr. Lackland, [Father] De La Grange and myself, on the following day went through the school building. Suggestions were made—and if carried out the lower floor and the sisters' house could be used. The suggestions were complied with. The entire first floor of the old school building and the lavatories in the basement were fixed up according to the suggestions made. This, of course, necessitated postponement of [the] opening of school 10 days.

Minutes of Mothers Club meetings shed some light on the situation. In June 1926, the women voted to have the school rooms plastered and painted at their own expense. "Mr. Wilhelm" and "Mr. Burkhardt" did the work. The mothers held bake sales and revived the paper drive to pay off the debt. Nevertheless, during his pastorate Father Ehrhard headed a fund drive for construction of a new school.

In January 1927 he organized the parish chapter of the St. Vincent de Paul Society, a foundation of Catholic laymen devoted to works of charity. That same month, Ehrhard began holding weekly classes for converts to the Catholic faith.

After January 1927 he added nothing to *Historia Domus*. Between 1927 and 1932 there was a rapid turnover in assistants; probably Father Ehrhard and his associates had little time to devote to the journal. Things changed in 1929 with the arrival of Father Joseph H. Wels, most recently from Prairie du Chien, Wisconsin. On September 26, Ehrhard installed Wels as his assistant and directed him to resume the history of the house.

Historia Domus

Father Wels wrote daily entries in *Historia Domus*. Like Father Henry Wolters, he described the regular administration of the parish, its people, and lay associations. He also revealed a little of the world around him. These excerpts from Wels' entries illustrate the changing roles of the laity and clergy, the separate treatment of black Catholics, the growth of the retreat movement, and the popularity of St. Louis's White House Retreat Center:

Oct. 16, 1929: Carnival of Nations under the auspices of the Y. L. S. [Young Ladies Sodality] & [the] Charlene Club in the evening in the basement of the church.
Oct. 21, 1929: . . . Fr. [Otto] Moorman [S.J., recently arrived from the Pine Ridge reservation of South Dakota] is going to stay with us as pastor of the colored parishioners of Anglum [now Robertson] and Kinloch and of the colored people in St. Charles and surrounding country.
Oct. 24, 1929: Fr. Moorman went to Ferguson to get a car for his missionary work among the colored people.
Oct. 25, 1929: Fr. Moorman returned with a new Durand.
Jan. 19, 1930: . . . According to Synodal decrees, sermons had to be preached on Matrimony. Fr. Moorman went again to Kinloch, his negro mission, and stayed at Florissant Seminary overnight. Fr. Ehrhard attended and spoke at the Catholic Western Union meeting in St. Peter's hall in the afternoon.
Feb. 12, 1930: Fr. A. Tallmadge of the Whitehouse retreat house . . . drove in with his car shortly before supper to stay here for some days in order to canvass the neighboring parishes for retreatants.
Feb. 25, 1930: . . . Frs. Ehrhard and Wels attended the Third Annual Banquet of the Laymen's Retreat League of St. Louis at Statler Hotel. 500 men were present.
May 8, 1930: Fr. Ehrhard went to Mexico, Missouri, to attend a meeting of the Rotarians.

On August 19, 1930, Father William B. Sommerhauser arrived from Mankato, Minnesota to replace Wels as associate pastor. Wels left that afternoon for Mankato to replace Sommerhauser. Father Sommerhauser was a native German who had moved as a child to California, Missouri. He entered the Jesuit order in 1899, three years after his ordination as a secular priest, and afterward received a Master's degree in Education. He

Joseph H. Wels, S.J., at the Holy Rosary Mission, Pine Ridge, South Dakota

taught Classics in various high schools and colleges before doing pastoral work in Mankato, Minnesota.

At Borromeo, Sommerhauser promptly took over *Historia Domus*. When he was not able, associate Father William Frain wrote in the journal. Sommerhauser frequently noted the details of parish administration as well as local and world events, even the oppressive weather of these "dust bowl" years. In the following excerpts he detailed the precarious condition of the school, rectory renovations, his own interest in liturgical music, current events, and some outspoken opinions:

Aug. 29, 1930: . . . Workmen began building roof-sheds over entrance to the [outdoor] toilets for the children at the school building.

Aug. 30, 1930: Frs. Ehrhard, Frain, Sommerhauser & Brother McGuire [Edward McGuire, the Jesuits' cook and sacristan] drove to Florissant to attend the funeral of Fr. John Otten [former superior at Borromeo]. . . . The sheds spoken of yesterday were finished today. It was again very hot, and the drought continues.

Sep. 11, 1930: Frs. Ehrhard, Frain & Sommerhauser took a drive to Weber Lake & a swim in old Mississippi. . . .

Sep. 18, 1930: Today School Boy Patrol was inaugurated in our parish as also in St. Peter's parish of this city. Six boys of the 8th & 7th grades respectively will see the school children safely across the streets in the school zone. . . . A pretty ceremony constituted the inauguration.

Sep. 28, 1930: Regular Sunday order, with a scandalous operatic & theatrical high Mass!

Sep. 29, 1930: Painters come to renovate the Fathers' rooms. The Grafton, Ill., Young Ladies Sodality visited our Y. L. Sodality this evening, and were almost to midnight before they got away!?

Oct. 7, 1930: . . . Fr. Ehrhard left for Kansas City, to buy *liturgical* church music, & "tackle" a friend for a fat donation for the much needed new parochial school.

Oct. 24, 1930: By grant of Very Reverend Fr. Provincial, the house enclosure was lifted today, & some 6 or 8 ladies of the parish entered to clean the house, especially mopping & scrubbing it. This was the first time for many a year that the privilege or permission was granted [for women to enter the rectory].

Oct. 27, 1930: . . . Al Smith handled the Republicans in a half hour radio talk.

Nov. 10, 1930: The Church Committee looked over our poor kitchen, with a view of renovating it. Deo gratias [Thanks be to God]; for the Lord knows it needs it.

Nov. 14, 1930: A great event in local Community: At last good Brother Kertz [Matthias Kertz, Brother's McGuire's successor in the rectory kitchen] has been prevailed upon to put away our hideous "catdom." Four nasty felines at last disappeared! Universal satisfaction!!

Dec. 7, 1930: . . . For first time we heard the splendid radio sermon of Rev. Charles E. Coughlin of Detroit on social evils of the day—"Little Flower" Radio Hour. [Coughlin was a popular radio speaker early in the Depression. In later years he became controversial for his anti-Semitic remarks and criticism of the Roosevelt administration, and eventually ceased broadcasting under orders from his bishop.]

Dec. 9, 1930: Busy day . . . Incidentally, Fr. Superior [was] lectured & insulted by the cook at the Sisters of Loretto. *O tempora, O mores!* [Oh, the times! Oh, the morals!] The scribe [Sommerhauser] thinks Sr. Anselma will go & that speedily!

Jan. 1, 1931: . . . At 1 P.M. today Benito

Mussolini gave a radio talk from Rome in English to America!

Mar. 27, 1931: Today a meeting was held of Pastor and Church Committee in the Rectory at which [were] submitted plans etc. for a new St. Charles Borromeo school. . . .

May 6, 1931: Fr. Superior held a meeting of the Church Committee [about] the new school. The hard times are not very propitious to the project.

May 21, 1931: Fr. Superior with 3 members of the Church Committee [went] to see the Archbishop [about] the new school & found him quite agreeable. Hence, it looks as though the new school may soon come.

June 1, 1931: The Bishop's permission came to build a new parochial school, making a maximum debt of $40,000. Deo gratias. Fr. Superior [went] to St. Louis, to consult with architects, etc.

June 3, 1931: Rev. Fr. Superior & Fr. Sommerhauser drove to Jefferson City, to inspect new school . . . a $60,000 addition with eight classrooms, etc. Our own new school of $40,000 is now as-

sured & ought to start soon.

June 10, 1931: A meeting with Church Committee this evening seems to suggest deferring the building of a new school, till better days arrive.

The plan to build a new school fell a victim to the Depression. "The scenes were pathetic," wrote Sommerhauser as he described the donation of Christmas baskets to Borromeo's poor in 1931. As the economic situation worsened, the Jesuits often commented on "hard times." On July 1, 1931, the parish circulated a report stating that "considering the condition of the finances at this time and realizing that the members of the parish are experiencing serious problems brought about by the present business depression, we have decided to defer the building of the school for the present." The people made do for another quarter of a century with the old building. Classrooms in the convent and in the old school hall helped contain the growing enrollment.

The Change in Religious Orders

In June 1932, Father Ehrhard entered St. Mary's Hospital of St. Louis for treatment of a sore eye. He stayed for over six weeks. Shortly after returning to Borromeo he was reassigned to Kansas City as an associate pastor, and Father Sommerhauser was named pastor of St. Charles Borromeo. Father Frain was reassigned to St. Louis University. Ehrhard remained at Borromeo for another three weeks, attending many dinners, picnics, and farewell parties. Frain described a celebration given by the parishioners on August 18, 1932:

At 8 p.m. [a] very fine entertainment in basement of church [was given] by children, directed by the unsparing work

of Leona Ehrhard. Farewell to Fr. Ehrhard & welcome to Fr. Sommerhauser, who was installed today at noon meal as Superior & Pastor. . . . Judge Dyer & Mr. Charles Mudd gave reminiscent and welcoming speeches to the New Superior . . . . The various sodalities and organizations gave Fr. Ehrhard a watch and other useful gifts.

Ehrhard left the next day. That same day, Sommerhauser spent several hours in St. Louis conferring with the archbishop and the Jesuit provincial over how to bring about a change of nuns for Borromeo school.

William Frain's last entries in *Historia Domus* suggest that Sommerhauser desired

*William B. Som-
merhauser, S.J.*

to replace the Sisters of Loretto because "for some years past they hold aloof & do not exert themselves much to please etc," and "have been acting very high-handed." Two weeks before Sommerhauser's installation as pastor, he wrote the Loretto superior from a retreat house in Kansas. His letter does not survive; he said that it contained a request for a full-time music teacher. A few days later the Loretto superior replied with the suggestion that he try to retain a different order.

Sommerhauser returned to town on August 17 and immediately consulted with Fathers Ehrhard, Frain, and De La Grange, then met with the superior of the St. Louis Notre Dame convent. The next day, according to Frain, the superior telephoned to say "that the Notre Dame sisters can probably replace the Loretto Sisters in our parish school, then they would have two schools in St. Charles & they like rivalry." Frain wrote his last entry in *Historia Domus* on August 20:

> Fr. Sommerhauser . . . after seeing in the afternoon the Provincial, the Archbishop, & the Sisters in Ripa of South St. Louis, sent a night telegram to Kentucky, [to] Mother General Olivette (Loretto Sisters) to this effect: At your suggestion I have arranged for six sisters & a music teacher of a different community; they will occupy the residence on August 29.

The *St. Charles Cosmos-Monitor* printed the story, as written by Sommerhauser, on August 26, 1932. Opening with a statement that the Loretto sisters had been withdrawn by their superior, the article went on to describe the sadness of Borromeo parishioners over the loss. It gave the following explanation:

> Nevertheless, there is no cloud without its silver lining. Circumstances such as in the present case will ever and again arise; and it behooves the intelligent observer to grapple with them in all kindliness and sincerity. We are losing at the Borromeo Church and in the city of St. Charles most beloved and cultured Religious of the great Order of the Lorettines. However, a benign Providence has almost miraculously provided worthy substitutes in the Sisters of Notre Dame, a well-known and efficient order with [a] motherhouse at Maria in Ripa, South St. Louis. These Religious will steer the canoe of happy school life at the Borromeo Parish in the future. The change has come so suddenly that the pastor gladly avails himself of this "statement" to spread before the people of the parish and city the brief facts leading up to the same. Upon his being appointed to the pastorate of the Borromeo Church, and being intensely devoted to children and their education, he forthwith wrote to Rev. Mother Superior inquiring about the possibility of bringing a suitable department of music into the school, particularly the well-known Ward Method of Liturgical Music, now so commonly in vogue and enjoying the well-deserved reputation of a high-class cultural instrumentality for both the school and the sanctuary.
>
> It was the inability of the Rev. Mother, owing to the great demand made upon her for Sisters from many quarters, to release a teacher of music for the St. Charles school that prompted her own suggestion, even at this late hour, if possible, to find Sisters of some other community who might be able to take the St. Charles school and furnish the musical department desired. Her satisfaction

By choosing the Notre Dame order, Sommerhauser brought to the parish religious women who specialized in parochial school instruction. The School Sisters of Notre Dame was founded in 1833 by Mother Theresa Gerhardinger. In 1847 the order established its first American school, in Pennsylvania. Within two years it opened another seven schools, and sent twenty-five European nuns to staff them. By 1860 over 200 American women had joined. Three years later the order opened Notre Dame College in Maryland, the first Catholic college for women in the United States. Notre Dame nuns taught in many St. Louis schools even before the 1897 opening of the St. Louis Motherhouse. By 1924 there were 882 Notre Dame sisters and 83 missions in the central and southern states.

Many parishioners did not greet the new nuns cheerfully. Some took up a petition to have the Loretto order reinstated and marched outside the church on Sunday with banners saying "We want our Sisters back." But the campaign did not succeed, and the Notre Dames stayed. Classes started on September 6, 1932. The school's 236 students were taught that year by three Notre Dame nuns, two lay teachers, and a candidate for the order named Verene Lueckenhoff, who was Father Sommerhauser's niece.

was plainly expressed at the possibility of using the St. Charles Sisters elsewhere in their vast system of schools.

Sommerhauser was indeed very interested in music, but how much of a factor this was in his decision is not clear. He was also related to some Notre Dame Sisters, and he had worked with the order in Minnesota. The Lorettines left St. Charles on August 26, and the Notre Dames moved into the convent early in September.

Father Sommerhauser

Schoolchildren sang at morning Mass for the first time on September 7, 1932. One week later Father Sommerhauser expressed his delight in *Historia Domus* over the beginning of a new financial system for the parish:

Sept. 14, 1932: Deo Gratias. At last we got our own bank account! Council meeting

agreed, etc. All O.K. The miserable old tradition of one pot for Church and Residence broken, & [the Jesuits] no long will pay the debts etc. of parish.
Sep. 15, 1932: Happily started our own bank account.

At about the same time, the pastor organized the first PTA (Parent-Teacher Association) of the parish. In October he embarked on a campaign to restock the Jesuits' library and to clean out the residence. One of Father Sommerhauser's new associates, Father John O'Connor, wrote in *Historia Domus:*

> *Oct. 12, 1932:* . . . Either the priests' libraries are shamefully neglected & destitute of theological works, as is ours of St. Charles Borromeo's, or the priests don't consult their authorities. In either case their ignorance seems to be *culpable.*
>
> *Oct. 25, 1932:* . . . They have been clearing the attic today of a lot of junk accumulated through the years by former occupants who were too lazy or negligent to dispose of useless things or were influenced by a mistaken notion of religious poverty or by a penurious instinct. . . .
>
> The basement of the church too was filled with junk which the workmen cleaned out some days ago. The library is still filled with junk—old missals, obsolete manuals of theology & ceremonials etc. —books that were old 50 years ago, not to speak of more ancient ones.

Several of Borromeo's Jesuits became sick in 1933. Associate James Paulus, who arrived in 1932, developed pleurisy and spent time in the hospital; John O'Connor went blind in one eye; and Sommerhauser came down with neuritis. During the summer of 1933 several parishioners and others, working gratis, repaired the school. In September an older Jesuit, Father Joseph Lynam, replaced O'Connor as chaplain to the Sacred Heart community. He also took charge of *Historia Domus.*

Lynam wrote his entries in black and red ink, in a spidery, wandering hand. He noted many topics affecting the parish: the Novena of the Little Flower, 40 Hours Devotion, Borromeo's participation in the October 24, 1933, centennial celebration of the founding of the School Sisters of Notre Dame, the continuing poor health

of Fathers O'Connor and Paulus, the November 5 performance in the school hall of "In the Good Old Summertime" by the Catholic Knights of America Players, and the Armistice Day parade, in which the parish float was decorated by the Notre Dame Sisters and carried a schoolgirl dressed as the Statue of Liberty.

In 1934 Lynam began gluing newspaper clippings into the journal instead of writing his own accounts. A series of clippings from March of that year details a famous Novena of Grace held at Borromeo. Charles "Dismas" Clark, S.J., who was known as an apostle to ex-convicts and the founder of Dismas House, gave the novena and also wrote the articles that appeared for several days in the *St. Charles Daily Banner News.* Clark's first report described the nine-day devotion for the intercession of St. Francis Xavier. At 2:30 and 7:30 P.M. every day, the priest opened the service with a prayer to the saint, then delivered the day's sermon. His themes included: "What it means to save your soul," "How to increase sanctifying grace," "What is a Christian?" "The result of mortal sin," "The Catholic idea of hell," and "The personality of Christ." Each succeeding article reported an increased attendance and many favors granted. The last, covering the March 12 closing of the novena, reported:

> . . . the church was crowded to capacity. For a time it looked as if even standing room would be at a premium. A spirit of happiness was almost something tangible. . . . Father Clark announced that fifty favors had been granted. There were sixteen positions secured . . . health was recovered in four cases, increases in wages was reported by two, successful business transaction were made, etc. If all the graces were known which were received during the Novena the record would be made in three figures.

The school building was renovated in the

A celebration marked the opening of the enlarged and renovated school, November 16, 1934.

fall of 1934. Archbishop Glennon returned to the parish on Sunday, December 2, to bless the structure, after which the parish held an open house and a bazaar. Eight classrooms now accommodated the 280 students enrolled.

Father Lynam recorded that the Jesuits bought a new Ford VH in May of 1935. On June 12 of that year: "Fine galvanized fence today is replacing a lot of the old wooden fences so often broken by boys. The new fences look like pure silver." Like his predecessors, he described the summer heat with much interest; electric fans and perhaps a dip in the Mississippi were the only relief available to the Jesuits from sweltering confessionals and poorly ventilated buildings.

In the middle of the 1930s Sommerhaus-

er had as many as four associates, but only two Jesuit brothers—Edward McGuire and Matthias Kertz. McGuire lived thirty-six years at the Borromeo rectory and celebrated his diamond jubilee in 1937. Although he began as the Jesuits' cook, he later retired from the kitchen and took over as sacristan. Kertz, who came to Borromeo around 1926, became cook. By the late 1930s, Kertz was in poor health and retired from the kitchen.

The community longed for good food. Sommerhauser asked his superior for permission to hire a woman cook, but to no avail. When Brother Kertz died in 1939 the Jesuits began to take meals with the Notre Dame community, who converted their music room into a dining room just for the priests. This arrangement was originally planned to last for three months but went on for about two years. Sommerhauser paid the nuns a hundred dollars per month for board, and a little extra to pay the "Catholic colored woman" hired by the convent to help the Notre Dame cook feed nine nuns and four Jesuits.

After several months of convent cuisine, Sommerhauser complained to the Jesuit provincial about the women's "mushy" food with "dainty little trimmings," and added that the men were ready for the plain cooking of a Jesuit brother. The matter was resolved with the hiring of Mrs. Hilda Borgmeyer as cook.

Church Decoration

Father Sommerhauser frequently submitted articles about the parish to the *Banner News* and *Cosmos-Monitor*. His topics included the various novenas and missions held in the church, holiday celebrations, graduations, and school entertainments and outings. Some of the articles carried the priest's byline, others simply ended with the word "Contributed." No matter; Father Sommerhauser's style was unmistakable. Not a native-born American, he did his best to leave the reader with a stirring impression, but occasionally had problems with English usage.

Shortly after coming to St. Charles in 1930, Sommerhauser became interested in researching and writing the history of the parish. Ben Emmons, the leading local historian, encouraged the scholarly priest, as did Jesuit author Gilbert Garraghan. Soon Sommerhauser embarked upon years of work. After becoming pastor in 1932 he had less time to devote to this pursuit, but he faithfully spent his spare hours tracing the intertwined roots of the parish and city of St. Charles.

One of Father Sommerhauser's related interests was the genealogy of Louis Blanchette, a topic previously unexplored to any depth. Mayor Adolph Thro put the priest in contact with Montreal genealogist Godfroy Blanchet, who had written for information on Louis Blanchette and his life in St.

Charles. Sommerhauser supplied information about Blanchette's contributions to the town, and Blanchet sent the priest a thorough genealogy of his family, tracing his ancestors back to French nobility of the 1500s.

During the 1930s Father Sommerhauser led a drive to have a monument to Louis Blanchette placed in the parish cemetery. In an article appearing in the August 26, 1936, *Cosmos-Monitor*, he announced that the St. Charles Borromeo Cemetery Board was seeking donations in order to erect a "large granite Cross surmounting a stone altar, and bearing the proper memorial tablet in honor of our Hero." One thousand dollars was needed. Miss Katie Shore stepped forward with the entire amount, but she requested that the altar and cross be dedicated to the memory of her late parents. The parish accepted her generous offer and erected in the cemetery a cross and altar in memory of the family of Dr. John Shore. For many years the altar served as the site for field Masses on Memorial Day and All Souls Day.

The interest in honoring Blanchette continued, and in December 1938 a large granite monument bearing a bronze commemorative plaque was placed in the older section of the cemetery. The exact resting place of Louis and Angelique Blanchette, however, is unknown.

In 1940, to prepare for the 150th an-

The church before the 1940 decoration. Note the bare proscenium arch, the scagliola finish on the pillars, and the clear clerestory window at upper far right.

niversary of the founding of the parish and the naming of the city of St. Charles, Father Sommerhauser and the congregation decided to have the church decorated. For several years the parish had been installing, one by one, huge art glass clerestory windows funded by various parishioners. Depicting the fifteen mysteries of the rosary, these windows still grace the church. The largest and most expensive of the group is the immense "rose" window, located over the central front door and overlooking the choir loft. This window was the last to be added, in part because the pipes of the church's organ first had to be divided and relocated in order to make room. The window was dedicated to the Holy Spirit in November 1944.

To launch the church decoration, the parish held a "Lenten Self-Denial Campaign," in which people saved a dime for each of the forty fast days. Because 1940 was the 400th anniversary of the founding of the Society of Jesus, which had administered St. Charles Borromeo since 1823, the improvements included the painting on the bare proscenium arch of a huge mural featuring eight Jesuit saints—Ignatius Loyola, Francis Xavier, Isaac Jogues, Peter Claver, John Berchmans, Aloysius Gonzaga, Stanislaus Kostka, and Peter Canisius. T. B. Kemner Studios of Quincy, Illinois, supervised by art critic Louis J. Tango, designed the mural and the other ornamentation. The studio employed local artisans to do the work.

These artisans painted the walls and ceiling of the church in flat shades of amber, gray, and other pastels, and painted the scagliola finish on the pillars a complementary shade. They added a frieze symbolic of the twelve apostles to the sanctuary walls high above the altar. All work was complet-

Kister family

Borromeo students in the 1941 historical pageant, "The Founding of the Catholic Church."

ed by Thanksgiving Day 1940, in plenty of time for the sesquicentennial of the founding of the parish and the naming of the city.

This two-fold anniversary opened with a Pontifical High Mass at the Academy of the Sacred Heart on the morning of Sunday, October 12, 1941. William A. Rice, S.J., bishop of British Honduras, celebrated the Mass with the assistance of Father Stephen McNamara as deacon and Father Henry Ehrhard as subdeacon. Sommerhauser served as a deacon of honor, and his associate, James Fallon, delivered the sermon. On Tuesday, October 14, parishioners marched next to a float depicting the "First Church, St. Charles Borromeo" in a parade that traveled from Main Street to Blanchette Park. Twenty floats in all commemorated themes from St. Charles' history, including the arrival of Louis Blanchette, the Lewis and Clark expedition, the founding of the Sacred Heart Academy, and the arrival of the Germans. On the next day the same floats regrouped and paraded via a different route to the park.

On Thursday, October 16, Father Sommerhauser met with representatives of some of the historical associations of Missouri for a dinner given in the basement of Borromeo church. Later that evening, many Borromeo schoolchildren enacted "The Founding of the Catholic Church" in a historical pageant at St. Charles High School. Several boys appeared in warpaint and feathers, many girls wore calico dresses and sunbonnets, and one boy with a painted mustache sported a top hat.

On Friday the city held a fair at Blanchette Park and a football game at St. Charles High School. The fair continued through Saturday. That afternoon, Missouri Governor Forrest Donnell, Congressman Clarence Cannon, and Mayor Thro dedicated a stone pedestal to Louis Blanchette at the entrance to the park. Years later, a statue of Blanchette was erected on the pedestal.

On Sunday, October 19, the Academy of the Sacred Heart wrapped up the festivities with a pilgrimage to the shrine of Philippine Duchesne. In May of the previous year, the Vatican had proclaimed the beatification of St. Charles' pioneer instructor. Soon work began at the Academy to construct a spacious shrine in honor of Mother Duchesne.

In the early 1940s, Father Sommerhauser submitted the first installment of his manuscript on the parish history to Jesuit authorities. He admitted in a letter to his superior that the work had taken a great toll on his health, causing him to suffer headaches, eye strain, and exhaustion. On June 25, 1942, after having the work checked by two experts, the provincial rejected the manuscript on the basis of numerous stylistic problems, but suggested that the priest enlist the writing skills of someone more familiar with the English language.

Sommerhauser's symptoms grew worse. He began having dizzy spells during Mass, and asked to be replaced as pastor. On July 24, 1942, he entered St. Mary's Hospital with symptoms of nervous exhaustion. He remained in the hospital until early August, then spent several months resting. In late November he resumed his pastoral duties. The next year he asked his superior to send an expert in the English language to help him rewrite the manuscript, but America had entered the Second World War and the Jesuits had no men to spare.

Father Sommerhauser's health continued to suffer. In September 1943, at the suggestion of the provincial, he gave up work on the book. Father Lawrence Cusack of Regis College in Denver replaced Sommerhauser as pastor on August 15, 1944.

Besides the manuscript, a curious memento remains of Father Sommerhauser's history. In the St. Louis Jesuit Archives is a thick clothbound book entitled *The Stones of Old St. Charles: 1791-1941*. The cover is embossed with a woodcut illustration of the log church. The title page lists Sommerhauser as author, and bears the date 1941. All the other pages are blank.

The nave after decoration

Pastors and Associates

Henry Ehrhard: As a hometown pastor, Ehrhard had the awkward task of ministering to his boyhood friends and neighbors. After having the condemned school building repaired and reopened, he led a campaign to have it replaced. The Depression began during Ehrhard's third year at Borromeo and put an end for a long time to the construction plans. Father Ehrhard's health suffered during his pastorate. He is remembered as a pious, simple priest who listened well to his congregation and tried his best to steer the parish through hard times.

Justin De La Grange: Born in Fort Wayne, Indiana, in 1874, De La Grange became a grocery clerk as a teenager, and later married. When his wife and daughter died, he resolved to become a priest and resumed his studies at the age of thirty-three. He first became a secular priest, then requested permission to enter the Jesuit novitiate without having to undergo additional years of advanced study. Permission was granted, and in his mid-forties De La Grange became a Jesuit. He worked as a hospital chaplain, then became pastor of a Detroit parish. He came to St. Charles as Father Ehrhard's associate in 1926, stayed three years, then spent the remaining four years of his life as a hospital chaplain in Cincinnati. He died in 1933.

William Frain: Born in St. Louis of Irish parents, Frain worked as an accountant before deciding to enter the Society of Jesus. He entered the Florissant novitiate at the age of twenty-seven. He later taught at St. Louis University High School and served as chaplain at Regis College. Frain had few equals in the confessional; in 1926 he heard 9,889 confessions at St. Francis Xavier College Church in St. Louis. During his first year at Borromeo he heard 6,776 confessions, and during each of his remaining two years his confessions totaled over 10,000. He left Borromeo in 1932 but returned eight years later. In 1945 he departed for St. Mary's College in Kansas, where he died in 1957.

Joseph Wels: A German educated in Holland, Wels longed to do pastoral and missionary work in the United States. He immigrated in 1898, studied in Wisconsin and Ohio, and completed his education at St. Louis University. Wels had a varied career as a Jesuit—teaching, doing mission work, serving as chaplain, and working in the library of the Florissant novitiate. He came to St. Charles in 1929 and left in 1930.

William Sommerhauser: Sommerhauser led the parish out of the Depression and through the worst of World War II. He had the decrepit brick school renovated and the church decorated, and involved himself in many civic concerns that won St. Charles Borromeo the support of non-parishioners. After leaving the parish in 1944, he became pastor of St. Joseph's parish in north St. Louis. Sommerhauser died in 1947.

Henry Grotegeers: A native German who studied for the Society of Jesus in Holland,

Henry Grotegeers, S.J.

Justin de la Grange, S.J.

Grotegeers spent part of his Jesuit preparation teaching at a mission school in Bombay, India. He immigrated to the United States and soon embarked on mission work at the Holy Rosary Mission of South Dakota. Grotegeers spoke English without an accent and mastered Lakota, the Sioux language in which he preached. He left the mission in 1923, worked at St. Joseph's church of St. Louis until 1932, then served at Borromeo as an associate pastor. While working as Father Sommerhauser's assistant he broke his hip. Handicapped for the rest of his life, Grotegeers retired in 1937 to St. Mary's, Kansas. He died of a stroke in 1951.

Brother Matthias Kertz: Born in Germany in 1863, Kertz came as a child to Ste. Genevieve County, where he became a farmer. After entering the Society of Jesus in 1905, he worked as a cook, and for the rest of his years enjoyed gardening as well. He cooked for Jesuit residences in St. Louis and Chicago, at Regis College in Denver, at Rockhurst College in Kansas City, and last of all in St. Charles. He made the Way of the Cross every afternoon in the church, but otherwise rarely left the rectory. During his last year at Borromeo he suffered from heart trouble. Kertz died in the Jesuits' kitchen on December 18, 1939.

Chapter 12
1942-57

World War II

In June 1939, a young German-born Jesuit named Engelbert Axer was stranded in St. Charles. Axer had been studying English and theology in the United States for several years when war broke out in Europe. Not wishing to return to Germany for his ordination, and unable to bring his family over to witness the event, Axer received Holy Orders at St. Mary's, Kansas, then moved for a time to St. Charles. This "man without a country" celebrated his first Mass in the parish church on June 25, 1939. He eventually left for Japan, and taught philosophy at the University of Tokyo for many years.

Several years before Axer arrived, St. Charlesans began to take part in the pre-war buildup. In 1932, to accommodate the many Catholics who worked at the new TNT plant in Weldon Spring, Father Sommerhauser added a 5:00 A.M. Sunday Mass to the regular schedule. He also began holding a special devotion after Sunday evening benediction for the young men of the parish in the armed forces. The names of these soldiers and sailors were written on a scroll and placed at the feet of the church's new Pieta statue, which had been donated around 1930.

Many Borromeo families attended a peace procession on the grounds of the Sacred Heart Academy on May 31, 1939. A crowd of about 3,000, walking four abreast, processed after dark carrying lighted candles, singing Marian hymns, and praying the rosary. The service ended a month-long devotion for worldwide peace, as requested by Pope Pius XII. After the United States entered the war, Memorial Day services involved the whole community. On the morning of May 30, 1942, Father Sommerhauser paid tribute to the city's soldiers, both past and present. After a rifle squad shot a salute and a bugler played "Taps," the multi-denominational crowd left Blanchette Park's Memorial Hall to decorate graves in the city's cemeteries.

As the war continued, St. Charles Borromeo members continued praying for peace. The Sunday evening services added prayers for the area's women serving in the armed forces. The Pope's special peace devotions were held each May in the church. On Memorial Day, the Borromeo Children's Choir sang at the field Mass held at the cemetery. Boy Scouts from the parish

German-born Engelbert Axer, S.J., flanked by priests and acolytes on the steps of the Jesuit residence, the day of his first Mass.

sounded "Taps" and directed traffic through the grounds.

The School Sisters of Notre Dame boosted prayers for the fighting men and women of the parish by awarding "military" rank on children who prayed for soldiers after school hours. A short prayer earned a child the rank of private; more devotions merited increasingly higher ranks. To become a general a child had to recite several prayers, attend Mass during the week, receive Communion on Saturday, and make a daily visit to the church. To keep interest high, the nuns kept a special bulletin board in the school headed by the campaign's motto: "An army on its knees to keep an army on its feet."

In early 1943, machinist mate William Vierling was reported missing in action after his submarine was sunk by enemy fire. The Borromeo parishioner had lived near Boschertown with his family. In February of the following year, navy lieutenant David A. Dyer drowned at sea. Father Sommerhauser and many other local priests, flanked by naval officers, celebrated Dyer's funeral Mass on March 9, 1944.

Borromeo priests were busy during the war years marrying young men and their sweethearts. Engagement periods were frequently short, and many couples asked to be married on short notice. Weddings were witnessed on all days of the week, frequently before the groom shipped out. Many couples delayed honeymoons or skipped them altogether.

Students from the second and third grade in 1914. **From left, front row**: Elmo Bernhoester, Frank Lawler, Ray Meyer, Tom O'Grady, Jim Tainter, Francis Schoene, Dalton Schreiber, Carlos Boschert, Chester Boschert, Ted Gross, Alfred Phillips, Earl Platz, Robert Phillips, Leonard LaBarge. **Second row**: Wilbur Heck, (?) Hunn, Francis Corrigan, Vincent Gilder, Roy Glosemeyer, Paul Kaemmerlen, Earl Smith, Agnes LaBarge, Delphine Dietx, Hazel Elder, Ursula Brockway, Leona Ehrhard, Stella Gilley. **Back row**: Herbert Bird, Alonzo Bizelli, Paul Feuerstein, Genevieve Beckmann, Elsie Huesgen, Loretta Ehlinger, Leaetta Ehlinger, Delphine Chrismer, Caroline Boschert, Adelia O'Grady, Olive Schreiber, Madeline Wilmes.

Grades six and seven on the church steps with Fr. McNamara in 1924. **From left, front row**: Agatha Wernart, Lucille Schrader, Catherine Wunsch, Ethel DuBois, Anna Vierling, Martha Bauers, Lorraine Young, Elsie Tayon. **Second row**: Mabel Moore, Bertha Chrismer, Rosemary Bernhoester, Mary Helen Huyg, Kathleen Thro, Albertine Bextermiller, Elizabeth Korte, Margaret Boschert, Pearl Wiechens, Ethel DeRoy. **Third row**: Stephen McNamara, S.J., Stella DeRoy, Irene Purler, Dorothy Wilmes, Glennon Ruckmann, William Honerkamp, Henry Burkhardt, Isabelle Honerkamp, Laura Bryan, Helen Young. **Back row**: Joseph Stratman, Elroy Schoene, Warren Alferman, Ollie Boschert, Melvin Driller, Jimmie J. Lawler, Lancelot Haislip, Chauvin Emmons, Joseph Wunsch, Glennon Beilsmith.

The marriage of Ensign Frank Rauch, Jr., and Mary Josephine Anderson, on Friday morning, May 22, 1942, was one of many wartime weddings performed in the church. The bride and groom had one attendant each, and after a brief reception departed for a west coast naval base. Similarly, after the Tuesday, August 3, 1943, wedding of Aleatha Bauers and Private Leroy Hollander, the couple was driven around St. Charles in a jeep. The bride's parents gave a reception in their home, after which the couple left for Hollander's army base.

The Young Ladies Sodality sponsored USO dances in the school hall for servicemen stationed at Smartt Field and other nearby bases. Many young men traveled by bus to dance the jitterbug with Borromeo's young women, to the tunes of the Jake Fischbach band and other local groups.

School Days

Borromeo School students of the 1920s and 1930s had much in common with students from the 1940s and later. For many years the students' morning began with Mass. Most children did not receive daily Communion; that privilege was reserved for special occasions and for First Friday Masses, after which the children ate the breakfasts they had brought from home. At that time, before receiving Communion all were required to abstain from eating and drinking from the previous midnight. The priests heard the children's confessions on Friday.

For many years the girls wore uniforms consisting of navy-blue pleated wool skirts and white blouses with rounded collars. Navy grosgrain ribbons, tied in a bow at the neck, completed the outfit. Although the boys did not wear uniforms until decades later, in the 1930s many young boys wore knickers or aviator pants, in the style of Charles Lindbergh. Church etiquette at that time required that boys and men uncover their heads in church, but that girls and women cover theirs. Borromeo's girls wore doily-like round mantillas made of lace, and later navy "beanies." Both were held down with bobby pins.

Children sat in desks that were attached to long wooden rails nailed to the floor. These desks were the old-fashioned sort, with writing boards projecting out from behind their seats. These boards contained a hole for an inkwell, which the teacher regularly filled. Young children learned to write with pencils, but later switched to ink. For many years, fountain pens were not used and ballpoints did not exist, so the children wrote with simple pens they dipped into the ink. To prevent staining their papers, some wiped excess ink from their pens with little flannel squares called pen wipers.

Boys sat on one side of the classroom and girls sat on the other. At recess, boys played on the yard to the south of school, and girls played on the yard to the north. Boys played with balls and marbles; girls played hopscotch, jacks, crack-the-whip, and ball games. Allowing balls and other playground equipment to drop into the deep window wells next to the church guaranteed a reprimand from the nuns on playground patrol.

Religious women, whether of the Loretto or Notre Dame order, staffed the school with little or no help from lay instructors. A Jesuit taught religion one day each week. The Loretto nuns led their classes in song, but the Notre Dames taught music according to the Ward System, by which students learned to read and interpret music using the "do-re-mi" method. The school offered

Borromeo sixth graders at their solemn communion in 1940. **From left, front row**: *Catherine Koch, J. C. Potts, Virginia Kreutzer, Fr. William B. Sommerhauser, Betty Jean Limpert, Fr. Eugene Monnig, Mary Elizabeth Wernart, Ray (or Roy) Boschert, Agnes LaBarge.* **Second row**: *Beatrice Slattery, Fred Feilner, Jr., Martha McMenamy, Muriel Hunter, Jacqulyn Fisher, Robert Powell, Velma Ziegemeier.* **Third row**: *Mathilda Vehige, Irvin Stephens, Doris Schoene, Betty Jean Boschert, John Trask, Gloria Fredenburg, Leroy Cleary.* **Fourth row**: *Lorraine Heckmann, Charles Silverberg, Martha Lenz, Alvin Boschert, Lucy Heck, Gerald Stewart, Marjorie Bernhoester.* **Back row**: *Norbert Vogt, Mark Heckmann, Janice Dryden, Joyce Heck, Jerry Beilsmith, Marvin Weseman.*

a solid curriculum, and many Borromeo graduates attended high school. Some went on to college.

For many years there was no hot lunch program. Children carried their lunches, wrapped sometimes in bread cellophane or newspapers, to school. Many who lived nearby walked home for lunch. In 1941 a surplus commodities lunch program began. Parents able to afford a contribution paid about ten cents each week so that the school could continue buying surplus food items. The purpose of the program was to feed children of the many parents on the WPA (Works Progress Administration). The menu on the first day consisted of scrambled eggs, mashed potatoes, slaw, cocoa, bread and butter, and apples.

Later that year, the parish sponsored a WPA garden in north St. Charles to raise vegetables for use in the lunch program. Two WPA workers tended the crop, and women WPA workers canned the vegetables during the summer so that the food could be served the following year in the school cafeteria. This saved the parish from having to buy vegetables from the surplus food commodities. The system worked well, except that occasionally the parish had over-supplies of certain fruits and vegetables. After the WPA was disbanded the school continued offering hot lunches.

For many years the children put on an annual entertainment, usually an operetta, in the church basement. Parents were expected to provide costumes, no matter how detailed or ornate. For example, in the 1942 operetta "Aunt Drucilla's Garden," the eighth grade girls dressed as roses, and a younger girl cast as a goldfinch wore an elaborate costume made of crepe paper. Props were also serious business. When the stars of "Hansel and Gretel" pushed the witch through a real stove front, young children in the audience believed that the wicked woman was actually inside a burning oven.

Until the early 1930s, black children were excluded from attending Borromeo School. Black Catholics in St. Charles had no choice but to send their children to Franklin School, which had once been the parish boys' school. Even after the children of black parishioners were admitted to Borromeo School, these children were not allowed for many years to participate in the school's social events. Instead, they staged their own plays and held their own parties, usually at the Academy of the Sacred Heart. For black adults, belonging to a lay association was no guarantee that all the members of that association would sit with them in church or process with them to the Communion rail. Black families, whether they wanted to or not, sat in the last two rows of the church.

The school's music students gave public

The graduating class of 1941. **From left, front row**: *Mary K. Fischer, Lorraine Purgahn, Marilyn Helling, Fr. William B. Sommerhauser, Joe Sebacher, Maggie Jackson, Fr. David Hamilton, Margaret Mary Rufkahr, Mary Alice Klutenkamper, Irene Vogt.* **Second row**: *Phyllis Sebacher, Arnold Becker, Joyce Heck, Ray Jackson, John Nacke, Charles Wyhs, Catherine Roedenback, Ken Ziegmeier, Louis Mueller.* **Back row**: *Bob McKay, Kilby Weber, Betty Bishop, Stanley Boschert, Jean Jeye, Beatrice Nelson, Danny Bishop, Virginia Simon.*

recitals from time to time. At the 1939 program, various students played the clarinet, violin, cornet, saxophone, guitar, trumpet, and piano, but a school band was not formed until the 1950s. Each May the entire student body marched to Blanchette Park for the school picnic. For many years, children brought their lunches in shoe boxes the day of the school picnic so that the lunches could be trucked out to the park and not get crushed. At different times throughout the day, the nuns rang bells to signal children to line up for treats of ice cream and soda, to play games, or to eat their lunches. Mothers made lunches for the nuns, who ate separately in Memorial Hall.

The girls' playground was the setting for the annual quilt social, held during the summer. The women of the parish quilted throughout the year in a structure called Sodality Hall. During the social, several dozen quilts were awarded as prizes to winners of a Bingo-like game called Lotto.

At May crowning, all the schoolchildren processed to a statue of the Blessed Virgin Mary in the Jesuits' garden. Until around 1960, the eighth grade girls wore long white formals (frequently borrowed from older sisters) and wobbled in high heels;

afterward they wore the school uniform. Children in the first or second grades made their First Communion. Older children, typically in the sixth grade, made their Solemn Communion, for which they wore white, repeated their baptismal vows, and received a decorated candle.

Children sold raffle tickets for the annual bazaar (later called the Fall Festival), which was held in October or November. Prizes sometimes included a ton of coal and live chickens, ducks, or geese from the Vogt Brothers' Poultry Farm. The prizes in 1949 included a $50 war bond, an embroidered quilt, and a year's subscription to the *Cosmos-Monitor*. The bazaar featured the ever-popular booths (fishpond, grab bag), games, food, and soda, and was a reliable source of extra money for the parish.

In May throughout the 1930s and 1940s, the upper classes frequently traveled to Pere Marquette State Park in Grafton, Illinois for a picnic. Choir girls and altar boys were rewarded during the summer with boat trips on the Mississippi River or picnic outings to other popular spots. A few days before Christmas the Mothers Club gave a party at which Santa Claus arrived, bringing candy and small gifts wrapped in brown paper.

Fathers Cusack and Fallon

Father Lawrence Cusack, most recently of Regis College in Denver, took over at Borromeo for Father Sommerhauser in August 1944. Father Fallon left St. Charles at the same time to become the pastor of St. Ferdinand parish in Florissant. The *St. Charles Cosmos-Monitor* reported: "Parishioners . . . were greatly shocked to hear of these transfers as both priests are very well-known and liked here."

Cusack began his pastorate with four assistants: David Hamilton, William Frain,

Bernard Miles, James O'Connor, and Brother John Reitzner, but not all were able to work hard for the parish. Frain helped out as chaplain to the Sacred Heart community but suffered chronic illness; O'Connor said Mass when his asthma allowed; Hamilton had a stroke; and Brother Reitzner returned to Florissant to recover his health.

Like many of his predecessors, Cusack began his pastorate by having the rectory renovated. His Latin report to the Jesuit provincial for the years 1942 to 1945 states

Lawrence Cusack, S.J.

James Fallon, S.J.

that the dining room was transformed from a cold and drafty room into a pleasant place. By this time the Jesuits were taking their meals at home once again.

Cusack's pastorate was remarkably uneventful. The parish continued to save toward the goal of replacing the old school, but construction did not begin for over a decade. Around 1947 Father Cusack and representatives of the parish decided that the Sisters of Notre Dame deserved a finer home than the old convent on Decatur and Fifth streets, so they began negotiating with Mary Theresa Wentker over the purchase of her residence at the northwest corner of Fourth and Decatur streets.

The widow of Benedict Wentker, Mary Theresa Wentker had raised a family of four children in the imposing Greek Revival house that had previously belonged to the Joseph Alexander family. By 1947 all four of her children had grown up, and she shared the house with her daughter Billye and son-in-law Gene Williams, and the couple's growing family. Mrs. Wentker found the big house too much of a responsibility, and Billye and Gene Williams hoped soon to move into a home of their own. Because one of her sisters was a nun who had lived in various shabby convent buildings, Mrs. Wentker offered the elegant residence to the parish with the provision that it be used as a convent. Father

Cusack and the parish accepted, and secured permission from the archdiocese.

The house was never used as a convent. Mrs. Wentker moved out, but Billye and Gene Williams asked Father Cusack after the sale whether they could remain another year as renters; Frank Rauch of the Rauch Lumber Company had advised the couple against building a new house with green lumber, the only kind of construction lumber that was readily available during the first years after the war. Rauch believed that better lumber would arrive within a year. Father Cusack did not answer, and the Williams family moved out. The parish rented the home to others for a short time, but for several years it stood empty.

When Father Sommerhauser left in 1944 no one took over *Historia Domus*. Few records from 1944 to 1949 survive in the parish archives, except those of baptisms, marriages, and funerals. Why the parish bought the Wentker house, then never used it as a convent, is not clear. One possible reason is that it could not afford to furnish the building for the Notre Dame community, which began to shrink during the 1950s. The building was renovated as a rectory in November 1957 and provided a home for the parish diocesan priests until 1991.

The old convent badly needed renovation. Sister Mary Arthen Casson, S.S.N.D., recalls that the nuns stepped on splinters if

The four ordained Thro brothers and family. Fathers Linus, Edward, William, and Thomas Thro flank their mother, Elizabeth, in the second row. Their father, Edward, stands behind their mother.

they went barefoot in the building. Except for Sister Superior, who had a small bedroom on the second floor, the women slept in two large dormitory rooms on the third floor. After Father James Fallon replaced Lawrence Cusack in 1949, he had the convent renovated.

A house journal kept by Borromeo's Notre Dame community details the progress of the renovations:

Aug. 11, 1950: Father Fallon had the third floor insulated. The workmen under Mr. L. Platte's guidance began to put new ceilings throughout the second floor. The electricians, too, were with us. They had rewired the entire convent. . . .

Dec. 19, 1950: The new parlor floor was laid. Thanks to Father Fallon.

May 23, 1951: Straightened and cleared the front attic room in preparation for the third floor renovation.

June 8-11, 1951: The roofers from St. Louis put an entirely new roof on our convent. Another proof of Father Fallon's thoughtfulness for the Sisters. No leak has been detected since the new roof is on.

June 27, 1951: His Excellency, Bishop Cody, came with Father Fallon to inspect our convent, school, church, and rectory. At first the Bishop was going to take all the Sisters off the third floor, but when he saw all the room up there, and when he realized how well the convent was built, he told the Pastor not to hesitate to spend from $27,000 to $30,000 for repairs. He recommended that provisions be made for twelve Sisters. He also emphasized the fact that the Sisters could only live on the third floor if an elevator were installed. We're all still praying against it because the two outside fire escapes could be installed more cheaply, and the balance could be used for furnishings needed. The Bishop said that the elevator would cost $9,000 and an outside fire escape $2,000. Father Fallon was quite satisfied and pleased with the

Bishop's visit.

July 3, 1951: At 6:30 p.m. Bishop Cody came with Arthur Stauder, the architect. The Bishop then said that the work could not begin before September, but the elevator and the furnace should be taken care of very soon.

Dec. 27, 1951: New refectory chairs and tables arrived. The purchase of these necessary items was made possible by the pastor giving us permission to sell candy and drinks and to keep the profit for house furnishings and needs.

July 9, 1952: The deep freeze and the new refrigerator which Father Fallon permitted us to select arrived at 7:30 p.m. Both were duly installed and the N.D.s are grateful and happy to have so much cold air at their disposal.

July 14, 1952: The workmen, carpenters, and heat men actually arrived, and the renovation of our third floor began. The job without the elevator will cost $40,000, with the elevator $49,000. These were the figures which the general contractor, Mr. Elmer Kolkmeier, gave me. Father Fallon made it sound cheaper, but that's his big-heartedness. We are praying very hard for many generous benefactors to help Father meet the expenses.

When the work was finished, the third floor had individual bedrooms for the women, a small bathroom, and a portable shower.

On June 17, 1951, St. Charlesan Father Thomas Thro returned to Borromeo to celebrate his first solemn high Mass. Assisting were his two brothers, Linus and Edward, who were Jesuit priests. His brother William, who was then preparing to be or-

dained, served as Master of Ceremonies. The four Thros were the sons of Mr. and Mrs. Edward Thro. Although the brothers had grown up near Borromeo, the family had belonged to St. Peter's parish for many years. Linus and Edward had celebrated their first Masses in St. Peter's church, but their family joined St. Charles Borromeo before Thomas's ordination.

In June 1952, Father William Thro celebrated his first Solemn High Mass in St. Charles Borromeo church, with the help of this three ordained brothers. Edward served as archpriest, Linus served as deacon, and Thomas assisted William as subdeacon. The brothers and co-celebrant Father Fallon used the main altar as well as the side altars dedicated to the Blessed Virgin and to St. Joseph. A few years after his ordination, Father Edward Thro became one of Father Fallon's associates and also taught at Duchesne High School.

During the 1950s, St. Charles was slowly losing its small-town identity. Large employers across the river such as McDonnell Douglas and automotive manufacturers beckoned, and many local people began to commute via the Highway 115 bridge. When Interstate 70 linked St. Charles with the expressways of St. Louis, the town became attractive to people seeking inexpensive housing and a pace slower than that of St. Louis. In 1950, 14,314 residents lived within the city limits of St. Charles. Ten years later, nearly 24,000 did. Many of these new residents joined St. Charles Borromeo and sent their children to the parish school.

Two journals kept by the Notre Dame Sisters—one for the convent and one for the school—detail the development of the educational program after the war and into the 1950s. In the late 1940s, as in previous decades, nuns taught all eight grades with little or no help from lay teachers. Borromeo School's enrollment totaled around 300 each year. Music stayed a mainstay of the curriculum, but the students excelled in other courses as well.

The nuns took advantage of new technologies for the classroom. In January of 1951, they bought a new Bell and Howell movie projector from the Pictosound Company, and later paid for it with proceeds from a magazine drive and a seed sale. On April 6, the school raised more money by showing benefit movies provided by Pictosound: *The Enchanted Forest;* W.C. Fields' *Hurry, Hurry;* an Andy Panda cartoon called *Nutty Pine Cabin;* a Woody Woodpecker cartoon called *Loan Stranger;* and the Abbott and Costello feature, *Oysters and Muscles.* Afterward, the school regularly used the projector to show family movies, including *Susannah of the Mounties, Five Little Peppers and How They Grew,* and *Rebecca of Sunnybrook Farm.* Borromeo students of the 1950s also watched films on bicycle and swimming safety, the lives of musician Franz Schubert and scientist Louis Pasteur, and a film about religious vocations called *God's Career Women.*

In November 1950, the school put on an operetta called *The Magic Piper* and bought band instruments with the proceeds. In February 1952, the PTA donated $100 to-

ward the purchase of more instruments after holding a "Pillow Slip Social." Several children signed up for band instruction, but so few came regularly for lessons that in October 1952 the band program was discontinued. In September 1953, Sister Harriet, the Notre Dame's music supervisor, resurrected band lessons by referring a music instructor named Gerald Wimer. The Borromeo nuns signed up Wimer and lessons began. Before 1954, the St. Peter's School band had led Borromeo children to Blanchette Park for the annual school picnic, but that year Wimer's students set a new tradition by providing march music for the Borromeo School parade. Afterward, parishioner Joe Weber trucked all the instruments back to the school.

The operetta and "Pillow Slip Social" were two of many fund raisers involving Borromeo students during the 1950s. During the Fall Festival, eighth graders worked at some of the booths. Each January and February, the younger children sold seeds and the older children sold magazine subscriptions. During Lent, all eight grades collected funds for the Jesuit Missions in "Mite" boxes located in the classrooms. Benefit movies partially funded a new reading program in 1951, and the school kicked off a bicycle raffle in 1952 by sending in bands from packages of Lucky Star loose leaf paper. The whole school took part in the annual March of Dimes campaign.

During the 1953-1954 school year, many contributed toward the purchase of the school's first television set, which arrived on March 27, 1954. The television spent lit-

Fathers William Puetter, James Fallon, and Francis Clerkin with the graduating class of 1954

tle time educating students. The school chronicle explains, "Because Channel 9 did not come in, and because it is too dangerous to keep the set in school during the summer months, some strong PTA men brought it to the convent where it is stored in the recreation room." Later entries fail to mention whether the set was returned in the fall.

Borromeo students in the 1950s participated in traditional as well as more modern devotions. October 24, 1950, was a Children's Sodality day of prayer, marked by the praying of the rosary throughout the day and the formation of the "living" rosary in the evening. Bells rang in honor of United Nations Day. Forty Hours devotion usually involved the whole school, and many children took part in the Corpus Christi procession and May crowning. Eighth graders had their own day of recollection at the end of the school year. Visiting Jesuits sometimes gave special missions just for the schoolchildren.

Enrollment figures for the first half of the 1950s show that the growth of the St. Charles area and the "baby boom" (a marked rise in the birthrate that followed World War II and lasted for the next two decades) put increasing pressure on the old school building. These factors also proved too much for the parish's six Sisters of Notre Dame. In 1950, 325 children were enrolled in Borromeo School. By 1956, 528 were enrolled, and the parish had begun to hire lay teachers on more than just a temporary basis. One of the first of these was Barbara Schwendeman, who began many years of teaching at Borromeo School in 1955.

By 1957 six nuns and five lay women taught 556 children. During that year, second and seventh graders attended classes in the Jesuit rectory, first graders learned their lessons in the convent, and Sister Mary Ferdinand taught her sixth graders in the loft above the parish garage.

While the first wave of "baby boomers" was straining the capacity of Borromeo School, their older brothers and sisters were attending classes in the rickety and unsafe St. Peter's High School building. Since 1924 many graduates of Borromeo and St. Peter's grade schools had furthered their education at St. Peter's High School, the only parochial high school in St. Charles. At first a two-year school, St. Peter's offered a four-year program for the first time in 1929, and gained state accreditation in 1934. Its students came from St. Peter's parish and Borromeo, and also from St. Charles and St. Louis counties. The high school building stood to the west of St. Peter's church. Constructed in 1900, it was dangerously crowded and a potential firetrap by 1952.

That year, Father Fallon and Monsignor Anthony Strauss of St. Peter's parish discussed building a regional Catholic high school with Arthur Stauder, whose architectural firm had designed the recent improvements to the Borromeo convent. The pastors contemplated having their parishes split the cost of erecting a new building on a fourteen-acre tract of farmland in the Prairie Haute common field just west of the city limits. The Boschert family, owners of the land, agreed to sell it for $30,500. Fallon, Strauss, and Stauder took the matter to the archdiocese, and soon had a loan for the entire sum plus the permission of Archbishop Joseph Ritter to build a high school for no more than $750,000.

In 1953 Fallon and Strauss hired the Kansas City firm of Thomas R. Finn and Associates to help raise $500,000. Finn pro-posed recruiting several hundred men from the two parishes to carry out the drive over an eight-week period. He planned that the campaign would publish several tabloid-style progress bulletins written by campaign members and would prepare sermon notes for the priests of both parishes, who would preach from each other's pulpits as well as their own. Finn also agreed to hold a kick-off dinner to be cooked and served by women from both parishes, and he set up a system for collecting funds and preparing the necessary forms. He proposed assigning two staff members to the job, and quoted a fee of $12,600. Finn assured the pastors:

> We have directed over 50 Archdiocesan and Diocesan campaigns in the United States and Canada, all of which have been at least 100 per cent successful. We have directed over 400 parish campaigns, only four of which have not realized the announced objective and in these, at least 75 per cent of the goal was obtained.

Finn's campaign swung into action in March 1954. Over 200 men from Borromeo joined the tightly organized effort as division heads, team chairmen, or team members. Frank Rauch served as Borromeo's campaign co-chairman with Father Fallon. Albert Kister headed the parish Special Gifts collections. Melvin Gravemann and Joseph Marheineke planned publicity, Randolph Briscoe set up meetings, and Lawrence Boschert, Oliver ("Sam") Denker, and Hugh Holmes planned the solicitation

Borromeo fund-raisers. Seated are Hugh Holmes and Frank Rauch. Standing are Oliver ("Sam") Denker and Lawrence Boschert.

strategy. Harry Miller and Charles Mudd headed the Endorsement Committee. Henry Pieper, with Fathers David Hamilton and William Puetter, kept track of payments. Monsignor Strauss and Father Fallon set forth the campaign slogan, "Pray, Work, and Give," which they explained in the first campaign news report, dated March 28, 1954:

> It is for us in the coming weeks to give of our time and substance to promote a cause so near and dear to the heart of Christ. We can derive a great personal joy by associating ourselves with this endeavor. But we must spend also of our prayers, giving here, too, a 'Fair Share.'
>
> It is a clear path that we must walk. We therefore ask your participation in this effort to the full limit of your abilities—your prayers, your work, and your sacrifice. Let no barrier halt a supreme effort to reaffirm Catholic leadership and establish its fidelity to God. Let us assist in every way possible so that our parishes may fulfill their divine mission in the Universal Church of Christ.

> The Crusade upon which we are embarked—and it is truly a Holy Crusade—is more than a mere collection of funds. Its successful accomplishment will be realized if we heed the watchwords—PRAYER, WORK, SACRIFICE. Let unity of purpose and enthusiasm inspire us to a new height of faith. Certainly with such an inspiration, we will achieve a glorious victory.

Archbishop Ritter spoke at the campaign kick-off dinner, held Thursday, April 22, at Borromeo hall. On the following Sunday, all campaign members met at their churches at 1:30 for Benediction, then began making house calls. During these visits to the homes of parishioners, volunteers stressed that the amount to be given should represent the individual parishioner's own "fair share," depending on his or her needs and income, not on any set amount or formula. They urged parishioners to spread payments over a thirty-month period rather than to give a lump sum. Before the house calls even began, the nearly 500 campaign workers had pledged close to $200,000.

Parishioners' pledges began rolling in during the last week of April 1954 and soon helped top the $500,000 goal. Aiming to build the best school possible, Fallon and Strauss reviewed bids and designs, but sometimes clashed with the Diocesan Building Committee, which kept a sharp eye on the total cost of the project. In April 1955, the pastors had campaign workers call again on those parishioners who had not pledged or who had not fulfilled their earlier pledges.

Archbishop Ritter broke ground for the new "Inter-Parish High School" on Saturday, May 28, 1955. The Borromeo School band and the St. Peter's School band took turns playing marches, the "Star Spangled Banner," and "Come Holy Ghost." Ritter, then priests, nuns, and laymen from the two parishes, and finally civic officials, each removed a spade of earth. Mayor Henry

In charge of the kick-off dinner, (seated) Mrs. Leo Vehige and Mrs. Randy Briscoe, (standing) Mrs. Albert Kister, Mrs. E. Feldman, and Mrs. M. Johannesman.

Vogt addressed the crowd, as did Ritter, the pastors, County Superintendent of Public Schools Fred Hollenbeck, and City Superintendent of Public Schools Stephen Blackhurst.

Work progressed during the summer and fall of 1955. On December 4, 1955, Father Fallon and Monsignor Strauss laid the cornerstone into which was cut the school's name, Blessed Philippine Duchesne High School. The pastors sealed in the stone current copies of the *Banner News, Cosmos-Monitor,* and *St. Louis Register,* along with an illustration and some relics of Philippine Duchesne, and a list bearing the names of the men from each parish who had chaired the High School Committee.

Work continued into the summer of 1956 under the direction of Plez Lewis and Sons construction company of St. Clair, Missouri. On June 24, 1956, the parishes held an open house in the nearly completed structure, which housed twelve classrooms, a chapel, gymnasium, cafeteria and kitchen, and several offices. Building continued on schedule and the new school opened its doors on September 4, 1956, to 356 students. Father Arthur Bromschwig served as the school's first administrator and headed the faculty, which included Fathers Edward Thro and Marion Budzinski from St. Charles Borromeo.

All told, the close cooperation between the parishes of St. Charles Borromeo and St. Peter's made the regional high school possible. Father Fallon reported to the Jesuit provincial in January 1957 that the parish had borrowed $120,000 from the Archbishop's Expansion Fund to build and equip Duchesne. The Archdiocese had also taken an option on six acres east of the high school, where it planned to build a new parish. Fallon approved the idea, explaining that it would be wise to have a church close to Duchesne, for Mass and the sacraments. Having topped all financial projections with the help of Thomas R. Finn and Associates, Fallon planned to retain a professional fund raiser to help finance construction of a new St. Charles Borromeo School.

People

Oliver ("Sam") Denker: A native of St. Charles, Denker grew up in St. Peter's parish but switched to Borromeo as an adult. He married Olive ("Peanut") Link, had six children, and lived at 712 Jefferson Street. For many years he owned and operated the Sunshine Bakery on Second Street. Denker oversaw the solicitation of funds to build Duchesne High School, promoted the White House Retreat League, sang with the Adult Choir, and aided the needy of St. Charles through the St. Vincent de Paul Society. He died in 1970.

Miss Leona Ehrhard: Born in 1888, the youngest of Casper Ehrhard's eight children, Miss Ehrhard was a cousin of Father Henry Ehrhard and an alumna of Borromeo School and the Sacred Heart Academy. She studied music at Lindenwood College, then played the Borromeo church organ for many years without compensation, supporting herself by giving private violin and organ lessons. Late in life she cared for some of the elderly members of the parish. Miss Ehrhard spent her last years at the Carmelite Home.

Sidney Ginger: The son of an immigrant from England, Ginger was born in 1901 and attended the parish school. He married Bonnie Skinner in the present church and worked nearly fifty years for the International Shoe Company. Ginger belonged to the Ushers Club and Men's Sodality, and served many years on the Cemetery Board. He presently lives at the Camelot Residence in St. Peters, Missouri.

Henry Hellrich: Manager of the Borromeo Cemetery Board from its inception in the 1930s, Hellrich supervised the upkeep of the cemetery and the administration of its perpetual care fund. He also called the annual quilt bingo. Hellrich grew up next to Franklin School and belonged to the parish throughout his life. He married Edna Weissenborn and had two children. He worked for many years as a city policeman and meter reader.

Joseph Marheineke: Born in St. Peters in 1893, Marheineke moved to St. Charles in 1916. For fifty-five years he was associated with the Kansas City Life Insurance Company, but he also spent much of his time working for charitable causes. Marheineke organized the St. Charles County chapter of the Red Cross, serving as its chairman from 1950 until 1971. For six years he chaired the local chapter of the National Foundation

for Infantile Paralysis. He belonged to the St. Charles County Historical Society and served as Grand Knight to Council #823 of the Knights of Columbus. For thirty-five years, Marheineke served as captain of the White House Retreat League. He belonged to Borromeo's chapter of the St. Vincent de Paul Society and to the Men's Sodality, and was a member of the Third Order of St. Francis. He died in 1974.

Frank Rauch: One of St. Charles' leading suppliers of lumber and building supplies, Rauch often donated the wood that went into the parish bazaar booths. Altar boys and choir girls going to Pere Marquette Park or other picnic spots frequently rode in the back of a Rauch Lumber truck. Throughout his life a quiet philanthropist, Rauch donated to many parish and civic causes and helped out needy people. He belonged to the Knights of St. Gregory, and was elected St. Charles Man of the Year. He died in 1972.

Vincent Schneider: A native of St. Peter's, Missouri, Schneider sometimes served as the Jesuits' physician. He established the St. Charles Clinic and frequently invited Borromeo's Notre Dame nuns to picnics held at his family farm in St. Peters. Schneider died in 1963.

Adolph Thro: Pressed into the role of mayor after the unexpected death of Charles Kansteiner, Thro worked at the family's clothing store when not running the city. He presided over the 1941 celebration of the 150th anniversary of the naming of St. Charles and the founding of Borromeo parish. Thro married Louise Schreiber and had five children, four of whom lived to adulthood. After he finished out Kansteiner's term he was elected mayor, but died in 1945 before the end of his term.

Lawrence Cusack: A quiet, scholarly priest who took little care of his appearance, Cusack seemed perhaps more suited to teaching at the university level than to pastoring a growing parish. Nevertheless, he guided Borromeo through the end of World War II and into the post-war era, from 1944 to 1949. No construction or renovation occurred during these years, but Cusack did supervise the purchase of the Wentker-Alexander home at the corner of Fourth and Decatur. During his pastorate the parish paid off its bonded indebtedness.

David Hamilton: For twenty-five years Hamilton was associated with St. Charles Borromeo. He entered the Florissant novitiate in 1897 and was ordained in 1912, having obtained his education at St. Louis University. He taught at Jesuit schools in Detroit and Cincinnati, then served for eight years at St. John's College in Belize, British Honduras. After Hamilton came to St. Charles, Father Sommerhauser noticed his success with people and suggested to the Jesuit provincial that Hamilton be allowed to do mission work. Although he remained stationed at St. Charles Borromeo, Hamilton ministered to many people in the midwest. He suffered a stroke in 1944, but continued living at the rectory until 1957. He died in May 1958.

James Fallon: One of Father Sommerhauser's most popular and energetic associates, Fallon first lived at Borromeo between 1941 and 1944. He was a burly, red-faced Canadian who loved cold weather. Having

grown up in a large family, he enjoyed visiting the homes of his parishioners. During these visits he frequently pitched in with chores, even hanging diapers out to dry on occasion. Fallon guided the parish as pastor between 1949 and 1957. He later moved to Denver, where he died of a heart attack in 1961.

James O'Connor: A chronic sufferer from asthma, O'Connor came to the parish as an associate in 1942. Ordained in 1913, he served as a missionary in Wyoming and also as a college prefect. He did pastoral work at St. Mary's, Kansas, and in Kansas City before coming to St. Charles. During

The scene of the 1953 train accident at Orchard Farm, Missouri, that killed Robert Kelley, S.J.

David E. Hamilton, S.J.

Jesuit Missouri Province Archives

Francis Clerkin, S.J.

Jesuit Missouri Province Archives

his eight years at Borromeo, O'Connor directed the St. Vincent de Paul Society and said Mass when his health permitted. Poor eyesight did not prevent the elderly priest from greeting parishioners after Mass, but he sometimes addressed all women, whether married or single, as "Mother." He died at St. Joseph's Hospital in 1950.

Francis Clerkin: Born in Akron, Iowa, in 1902, Clerkin grew up in Madison, Wisconsin. He entered the Jesuit novitiate at Florissant and studied at St. Louis University and St. Mary's College. Clerkin was ordained in 1934 and spent most of his career doing pastoral work all over the West and Midwest. He spent seven years at Borromeo, between 1950 and 1957, and afterward moved to Mt. Carmel Church in Trinidad, Colorado. Parishioners remember Father Clerkin as a humble but warm and friendly man who loved people. He

died in 1979.

Robert Kelley: Born in 1877 in Iowa, Kelley moved to St. Mary's, Kansas in 1892. Five years later he entered the Florissant novitiate. As a priest he taught English and classics and served in various high positions at Creighton University in Omaha. In the 1920s he served as president of Regis College in Denver and Loyola University in Chicago. Kelley later worked at St. Mary's College in Kansas and was acting president of St. Louis University. During World War II he directed retreats at the White House Retreat Center in Lemay, Missouri. In 1949 he came to St. Charles Borromeo as chaplain of the Sacred Heart convent and also served as confessor to nearby religious communities. On August 22, 1953, while driving to hear the confessions of the nuns of St. Francis parish in Portage des Sioux, Kelley was killed in a collision with a train.

Part 5
The Present Church: Diocesan Era

Chapter 13
1957-70

Father Owens

One day in the spring of 1957, Frank Rauch and his son Henry were returning by rail to St. Charles from a lumber convention in Kansas City when they noticed that two young priests were traveling on the same train. The Rauchs introduced themselves and invited the young men to join them for dinner. The priests accepted. In the dining car, Frank Rauch asked the men who they were and where they were stationed. One of the priests, a tall and handsome man, replied that he was Father Michael Patrick Owens and that he had just been assigned pastor of St. Charles Borromeo. "The hell you are," snapped Rauch, "you're not a Jesuit."

Other parishioners reacted in the same manner when they learned that their beloved Jesuits were leaving to make way for diocesan priests. The news came without warning. The St. Louis Chancery explained that Jesuit Provincial Joseph P. Fischer had proposed moving his priests from St. Charles Borromeo and Sacred Heart parish in Florissant so that the men could staff needier schools and parishes in the province. Because he wished to issue new appointments by Easter of 1957, Fisch-

er asked his superiors for a swift change, and he got it. The story broke in late April.

The *Cosmos-Monitor* described the situation:

> The recent announcement of the coming departure of the Jesuits from St. Charles Borromeo parish . . . was met with sorrow by all, particularly by the people of the parish who have known and loved them for so long. The experience is a little like a death in one's family. Someone said, "It's like losing your right arm!"

On the evening of May 6, over a hundred parishioners and friends held a farewell party for Father James Fallon and his assistants David Hamilton, Francis Clerkin, Edward Thro, James Preuss, and Marion Budzinski. Each priest received a wristwatch, a leather wallet, and a gift of cash. As the party drew to a close, the Jesuits shook hands with their St. Charles friends, many of whom had tears in their eyes. Fallon soon departed for St. Malachy parish in St. Louis, Hamilton retired to St. Robert Bellarmine Hall in St. Louis, Edward Thro and Marion Budzinski left for St. Ferdinand parish in Florissant, Francis Clerkin went to

Fr. James Fallon at the last Mass under the Jesuit administration, May 9, 1957.

a parish in Trinidad, Colorado, and James Preuss moved to St. Francis Xavier College Church near St. Louis University.

The departure of the Jesuits from St. Charles Borromeo foreshadowed their departure a year later from St. Ferdinand. Both parishes dated back to the Spanish regime. Both had shared Pierre Joseph Didier, their first pastor. In 1823 Borromeo and St. Ferdinand became two of the first Jesuit missions in Missouri. For the next 134 years they maintained close ties; it is fitting that they became diocesan parishes at nearly the same time.

On the evening of May 9, Father Michael P. Owens was installed as pastor, and Fathers Francis Holterman, William Kraemer, and Joseph Meisner were installed as associate pastors. The new staff moved into the parish residence at the corner of Fourth and Lewis.

St. Charles Borromeo was Father Owens's first pastoral assignment. The son of Irish immigrants, he grew up in the Kerry Patch neighborhood of north St. Louis. Owens attended St. Louis Preparatory Seminary and Kenrick Seminary, and was ordained in 1941. That year he became assistant pastor at St. Teresa of Avila parish in north St. Louis. He served as such until

1945, when he became an army chaplain to American troops in Burma and India. After the war, Owens spent several years as assistant pastor to Most Holy Rosary parish in St. Louis, then served nearly two years as an army chaplain in Korea. He returned in 1952 as administrator of Annunciation parish in Webster Groves, Missouri, where he served until being named pastor of St. Charles Borromeo.

Things happened fast when Father Owens took over at Borromeo. The new pastor ratified Fallon's plan for a large, two-story school building containing fourteen classrooms, two multi-purpose rooms, a principal's office, a library, and medical rooms, and endorsed the renovation of the church basement and the building of a new cafeteria, retaining Rime A. Dusard as the architect. Owens then set about organizing financial support, anticipating that the new building would cost about $350,000. He carried out Fallon's plan to hire a professional fund raiser, with good results. He also decided that the building would be constructed south of the brick school.

Before construction began, however, Father Owens decided to move the priests out of the dilapidated rectory and into the unoccupied Wentker house at 709 North Fourth Street. The parish had owned the Wentker house since 1947, but had decided not to use it as a convent. During the summer of 1957, Father Owens directed the modification of the house into a pastoral residence and had the first floor fitted with meeting rooms and offices.

Between November 1957 and March 1958, workmen divided the house's large rooms into smaller units and removed many of its embellishments. Wall stencils were covered over and high ceilings lowered. An upstairs solarium was eliminated. Fireplace mantels, Dutch tiles, chandeliers and beveled plate glass mirrors were removed. Several healthy hardwood trees that shaded the house were cut down.

Shortly after the priests moved into the house in March of 1958, the old Jesuit residence was torn down and its site paved over. The new administration did not replace the bell that connected the church's confessionals with the old rectory.

On December 1, 1957, Archbishop Joseph Ritter broke ground for the new school, in the company of Father Owens, Father Fallon, and Monsignor Anthony Strauss of St. Peter's parish. Other dignitaries attending were Mayor Henry C. Vogt, superintendent of St. Charles public schools Stephen Blackhurst, Notre Dame Sister Superior John Louis, and Father Arthur Bromschwig of Duchesne High School. Builder John A. Ditenhafer began construction work the next day. Subcontractors were the Connors Heating Company, E. J. Fischer Plumbing Company, and Dickherber Electric Company.

Work proceeded during the school year. Students in classrooms on the south side of the old building frequently stole glances out the windows to watch the building going up. Extremely cold temperatures during the winter of 1957-1958 delayed the pouring of concrete, and a strike delayed steel work, but enough progress was made by the summer that the cornerstone could be laid. In a simple ceremony on July 4, 1958, Monsignor Strauss presided over the setting of the cornerstone, which contained the names of all Borromeo School students, re-

Eileen Owens

Fr. Michael P. Owens as a chaplain during World War II.

ligious medals, and relics of several saints.

In September 1958, classes began in the old building for all students except first graders, who attended classes in the convent. Fire drills were waived because the old school would soon be abandoned. On September 22 classes for the seventh, fifth, and fourth grades moved to the basement of the new school building. On November 17, bells rang for the last time at the old school. At 11:00, Fathers Owens, Meisner, Kraemer, and Holterman opened the doors of the new school to students, who brought over their own books. When all children had settled in their new, modern desks, Owens and the other priests walked the halls and sprinkled holy water into each classroom. Library books and teaching equipment were carried over later that day. After Thanksgiving, the old building was torn down.

On April 12, 1959, the parish held an open house at the new school. The Borromeo band played on the stage in the church basement, and the new cafeteria kitchen served refreshments. One week later Archbishop Ritter dedicated the building. With some of the same dignitaries who helped break ground in 1957, Ritter presided over a short ceremony in the church, then led the crowd outside to a speakers' platform at the main entrance of the school. After addresses by Ritter, Owens, and Stephen Blackhurst, the archbishop blessed the interior of the building and placed a crucifix inside the main entrance. Afterward, the ladies of the parish served a meal in the church basement.

Groundbreaking ceremony for the new school. From left, Fr. Arthur Bromschwig, Fr. Michael P. Owens, Archbishop Joseph Ritter, James Fallon, S.J., and Monsignor Anthony Strauss. At the far left are the Notre Dame sisters wearing the old habit.

Throughout their administration, the Jesuits had lacked a comprehensive system for collecting financial support. When unable to pay a parish expense such as the coal bill, they often had asked the congregation for help, adding that those unable to contribute should excuse themselves. For many years, collections were too low to fund much-needed capital improvements.

Father Owens soon established a more reliable system of financial administration, based on the collection of weekly tithes. He unveiled a new program for church support on November 10, 1957. A flier distributed to parishioners on that date explained that each employed parishioner should pay one hour's wage per week, or one-fortieth of his or her income. This amount soon proved unsatisfactory. In an open letter to the parish dated October 27, 1959, Father Owens announced a new goal for church support:

As we dedicated our beautiful new school building last year, it was apparent that a serious financial problem existed. Our $400,000 parish investment had us burdened with an enormous debt. A new era of parish financing was of necessity upon us.

Through your generosity last year, we were able to reduce our debt by $52,000. We expect to lower the debt by another sizeable amount this year. But, as you all know, the bulk of the funds used to reduce our indebtedness came from the new grade school pledges. Unfortunately, most of these school pledges will be paid in full by the end of this year. The obvious and alarming conclusion is that practically all of the ordinary income to be realized next year will be required to pay the ever-increasing ordinary parish expenses—very little income will be left

Monsignor Anthony Strauss blesses the school cornerstone as Fr. Joseph Meisner and Fr. Michael P. Owens look on.

Fathers William Kraemer, Joseph Meisner, Michael P. Owens, and Francis Holterman with the first class to graduate under diocesan administration, 1957

to lower our debt.

The situation must be remedied. We have no alternative but to turn to our people for increased financial assistance. We are therefore inaugurating a parish program to increase our regular weekly income. Each wage-earning parishioner is asked to budget, for parish support, approximately 5% of his annual income.

The letter went on to suggest that payments be made in weekly installments. An accompanying brochure stated that such support would nearly eliminate the need for additional appeals throughout the year. The new program ended pew rents and holy day collections. To boost support, campaign workers made home calls and signed up parishioners who promised five percent of their income for the next three years. Members of the congregation, even the youngest school children, received weekly payment envelopes. The campaign soon began to get results. To keep up the momentum, Father Owens erected in the rear of church a wooden signboard showing the latest reductions of the parish debt and future projections.

Part of the success for the financial program was no doubt due to Father Owens's persuasive oratory. A gifted speaker with a rich, baritone voice, he threw his energy into persuading his parishioners to support the church as they would their family or business. He soon prompted nearly a tripling of regular income to the parish.

Another of Father Owens's early administrative decisions was to surrender control of Borromeo Cemetery to the archdiocese. For many years, Henry Hellrich and a board of laymen had run the cemetery, employing a sexton who lived in a small house on the grounds, arranging for perpetual care, and investing the cemetery's revenues. Families were expected to maintain the appearance of their relatives' graves, but some did not. The Cemetery Board had accumulated a perpetual care fund of about $12,000 by 1960. That year, Father Owens turned over control of the burial ground and the perpetual care fund to Catholic Cemeteries of St. Louis and dissolved the Cemetery Board.

Catholic Cemeteries agreed to send its own crew of maintenance workers from St. Louis out to St. Charles at regular intervals. But because Borromeo Cemetery was one of the most remote burial grounds of the archdiocese, sending workers to St. Charles instead of to cemeteries in St. Louis cost more in money and manpower. Maintenance became less frequent. Parishioners complained to the archdiocese, but the problem lingered for many years.

Vatican II

The archdiocese granted Father Owens three young associates to help him get started in St. Charles—Fathers Francis Holterman, Joseph Meisner, and William Kraemer. Winning over the parishioners was not easy. The Jesuits and their administration had been so popular that many greeted the diocesan priests with resentment, just as many had resented the arrival of the Notre Dame nuns in 1932. One of Father Owens's first pastoral acts was to erect a plaque in the church vestibule in honor of the Jesuit pastors and the transfer of the parish to diocesan clergy.

Thirty-three years of age in 1957, Father Francis Holterman was the youngest of the group. Born in Loose Creek, Missouri, he attended St. Louis Preparatory and Kenrick seminaries and received Holy Orders in 1951. He worked for three years at a parish in Ste. Genevieve, then spent another three assisting at St. Aloysius parish in St. Louis. Holterman's health suffered in St. Charles and he was transferred in 1959 to Incarnate Word Hospital as resident pastor. Placed on sick leave in 1961, he died in April 1962.

Father William Kraemer stayed at Borromeo for five years. In better health than

Holterman, he performed many of the baptismal, matrimonial, and funeral duties. Kraemer was transferred in 1962 to the St. Engelbert parish of St. Louis. His replacement at Borromeo was Father Robert Clarke, who stayed until 1971.

The original diocesan assistant who served the parish longest was Father Joseph Meisner, a tall, lumbering priest. Like Kraemer, Meisner administered the sacraments frequently, and he also devoted much time to personal and ecumenical ministries. He continued the practice of visiting parishioners in their homes, and involved himself in civic causes. Meisner rang the Christmas bell for the Salvation Army, made frequent hospital and sick calls, and kept in close touch with the Sacred Heart community. After Holterman and Kraemer left, Meisner's duties increased, but he remained energetic during his seven years as an assistant pastor. Father Robert Gettinger replaced Meisner in 1964.

With the help of his three, and then two, assistants, Father Owens settled in to his role as pastor. His interests often complemented those of his assistants, making for a balanced ministry. Because Father Meis-

The church decorated for Christmas 1960

ner and then Father Gettinger enjoyed working with people, Owens gave each man a great deal of autonomy. They led discussion groups, joined civic organizations, and taught religion in grade school and high school, in addition to administering the sacraments.

Toward the end of Father Owens's first decade at Borromeo, the parish grappled with numerous liturgical changes brought about by the Second Vatican Council. Like other pastors, Owens had little choice but to modify Masses and other services according to official guidelines. Parishioners learned in the middle of the 1960s to follow the Mass in English rather than in Latin and to sing English hymns, some with Protestant origins, instead of Gregorian chants. Guitars occasionally supplemented the pipe organ. Facing the congregation, the priests said Mass on an altar placed in the front of the sanctuary, and distributed Communion to standing parishioners. Women stopped covering their heads in church. Father Owens and his associates encouraged people to pray the rosary before and after, but not during, Mass. Because many found these developments bewildering, Father Gettinger led parish discussion groups and maintained close ecumenical ties with other religious leaders.

When parishioners had become somewhat accustomed to the liturgical changes, Owens directed the renovation of the church, retaining a St. Louis architect to design a spare, modernistic interior in keeping with the changes of Vatican II. A quarter of a century had passed since the 1940 decoration; years of dust coated Father Sommerhauser's earthy pastels. Jesuit saints in paintings and statuary ornamented a church no longer under Jesuit administration.

In addition, the building badly needed air conditioning, rewiring, and an improved sound system. For many years, small oscillating electrical fans attached to the pillars had buzzed during summer Masses, but did little to relieve parishioners from the humidity. Although tilting open the lower windows allowed a little air to circulate, people often fainted from the heat. The church's lighting was obsolete and its wiring failed to meet code standards. A few speakers perched on top of the pillars made up the sound system.

Scaffolding went up in November of 1967. The work progressed in stages, allowing the parish to continue using the church for Sunday Mass, but the 8:00 daily Mass for the children was suspended. First, workmen took down the main altar and the two side altars, removing most of the statues, among them the two adoring angels, St. Charles Borromeo, St. Joseph holding the Child Jesus, St. Theresa, St. Francis Xavier, and St. Ignatius Loyola. Out went the pulpit and the Communion rail. Just as Edna McElhiney Olson had sal-

The church after the 1967-68 redecoration

pale blue wash. To highlight the church's many interior arches, the painters applied gold accents in overlaid geometric designs. Red plush carpet went down over the terra cotta linoleum of the nave floor and the terrazzo of the sanctuary. The original hardwood pews received a coat of grayish wash.

To the lower sanctuary walls, workers applied a black and white marble-like finish. These colors complemented the sanctuary's focal point—a soaring baldachino that canopied the altar with a golden dome. Two lecterns flanking the altar replaced the pulpit, and marble Communion stations took the place of the Communion rail. Behind the altar hung a tapering black cross, to which workers attached the whitewashed figure of Christ crucified that had hung for many years in front of the St. Joseph altar. A simple shrine replaced the former altar of Our Lady. To the opposite side of the church, a tabernacle niche took the place of the altar of St. Joseph. The redecoration ended at the end of the 1967-1968 school year, just in time for graduation exercises.

vaged the discarded painting of St. Charles Borromeo and another of the Sacred Heart in 1963, several other parishioners claimed some of these unwanted items, a few of which found their way back into the church during the 1991 renovation.

Painters then covered the earth tones of the walls and ceiling, the proscenium mural of saints, and the sanctuary frieze with a

The Baby Boom

Enrollment jumped when the new Borromeo School building opened. By September of 1960, 729 students attended. The next fall 792 signed up, and 810 did the following year. Enrollment peaked at 817 for two successive school years, 1964-1965 and 1965-1966. In later years it dropped gradually, but continued to put pressure on the school building and the resources of the parish.

In the fall of 1957 Father Owens hired five lay teachers to assist the six School Sisters of Notre Dame. At the start of the 1959-1960 school year, lay teachers outnumbered nuns for the first time ever. Two more teaching

Sisters arrived in 1962 and one more in 1963, but after the early 1970s the number of nuns began to dwindle. In 1959, the school opened another two classrooms. The next year it pressed into service the two multi-purpose rooms, bringing the total number of classrooms to sixteen. As enrollment increased, the number of children per teacher also increased, averaging nearly fifty-to-one by the middle of the 1960s.

As in previous years, students sat in long rows stretching from the teacher's desk to the cloak room. Girls wore uniforms consisting of white short-sleeved cotton blouses and navy pleated skirts. Boys still did not wear uniforms, but dressed somewhat alike in light-colored cotton shirts and dark trousers. Blue jeans and tennis shoes were forbidden. Older girls in the 1950s and early 1960s wore teased hair, but girls a few years later wore long, straight hair with bangs. The style soon caught on with boys. Teachers responded by checking hair length: girls whose bangs hung below their eyebrows or boys whose hair touched their collars were sent to the principal's office. While miniskirts were in fashion, teachers sometimes measured the distance between the hem of a questionable skirt and the wearer's knees.

At lunchtime, children had three options: to buy a hot lunch, eat a sack lunch from home, or walk home if they lived nearby. Those who bought usually had weekly lunch cards, which cost between one and two dollars. A typical lunch consisted of a meat dish, such as chili or a hot dog, a fruit or vegetable, milk, and raisins or cookies. Children received only one serving of each course, but were allowed extra helpings of white bread spread with margarine. Teachers patrolled the cafeteria to make sure all children ate their lunches.

Boys and girls still played separately. Girls spent lunchtime recess on the upper parking lot, jumping rope or playing volleyball, tetherball, or foursquare. Boys played ball games on the lower playground. Asphalt now covered the site of the Jesuit residence at the southeast corner of the block, and early in the 1960s the parish paved over what had once been the Jesuits' garden on the northeast side of the block. Increased traffic on Fourth and Fifth streets prompted the school to erect a steel fence around the upper and lower lots.

Borromeo students in 1958 participated in the first St. Charles Science Fair. An entry in the convent chronicle for March 10, 11, and 12 of that year reports, "A number of our children won prizes or ribbons on their projects. It was such a huge success

that it was decided to make it an annual affair." In March 1961, Borromeo School held its own science fair and awarded prizes to all participants. That same month, 197 students took part in the St. Charles Science Fair. The top winners competed during April of 1961 in the Greater St. Louis Science Fair, which awarded Borromeo School more ribbons than it awarded any other school in the metropolitan area.

The 1960s brought many "firsts" to the students. The St. Charles Bookmobile began making regular calls at Borromeo School in February of 1961. A new AAA-approved safety patrol system signed up boys and girls from the seventh and eighth grades. In May 1961 the school bought a portable electric piano, which enabled music instructors to teach in all classrooms. The Home and School Association funded a public address system for the school building in September of that year. Borromeo students entered the annual St. Charles County Soil and Water Conservation District poster and scrapbook contest and the annual spelling bee sponsored by the *St. Louis Globe Democrat* and Radio Station KMOX.

Under the direction of Marvin Hohman, the St. Charles Borromeo marching band won various competitions. Sister Angela's music students held recitals every year, and sometimes hosted music festivals for other schools. Sister Miriam Michael, who had previously worked as a missionary in Central America, taught Spanish to third and fourth graders in 1963. The children put on a performance in Spanish for a meeting of the PTA in January 1964. Spanish instruction continued for several years, and gave parish children perhaps the only opportunity then offered by St. Charles grade schools to learn a foreign language.

On March 25, 1963, the School Sisters of Notre Dame gained permission to wear a new style of habit. Like the old habits, the new ones consisted of long, black dresses with ear-covering wimples, but they hung closer to the body and freed the women from wearing large, dangling rosaries. The nuns' old veils had projected out from their wimples like blinders, but the new veils hung like scarves behind their faces, and made turning corners easier. In April 1963, the Ladies Sodality donated $100 toward the purchase of material for the new habits.

The 1960s expanded the nuns' horizons. During the summer, many took "geography tours" of the United States. Hosted by St. Louis University Professor of Geography John Conoyer and funded by the school's parents, the tours took Sister Herman Marie to the Pacific Northwest and Sisters Robertus, Miriam Michael, and Martin de Porres to the desert southwest. In July 1970, the parents sent the principal,

Sister Maura, on a tour of Europe.

Father Owens carried on the Jesuits' tradition of generosity toward the Notre Dame community. In January 1961 the pastor bought the old convent a forty-gallon water heater and a Whirlpool RCA combination washer and dryer. That spring he purchased living room furniture for the convent parlor. Occasionally he sent over the makings for special meals, such as on Christmas, Thanksgiving Day, and Mardi Gras. The Sisters observed the feast day of St. Michael each fall. In March they honored the pastor's Irish heritage by directing the schoolchildren in a St. Patrick's Day performance. The students decorated the stage with paper shamrocks and leprechauns, then put on a skit about Ireland and sang

Fr. Owens in 1958 with the first class to graduate from the new school

"Danny Boy," "When Irish Eyes are Smiling," and other Irish-American tunes. The climax of the show came at the end, when Father Owens opened his black shirt to reveal a green garment underneath, then granted the children a holiday.

On November 22, 1966, Father Owens took the Notre Dame community by surprise. After notifying the teachers to assemble the school children on the upper parking lot at 1:00, the pastor delivered a new Chevrolet nine-passenger station wagon to the nuns, who handed over the keys to their old 1957 sedan. Owens then blessed the new vehicle. The scene was repeated on October 3, 1971. One of the nuns wrote the next day in the house chronicle, " . . . Father Owens, our Pastor, and Mr. Henry Elmendorf drove up to our back door and said, 'We'll trade your station wagon for this new one.' There it was, a beautiful dark blue 1972 Townsman Wagon. A hearty 'Thank you' to our generous Pastor."

On March 28, 1969, Sister Maura, Monsignor Anthony Strauss, and St. Charles Borromeo Finance Committee Chairman Douglas Boschert broke ground near the corner of Fourth and Lewis streets for a new convent. The old convent was now beyond affordable repair. Construction of the new building progressed during the spring and summer of 1969, and the

Fr. Michael P. Owens exchanges cars with the Notre Dame community. From left, Fr. Robert Gettinger and Fr. Robert Clarke, Sr. Miriam Michael, Fr. Owens, Henry Elmendorf, and Sr. Maura.

women moved into their new residence in September. To make up for the lost parking space, the parish had the old convent torn down.

The blond bricks of the new convent matched those of the new school. After the old convent was razed, none of the block's original red brick buildings remained. The L-shaped new convent provided quarters for twelve nuns as well as a chapel, kitchen, and recreation room, but the Notre Dame community shrank during the next two decades. In 1990, the parish modified the lower level of the convent into an office and meeting rooms. The next year, the two remaining Sisters of Notre Dame moved out to different quarters, and Borromeo's priests moved in.

Events of the 1960s

In 1961 Father Owens accompanied Cardinal-elect Joseph Ritter to Rome for Ritter's elevation to the rank of prince of the Catholic church. Just before leaving on the morning of January 10, Owens received the best wishes and congratulations of Borromeo School students, Monsignor Anthony Strauss, Mayor F. L. Harrington, City Superintendent of Public Schools Stephen Blackhurst, and Henry P. Rauch of the St. Charles Chamber of Commerce. While awaiting their flight at Lambert Airport, Owens handed Ritter a scroll from the people of St. Charles wishing the cardinal-elect

School Sisters of Notre Dame Principals	
Date	**Name**
1932-1938	Sister Bernard Brennan
1938-1944	Sister Ilona Pfeiffer
1944-1946	Sister Sarita Pruemer
1946-1950	Sister Laurissa Mertensmeyer
1950-1954	Sister Anne Catherine Boschert
1954-1955	Sister Theodore Markus
1955-1956	Sister John Louis
1956-1964	Sister Herman Marie Siebenmorgen
1964-1970	Sister Maura Owens
1970-1971	Sister Caroline Kramer
1971-1976	Sister Rosanne Marie Mock
1976-1982	Sister Berenice Hartke
1982-1985	Sister Bernita Wasinger
1985-	Sister Barbara Bitter

a happy journey.

Father Owens traveled abroad on many occasions, but his most celebrated European tour occurred in 1966, on the occasion of his silver jubilee as a priest. On May 1 of that year, the parish honored the pastor's anniversary with a special party. Owens opened the festivities with a Mass of Thanksgiving, which featured the singing of the Adult Choir and a homily by Owens's close friend, Monsignor George Lodes. A reception and entertainment by the Adult Choir followed in the school cafeteria. A short time later, Owens embarked on a twenty-four day "Jubilee Journey" of Europe. The tour covered seven countries and ended in Rome for the 100th anniversary of Our Mother of Perpetual Help.

In 1969 Father Owens accompanied Cardinal-elect John Carberry to Rome for Carberry's elevation. Photographs of the send-off party appeared on the front page of the April 28, 1969, *St. Charles Journal*. On hand to bid the pastor farewell were the 700 students of Borromeo School, the Notre Dame community, Father Gettinger, parish officers Henry Elmendorf and James Golden, and John Witte of the St. Charles Chamber of Commerce.

The parish paid tribute to its long history during the 1969 bicentennial celebration of the founding of the city of St. Charles. The main events began on Sunday, August 17, with a day devoted to the city's religious heritage. Local churches held services with an historical emphasis, and during the afternoon, St. Charles Borromeo and other churches displayed historical exhibits at the Boys' Club gym in Blanchette Park. The day closed with a special address by Dr. Homer Clevenger, Lindenwood College professor emeritus of history.

Other bicentennial festivities included tours of the older section of town, a German beer garden and a "costume stroll" at Blanchette Park, a pageant entitled "The Way West," a reenactment of the landing of Louis Blanchette, and a "giant bicentennial parade," that formed in front of Borromeo church and looped around the older section of town, ending near the Academy of the Sacred Heart. The Knights of Columbus sponsored the parade's prize-winning float in the religious category—a small-scale horizontal log replica of Borromeo's vertical log church.

St. Charles Borromeo played host to a special visitor during the bicentennial. A distant relative of Louis Blanchette, Bishop Romeo Blanchette of Joliet, Illinois, flew to Lambert Airport on Monday, August 18. Father Owens, who had arranged the bishop's lodging and transportation, invited Blanchette to say Mass in the church. Accordingly, the bishop celebrated a pontifical low Mass at 9:00 on Tuesday morning, then unveiled a statue of his cousin Louis at the bicentennial hospitality center set up in the St. Peter's parish cafeteria.

One of the organizers of the bicentennial celebration was Edna McElhiney Olson, who for many years wrote historical articles for the *St. Charles Journal*. A series of these articles earlier in the 1960s suggested that the people of St. Charles honor Jean Baptiste Point Du Sable, the founder of Chicago who was buried in the original parish cemetery, with a suitable grave marker in the present cemetery. Lacking cooperation from Catholic Cemeteries, Mrs. Olson turned to the public for support. On Saturday, October 26, 1968, a contingent of over 100 people, many from Illinois, watched Chicago Auxiliary Bishop Michael Dempsey, St. Louis Auxiliary Bishop George Gottwald, and Father Owens dedicate a large marble stone commemorating Du Sable. The stone was then placed in the old section of the cemetery.

Chapter 14
1970-91

Boundary Changes

Parish life of the 1970s continued in the pattern set during the 1960s. Father Owens and his associates enjoyed several years without having to oversee a building project. The parish debt shrank on schedule, with occasional help from a fund-raising program called "God's Plan for Church Support."

Father Robert Gettinger came to St. Charles Borromeo just after his ordination in 1964, a self-described "baby priest" full of "reckless abandon." For several years before his 1970 transferral he led the "Operation Renewal" group, which gave parishioners a chance to study and discuss the many changes sparked by Vatican II. Like Father Meisner, Gettinger led other parish groups and joined civic organizations, among them the Kiwanis Club and the Jaycees. He maintained contact with local Protestant ministers, taught religion in the school, and moderated the CYC (Catholic Youth Council). He also loved to socialize. During hot summer weekends, Gettinger often went skiing on the Mississippi River with parishioners and attended family gatherings.

Father Robert Clarke remained associat-ed with the parish until 1971, when he was replaced by Father Donald Buhr. Older than Gettinger and not as outgoing, Clarke left St. Charles to become pastor of the Sacred Heart parish in Ozora, Missouri. In 1972 he was named associate pastor of St. Paul parish in Fenton. Clarke later served as pastor of St. Agnes and St. Liborius parishes of St. Louis. Late in life he became associated with St. Ferdinand parish, and served as chaplain to the nearby St. Patrick Retirement Apartments. He died in 1985.

During the 1960s and 1970s a controversy brewed over parish boundaries. Unlike most St. Louis parishes, St. Charles Borromeo had developed without a tightly-defined territory. After the creation of St. Peter's parish, St. Charles Catholics, no matter where they lived, were able to choose between the "English" church (Borromeo) and the "German" church (St. Peter's). Father Joseph Rielag had described Borromeo's territory in 1914: "No boundary lines in [the] City or County between the English and German churches; half the way to Portage, All Saints at St. Peter's, six miles south, by the Missouri River on the east."

When the archdiocese bought the acreage east of Duchesne High School in the 1950s, it intended for the land to become the seat of a new parish. Subdivisions were then springing up all around the high school and many Catholic families were moving in. The same was happening to the south along Highway 94, and in response the archdiocese established St. Robert Bellarmine parish in 1963. Its boundaries cut through territory formerly considered St. Peter's.

The new parish near Duchesne High School opened in 1965 under the guidance of St. Cletus. For its eastern boundary the archdiocese chose College Drive and Boschert Creek, roughly dividing the older section of town from the newer developments. This new boundary prevented Borromeo from gaining the membership of many young families, in effect limiting the parish to its own aging population. Father Gettinger summed up the problem in 1969 in his answer to an archdiocesan survey. To the question, "Is the age of your parishioners a significant pastoral factor in your parish?" he replied, "[We have] many elderly people . . . no families [are] growing up, [fewer] really young families—they are moving into the new sections of town outside the parish." Further in the survey he restated the issue: " . . . the old section of town which we are located in [is] becoming slum-looking and more poor people are moving in. The young people are moving out to the new section of town."

During the late 1960s and the 1970s, the neighborhoods around Duchesne and St. Cletus rapidly filled, and the building boom moved farther to the west. Borromeo and St. Peter's once again cooperated in financing a new wing for Duchesne High School. This addition added greatly to the school's classroom space and encouraged a jump in enrollment. By the late 1970s, the high school needed further room for expansion.

J. B. Forbes

Bishop John N. Wurm demonstrates proposed parish boundary changes with an overhead projector as Fr. Robert Jovanovic, Archbishop John L. May, Fr. Michael P. Owens, and a crowd of about 700 look on.

By the same time, St. Cletus church sat far to the east of the newest subdivisions. Its membership totaled just over 600. The expansion to the west of town led the archdiocese to plan for a new parish, to be located near the intersection of Zumbehl and Droste Roads. In March 1981, Archbishop John L. May met with about 700 Catholics at Duchesne High School. After announcing that the archdiocese would soon redraw parish lines, May asked for opinions about relocating St. Cletus parish to the new site along Zumbehl and Droste Roads. This, he explained, would allow St. Cletus to expand its own territory and take in more young families, while freeing Duchesne High School to make use of St. Cletus's original church/rectory building on Duchesne Drive, and returning to Borromeo and St. Peter's much of the territory they had lost to St. Cletus in the 1960s. Though some opposed the plan, most St. Charles Catholics supported it. The archdiocese soon moved St. Cletus parish to the new site and gave back to the older parishes much of their lost territory.

A related controversy affected St. Charles parochial schools in 1972. Because St. Robert Bellarmine parish lacked an adequate school building, many of its children attended classes at St. Peter's, which housed several grades in the condemned high school building. Similarly, many children from the St. Cletus parish attended Borromeo. In early 1972, the School Sisters of Notre Dame from both Borromeo and St. Peter's announced that their order would soon withdraw a total of seven Notre Dame nuns from St. Charles. The nuns proposed consolidating the educational programs of all four parishes—Borromeo, St. Peter's, St. Robert, and St. Cletus— into a regional, inter-parochial school. Although St. Robert and St. Cletus lacked large school buildings, they possessed structures large enough to accommodate a few hundred children.

The nuns proposed that each parish educate children of nearly the same age from all four parishes. Hypothetically, St. Peter's would take over primary education, Borromeo would teach the middle grades, St. Robert would accommodate the seventh grade, and St. Cletus, the eighth. This system would allow each school to concentrate its resources on the specific needs of a particular age group, and would spread the remaining Sisters more effectively in the schools, saving the parishes the expense of hiring additional lay teachers. The nuns asked for parishioner input.

Father Owens and the three other pastors studied the proposal as well. Because the existing schools did not charge tuition but relied instead on support from parishioners, a question arose about financing. Another question concerned transportation: some parents feared having to drive their children to three or four different schools. The issue of parish identity also surfaced. In the end the matter was dropped, and each parish remained in charge of its own school. The seven Sisters of Notre Dame left in 1972. From then until 1976, other nuns from St. Robert Bellarmine and from the new St. Elizabeth Ann Seton parish lived at the Borromeo convent, under a financial agreement with Father Owens.

The Dyer Memorial Center

Until the late 1970s the parish lacked a gymnasium. For many years Borromeo students formed basketball and volleyball teams, but they played in the facilities of other schools. After the Academy of the Sacred Heart closed its high school in May of 1972, Father Donald Buhr worked out a rental agreement with the Society of the Sacred Heart. This agreement allowed Borromeo students to use the Academy's old gym for intramural and varsity sports. A few years later, the Academy's grade school and the new Perier Elementary for boys were booming, and the Society withdrew the old gym for the use of its own students.

In February 1977, the parish considered buying the old Franklin School and its gymnasium from the St. Charles Board of Education, which for many years had used the facilities for storage. Borromeo had the buildings appraised at $40,000, then estimated that the cost of equipping the gym with showers and other improvements, tearing down the school, and paving over its site for a parking lot would reduce the total cost to $22,000. The Board of Education, however, estimated that the cost of building a similar storage facility would exceed $80,000. Negotiations stalled.

In March 1977, Mrs. Adelaide Dyer and her daughter, Mrs. Margaret Ohrman, proposed a new idea: helping the parish build its own gymnasium by donating over $100,000. Cardinal John Carberry approved the generous offer and Father Owens worked out the details with the donors, agreeing to name the facility the "St. Charles Borromeo Parish Dyer Memorial Gymnasium," and to construct it on the southeast side of Fifth and Lewis streets. The parish dropped all plans for buying the Franklin property.

Because the intended site for the construction lay across Lewis Street from the school, Father Owens petitioned Mayor Frank Brockgreitens and the city council for permission to close off that section of Lewis Street. He pointed out that the street already dead-ended just east of the site at the Academy property, and soon had the support of the Religious of the Sacred Heart, who wished to discourage drivers from cutting through their campus. Owens nominated Parish Board officer Henry Elmendorf to handle negotiations concerning the Dyer Center.

During the summer of 1977, Mrs. Dyer more than doubled the size of her donation, and Father Owens requested permission of the archdiocese to increase the size of the proposed building. The Archdiocesan Building Commission approved. The architect selected was the St. Charles firm of Harry C. LePique and Associates. LePique designed a building of reinforced concrete and steel with a brick and masonry facade and enough space to house a 2,100 square foot ground floor, with locker rooms, a sewing room, and restrooms, below a 12,000 square foot main floor equipped with a 98' x 68' gymnasium/multi-purpose room, storage, kitchen, snack room, and a large foyer. Mr. Paul Ohrman and his wife, Margaret, funded the addition of a small stage and a podium.

Four houses occupied the site of the proposed Dyer Memorial Center. Built many years earlier, they had all fallen into disrepair. Two elderly sisters from the Poese family remained in one of the houses for a time, then agreed to move, rent-free, into the brick duplex at the southwest corner of Fourth and Lewis Streets. The occupants

of the other houses moved elsewhere, and soon a demolition crew cleared the land.

The parish broke ground for the Dyer Memorial Center on Sunday, August 21, 1977. Representing her mother at the ceremony, Mrs. Ohrman dedicated the building project to the memory of her father, Bernard H. Dyer, and her late brother, David A. Dyer, who had served as prosecuting attorney for St. Charles county before his death in World War II. Mayor Frank Brockgreitens gave the welcoming speech, State Representative Douglas Boschert introduced the speakers, Mrs. Ohrman unveiled an artist's conception of the center, Father Owens provided closing remarks, and Borromeo associate Father Donald Johanningmeier led the crowd in a prayer of thanksgiving.

Father Owens laid the cornerstone on October 20, 1978. After placing inside it several mementoes of the Dyer family, a list of the members of the parish, another list of the students and faculty of Borromeo School, several 1978 coins, and various parish documents, Owens blessed and sealed the stone, then helped position it into the wall. A crowd of schoolchildren and adults watched.

At last, on September 26, 1979, Bishop John N. Wurm, assisted by Father Owens, dedicated the completed Dyer Memorial Center. Henry Elmendorf served as Master of Ceremonies, and Mayor Douglas Boschert gave the welcoming address. Other speakers were Kenneth Kapeller, the president of the School Board, Borromeo School principal Sister Berenice Hartke, Father Owens, City School Superintendent Alan Henningsen, and Sister Patricia Steppe, the headmistress of the Academy of the Sacred Heart. A reception followed in the school cafeteria.

Three ramshackle houses remained along Fourth Street behind the Dyer Center, including the corner house into which the parish had moved the elderly Poese sisters. Although the parish wished to buy these houses and raze them for more space, it could not afford to do so immediately after the construction. In response, Henry Elmendorf and twenty-three parishioners formed the "Fourth Street Partnership" and bought the properties, intending to retain them until a more opportune time for the parish.

Although they rented the houses to several needy families, the partners encountered problems related to the condition of the buildings. They had two of the houses torn down in 1980, and donated the parcels to the archdiocese for the use of St. Charles Borromeo on May 10, 1981, in recognition of Father Owens's fortieth anniversary as a priest and his upcoming twenty-fifth anniversary as pastor of St. Charles Borromeo. The corner house remained the home of the Poese sisters as long as the women were able to live independently, and was torn down in 1990.

Changes

Just as the Sisters of Notre Dame shared convent space with nuns from neighboring parishes, the Borromeo rectory became the home of Father John Hickel, then Father Robert Jovanovic, both of whom helped out part-time at the parish and also served as administrators of Duchesne High School. After Father Donald Buhr left, associate Father Donald Johanningmeier arrived. During his years at Borromeo, Johanningmeier often wore boots and bib overalls, and endeared himself to parishioners by blessing their pets on the feast day of St. Francis of Assisi and by carefully maintaining the cemetery. Other associates during the 1970s and 1980s included Fathers James Edwards, Stephen Randall, Donald Straub, Peter Blake, and Stephen Bauer. Father John Abels came to Borromeo in 1987 as the first senior priest-in-service of the parish.

As the enrollment of Borromeo School shrank, the administration converted several classrooms to other uses. Around 1970 the school developed a Speech Club. In later years it inaugurated a student council and formed a yearbook staff. Borromeo children of the 1970s and 1980s played in the band, sang in the choir, served at Mass, studied French, and joined the safety patrol. In the fall of 1977, the school introduced a popular kindergarten program.

Construction of the Dyer Memorial Center helped physical education flourish. Since then, the St. Charles Borromeo Athletic Association has provided physical challenges for all of the school's children. Boys and girls from kindergarten to the eighth grade play soccer on Borromeo teams. The school's volleyball teams, consisting of girls from the fifth through the eighth grade, have been in the forefront of competition in the St. Charles area. Boys and girls from these grades also make up the school's basketball team. After graduating, many talented Borromeo athletes play for Duchesne and other high schools.

The school's scouting programs have also prospered. Established just after World War II, Troop 351 of the Boy Scouts was named the "Archbishop's Outstanding Unit" in 1990 and the "Archbishop's Honor Unit" in 1991. Although a sizeable minority of the scouts over the years have not been Catholic, troop leaders urge all to pursue the religious awards for their particular faiths. Many young parishioners in the Cub Scouts have earned the Parvuli

Dei (Children of God) Catholic award, and numerous older boys have merited the Boy Scouts' Ad Altare Dei (For the Service of God's Altar) Catholic award. The boys enjoy plenty of opportunities to hike and camp, and also take part in parish activities. Since the start of the Boy Scout program at Borromeo, nearly fifty boys have risen to the rank of Eagle Scout.

Girls from kindergarten to the eighth grades join the various divisions of the Girl Scouts: Daisies, Brownies, Juniors, Cadets, and Seniors. The youngest work toward badges called "Try-Its" in many fields including safety, earth sciences, music, and outdoor activities. Older girls work toward more demanding badges and gain experience in the outdoors. Like the Boy Scouts, members of Borromeo's Girl Scouts earn religious awards and sometimes take part in special Masses.

Around 1980 the parish made the church accessible to wheelchair-bound parishioners by installing a concrete ramp. Parish records became computerized in 1986. The organ received an overhaul in 1976, the year of the national bicentennial. To celebrate, Father Owens invited Dr. Mario Salvador, the noted organist of the St. Louis Cathedral, to give a concert in the church. Dr. Salvador obliged on May 23, 1976, presenting a well-rounded program of many selections, including Bach fugues, Schubert's "Ave Maria," *Tu es Petrus* ("You are Peter") by Mulet, and two toccatas. The concert was free and open to the public.

In 1978 Cardinal John Carberry appointed Father Owens dean of the St. Charles Deanery. Four years later, Owens became the first monsignor in Borromeo history. The parish celebrated with a Mass of Thanksgiving on November 14, 1982, and held a reception afterward in the Dyer Center. The pastor thereafter wore the purple cassock and white sash of a monsignor.

In 1981 Father Owens received the assistance of Donald Boschert, the first deacon of the parish. Boschert's ordination to the service of the church enabled him to witness weddings, baptize, and perform certain other sacramental functions. Although ill health influenced Boschert to retire several years later, parishioner Raymond Dickerson began serving the church as Borromeo's second deacon upon his 1987 ordination.

After several months of illness, Father Owens died on February 24, 1988. He had served as pastor nearly thirty-one years, longer than any other priest in the history of the parish. His funeral Mass on February 27 drew perhaps the largest crowd ever to Borromeo church. Archbishop John L. May attended, as did Cardinal John Carberry and Bishops Glennon Flavin, George Gottwald, and Charles Koester. Numerous priests and deacons from St. Charles and the St. Louis metropolitan area paid their respects, as did hundreds of parishioners, friends, and family members.

Father Timothy Michael Dolan gave the homily. Opening with a eulogy for Father Owens's years as a priest, Dolan summed up his life:

> There seem *three distinctive features* about him so obvious to those who knew and loved him:
>
> First are those *natural* characteristics that made him such *a good man:* his deep love for his family, his loyalty to friends, especially when they were sick or in need, and even after death, a sparkling sense of humor based probably on an awareness of his own shortcomings. . . .
>
> Secondly, a *good priest!* Monsignor Owens placed these sterling natural talents at the disposal of the Church he loved in the priesthood, and grace indeed built upon the nature he provided! He had an infatuation with the priesthood, a respect for the dignity of Holy Orders, a confidence, pride, and comfort in his priestly identity, and a fierce allegiance to the sacerdotal fraternity. . . .
>
> Thirdly, we note *his devotion to the*

Mass. . . . He never lost that childlike awe of the miracle of the Mass. . . .

And so we entrust him to Jesus, and to Our Immaculate Mother Mary, to whom he had such a tender piety. . . .

Father Owens was buried in the priests' section of Calvary Cemetery.

Owens died several months before the long-awaited canonization of Philippine Duchesne, on July 3, 1988. The pioneer educator's road to sainthood, however, had begun over a century earlier. Shortly after she died in 1852, Archbishop Peter Kenrick declared her "the noblest and most virtuous soul he had ever known." In 1895 Kenrick asked Mother Elise Miltenberger, R.S.C.J., of the old St. Louis City House school, to gather depositions about the sanctity and character of Mother Duchesne. Two years later, the Vatican received the results of her investigation. Pope Pius X declared Mother Duchesne "venerable" in 1909, and Pope Pius XI declared her to have "heroic virtue" in 1935. In 1939 the Vatican reviewed two miracles attributed to Mother Duchesne: the 1932 cure of a gardener who had worked at a Sacred Heart convent in Puerto Rico before falling seriously ill with cirrhosis of the liver; and the 1930 cure of an Italian Sacred Heart nun who suffered from mastoiditis. In 1940 Pope Pius XII accepted the cures

as miraculous and beatified Philippine, assigning November 17 as her feast day. Because of the great expense involved in promoting a candidate for sainthood, the Society of the Sacred Heart for a time relaxed its drive to have Philippine canonized. But when the Vatican recognized as miraculous a third cure—that of a Sacred Heart nun who had suffered from cancer of the thyroid—the cause gained momentum. The Congregation of the Causes of Saints decided unanimously on July 15, 1987, that Philippine should be canonized. Pope John Paul II ratified the decision in October of that year, and a board of cardinals gave final approval to the canonization in May 1988.

More than 700 people from the St. Louis area traveled to Rome for the event, including Archbishop May, Cardinal Carberry, Father Bauer, numerous parishioners, many local Sacred Heart religious and alumnae, and a large contingent of students from Duchesne High School and the Academy of the Sacred Heart. Those unable to attend crowded into the shrine of St. Philippine on the Academy grounds for a special Mass. On November 17, 1988, the first feast day of the new saint, Archbishop May celebrated a well-attended Mass at St. Charles Borromeo church in her honor.

Bishop Paul Zipfel

Father Paul A. Zipfel took over as pastor in March of 1988. A native St. Louisan, Zipfel received Holy Orders in 1961. Over the years he devoted himself to teaching and to parish ministries, and also developed a reputation as a masterful amateur magician. Father Zipfel brought to St. Charles Borromeo enthusiasm and a collaborative style of leadership.

He began his priestly ministry as an assistant pastor of St. Simon parish in Concord Village. Later, he taught and worked as a part-time associate pastor at Ascension, North American Martyrs, and Our Lady of Good Counsel parishes in north St. Louis county. Zipfel earned his master's degree in education with an emphasis on counseling from St. Louis University in 1965. He

Borromeo children and adults sing with others from parishes once served by Fr. Paul Zipfel, at Zipfel's episcopal ordination.

Richard C. Finke

taught at the old Laboure and Aquinas high schools, serving as administrator of the latter from 1968 to 1971. He became administrator of Holy Cross parish in Baden in 1972 and four years later became its pastor. In 1982 Zipfel was appointed pastor of Holy Family parish in south St. Louis. One of his assistants there was Father Stephen Bauer, who came to St. Charles Borromeo in 1987.

One of Father Zipfel's first pastoral acts at Borromeo was to form the Parish Council. First, a steering committee met for nearly a year to pray and plan the role of the group and its members. The committee debated many issues, including how to make the parish a more Christian community, how to involve young people in parish matters, and how to reach a consensus on decisions. The committee closed the October 24, 1988, meeting with this statement:

We might look on this steering committee and the future council as a rebirth. Talking about "who we are" is radical. We are creating a model. We build a community by looking at the plan of the Master in the gospels. Right

now, we, as a parish, have no common goal. In the past we have pulled together when there was a common goal, usually a building project, and we needed money. We need to be calling on our parishioners to meet human needs, not monetary [needs]. Visiting the people is the responsibility of us all, not just the clergy, and not just to visit shut-ins or collect money. Then, when needs are discovered, they must be met. Let them know someone from the community cares.

In January 1989, the committee stated the council's mission: "We, the St. Charles Borromeo Parish family, are called by virtue of our baptism to be a sign of Jesus Christ. We are sent to foster the growth of God's kingdom by praising God, serving others, and proclaiming the Gospel." The committee then formulated its purpose and functions, among them: to coordinate, encourage, and promote all apostolic parish activities, to implement needed programs, to establish dialogue among the clergy, religious, and the laity, and to further the goals of the parish according to archdiocesan guidelines.

Richard C. Finke

The newly ordained Bishop Paul Zipfel, followed by Archbishop John L. May

In February the committee decided that the council would consist of several ex officio clerical or religious members, nine elected and three appointed adult lay members, and one elected high school-age member. All except the pastor would be able to vote. Over the next few weeks, the committee formulated rules for the nomination, election, and terms of council members, the scheduling of meetings, and the setting of agendas. Although decision by consensus remained the council's ideal, the group provided for majority decision-making by a quorum of twelve members.

Father Zipfel called to order the first meeting of the Parish Council on June 12, 1989. The group elected its first board of members to terms of one, two, and three years, then named Joe Briscoe chairperson, Ann Johannesman vice-chairperson, and Melanie Wilkison secretary. Each member

was asked to serve on a particular commission, which included: Community Building, Worship and Spiritual Life, Administration, Education, and Outreach. These commissions soon got to work handling such diverse matters as setting the parish budget, moderating the Scout programs, ministering to Borromeo's unmarried adults, arranging blood donor programs, running the school, and planning liturgies.

Father Zipfel oversaw the hiring of Sister Helen Brewer, D.C., the parish's first director of religious education. He also endorsed the taking of a monthly collection for the benefit of the St. Vincent de Paul Society. Formerly dependent on private donations, the Society struggled to serve the needy of St. Charles city and county. After the collection became established, the Society agreed to share ten percent of the proceeds with the local chapter of Birthright, which cares for the needs of expectant mothers and their children. This outreach program supplemented another ongoing ministry which involves many parishioners: the cooking and distribution of casseroles for the poor and homeless of St. Louis. The St. Patrick Center on that city's near north side has fed 400 hungry people at a time with the casseroles prepared and delivered by Borromeo parishioners.

In May 1989, St. Charles Borromeo received some unexpected news: Archbishop John L. May had asked Father Zipfel to succeed George Gottwald as an active auxiliary bishop of the Archdiocese of St. Louis. Although this meant that Zipfel would become the first bishop from the ranks of the parish clergy, it also meant that he would leave St. Charles.

The story broke on Monday, May 22. The next day, the *St. Charles Post* quoted parishioners concerned over losing their pastor. Ethel Elmendorf explained that Zipfel was considered a "warm, kind, nice person who touched everybody here." Charles Boswell continued, "As thrilled as we are, our wish-

The 1989-90 Parish Council. **Standing, from left**: *Fr. Stephen Bauer, Fr. Richard Tillman, Vince Luetkenhaus, Bob Lanigan, Tom Pallardy, Chairperson Joe Briscoe, Joe Hensley, Tom Hayden, Jack Goldkamp, Deacon Ray Dickerson.* **Sitting**: *Sr. Barbara Bitter, Harriet Pallardy, Mary Conoyer, Vice-Chairperson Ann Johannesman, Secretary Melanie Wilkison, Sr. Helen Brewer, Barbara Bott.*

es are that he will be assigned a parish and [that] it will be our parish, because we think so much of him."

The date picked for Zipfel's episcopal ordination was the feast of St. Peter and St. Paul, June 29, 1989. On this date, a crowd of 2,000 packed the St. Louis Cathedral for the Mass and ordination rite. Before the Liturgy of the Eucharist, Archbishop May, Bishop Edward J. O'Donnell, and Bishop Terry Steib imposed hands upon Zipfel. All the bishops then joined in a prayer of consecration. After Zipfel's head was anointed, he received the symbols of his new ministry—the Book of the Gospels, the ring, the miter, and the staff.

Soon after returning to St. Charles Borromeo, Father Zipfel was reassigned to work out of the chancery and to reside close to its offices. In the July 2, 1989, parish bulletin he explained his imminent departure:

> You have been very supportive and encouraging in these past weeks although I think you knew that this appointment to the Episcopacy would mean my departure from St. Charles Borromeo. I did not know for certain until last Friday. . . . The Archbishop intends to divide the Archdiocese into three vicariates (regions) and Bishops O'Donnell, Steib, and I would be given certain responsibilities in each region. . . .
>
> I will be with you for the remainder of the summer so that my transfer can take place when other personnel changes would normally occur. . . . I promise not to be a "lame duck" in these last two months but you will understand if I would want to leave any major decisions

The Diocesan Era † 199

to your new pastor when he arrives. Seventeen months has not been very long but I would not trade it for anything because I have come to know some beautiful and loving people here at St. Charles Borromeo.

The Bicentennial Celebration

Father Zipfel's replacement arrived at the end of the summer. Monsignor Arthur V. Peet, the dean of the St. Charles Deanery, installed Father Richard J. Tillman as pastor of St. Charles Borromeo parish during the 10:30 Mass on September 17, 1989. Father Tillman came to St. Charles from the St. James parish of Potosi, Missouri, where he served as pastor and as Catholic chaplain to the maximum security Potosi Correctional Center. Earlier assignments included work at Catholic Charities and the Human Rights Office of the archdiocese. Father Tillman served at St. Ann's Shrine and the St. Philip Neri parish in St. Louis, and earned a master's degree in social work from St. Louis University. He was ordained in 1965.

Among his many responsibilities at Borromeo, Father Tillman inherited the task of preparing for the 200th anniversary of the parish, beginning on November 7, 1991. Father Owens had begun planning for the event, and Father Zipfel and Father Bauer had organized three groups of parishioners to coordinate preparations: the Celebration Committee, the Restoration Committee, and the Capital Campaign Committee. Father Tillman worked with Capital Campaign chairman Henry Elmendorf in launching the fund-raising effort. The preparations began in earnest.

At first, the committee aimed to raise $700,000 to fund the $900,000 restoration of the church, and soon had over $700,000 in pledges. Although Archbishop May had recently frozen most archdiocesan construction projects, he approved Borromeo's renovation, but asked that the parish trim ten percent from the total cost of the project and conduct a follow-up appeal to raise the balance. Accordingly, the Renovation Committee reduced the project cost to near $800,000. To collect the remainder, the Capital Campaign sent out volunteers to call on previous donors as well as new members of the parish.

During the pledge campaign, Father Stephen Bauer began collecting parish-related photographs, documents, and memorabilia for the St. Charles Borromeo archives. He also arranged for University of Missouri Archaeological Survey directors Joe Harl and Colleen Hamilton to excavate at the Academy of the Sacred Heart for traces of the 1858 parish school for girls and at the northeast corner of Block 28 for signs of the log church and the original cemetery. Harl and Hamilton directed a student dig at the sites during the summer of 1990. Their crew unearthed the outline of the parish school and many school-related items. Although it failed to turn up evidence of the log church or the first cemetery, it found the lot rich in nineteenth century artifacts. The next year, the Archaeological Survey excavated deeper at the school site.

Father Tillman authorized Celebration Committee chairman Richard Johannesman to oversee plans for the year-long festivities and the writing of the parish history. The committee retained Academy of the Sacred Heart French instructor Sara Gaylor to translate Borromeo's earliest baptism, marriage, and burial registers. As

Gaylor finished the translations, parish secretary Peggy Dupree entered the information into the computer system.

Lucy Rauch headed the Restoration Committee, which oversaw the redecoration of the church. Because nearly a quarter of a century had passed since the last redecoration, the church's interior badly needed cleaning and painting. The parish wished to incorporate acoustical and electrical upgrades and to add a multi-purpose section to the vestibule area.

At the same time, many wanted to bring the decor back to the original intent of architect Louis Wessbecher. Father Sommerhauser had introduced the first deviations from Wessbecher's design by painting over the marbleized pillars and by introducing the predominantly red and blue clerestory windows into the earthy color scheme. Although Father Owens's 1967-1968 redecoration had brought the church into compliance with Vatican II guidelines, it had also strayed far from the dominant Romanesque design and had further obscured the original coloration.

The Restoration Committee and architect Art Stauder of Stauder Architecture divided the work into three basic areas: general repairs and maintenance, historic restoration, and functional or liturgical upgrades. Contractor Hof Construction coordinated the work, including the spot cleaning of the exterior, roof repairs, caulking and shielding the windows with protective glass, rewiring, renovating the air conditioning system, pouring new front steps, and landscaping the square in front of the church.

Historic restoration involved bringing back the old main altar, sanctuary lamp, and tabernacle enclosure. The parish regained the painting of Charles Borromeo and hung it in one of the alcove shrines, formerly the site of a confessional. Workmen hung a San Damiano crucifix above the sanctuary. To tie all the elements together, decorator Tom Sator chose beige tones with gold and raspberry trim for the walls and ceiling, and forest green for the restored scagliola-covered pillars.

The parish achieved functional and liturgical upgrades by enlarging the vestibule and enclosing it with a glass wall and doors, installing a rest room and ushers area in the back of church, moving the baptismal font to the former St. Joseph side of the sanctuary and installing the old tabernacle in the former Blessed Mother side of the sanctuary, making the three confessional alcoves into shrines (one of which was dedicated to St. Philippine Duchesne), and building reconciliation rooms in the work sacristy. The church also received state-of-the-art acoustical and electrical improvements. Hof's subcontractors finished the work in early September.

People

John Becker: Chosen the St. Charles Chamber of Commerce Citizen of the Years in 1989, Becker has served as the only non-Catholic president of the Borromeo School PTA. He helped found the St. Charles Boys Club, commanded the city's American Legion Post, and has worked for the American Red Cross Disaster Assistance Program and the Daniel Boone District of the Boy Scouts. Becker served on the St. Charles Board of Adjustments for nearly three decades and has worked on the Architectural Review Board. He is married to the former Mary Louise

Schreiber and has two sons.

Hilda Borgmeyer: A young widowed mother when she began cooking for Father Sommerhauser and the Jesuits, Hilda Borgmeyer continued cooking for Fathers Cusack and Fallon and their associates, then cooked nearly thirty years for the diocesan priests. During Father Owens's pastorate she occupied a room behind the kitchen in the rectory at 709 North Fourth Street. Though originally employed to prepare meals, she later kept house for the priests, worked as a sacristan, and counted collection money on Sunday. She died in 1989.

Douglas Boschert: A lifelong parishioner, Boschert attended Borromeo School and served as an altar boy to the Jesuits. He has belonged to various parish groups, including the Ushers Club and the church board. Boschert has served the public as a state representative and worked as mayor between 1979 and 1983. He led the drive to replace the old convent and has worked many years for the Archdiocesan Development Appeal. He is married to the former Leathe Huffmeier.

Helen Briscoe: Called "the right arm of the parish" by Father Owens, Helen Briscoe served as Borromeo's executive secretary between 1966 and 1988. She replaced Elizabeth Meiser, who had served as secretary under Fathers Fallon and Owens until leaving St. Charles in 1966. Helen and her late husband, Randolph Briscoe, represented the parish at the St. Charles celebration of the national bicentennial in 1976. She is a charter member of the Zonta Club, an association of business and professional women. For many years, she, Billye Williams, Mary Prinster, and others have welcomed new members into the parish.

Sister Mary Arthen Casson, S.S.N.D.: A native of Marinette, Wisconsin, Sister Arthen came to Borromeo as a newly-professed School Sister of Notre Dame in 1936. She taught music in the school and played the organ until her transfer in 1950. After ten years of teaching in Chatawa, Mississippi, and another ten in Quincy, Illinois, she returned to the St. Louis area to teach music at Rosary High School. She partially retired in 1981, then moved back to St. Charles. She teaches singing as a part-time instructor at Borromeo School.

Henry Elmendorf: Starting as parish chairman of the Archdiocesan Development Appeal, Elmendorf went on to chair the Appeal for the St. Charles Deanery and then directed the entire campaign for the Archdiocese, being named an Honorary Life Member of the Development Council in 1985. He belongs to the papal order of the Knights of Malta, and in 1984 was named a Knight Commander With Star in the Equestrian Order of the Holy Sepulchre of Jerusalem. For many years Elmendorf was Father Owens's good friend and advisor, and has taken part in numerous parish decisions. Elmendorf has directed the Missouri-St. Louis Metropolitan Airport Authority, the Convention and Tourist Board of the city of St. Charles, and was named St. Charles Man of the Year in 1964 and 1966. He is married to the former Ethel Wiechens and has two daughters.

William ("Red") Freise: Active in the Boy Scouts for over sixty years, Freise served as scoutmaster of Borromeo's Troop 351, in which capacity he won the Duchesne Award. Freise worked in many different phases of the scouting program, specializing in training others to serve as den and pack leaders. An executive chef in several St. Louis restaurants and institutions, he also served as a buyer for the Borromeo School cafeteria. He died in 1989.

Jack Heck: A member of the parish all his

life, Jack Heck has been active in the St. Vincent de Paul Society for many years. He also does volunteer work for the St. Joseph Health Center hospice program, helping to relieve the caregivers of terminally ill patients by running errands, helping with meals, providing a break, or just keeping patients company. A fourth degree Knight of Columbus, Heck has taken part in many parish and school-related activities. He served on the 1990-91 parish council. Retired from Rauch Truck Lines, he is married to the former Emily Schneider and has four sons.

Richard Johannesman: A member of the parish since 1945, Johannesman has been active on the boards of both Borromeo School and Duchesne High School, and has served on the Archdiocesan School Board. He helped create the Duchesne High School Endowment Fund, and has served on the Archdiocesan Development Appeal. Johannesman has also promoted the White House Retreat League, helped organize the Parish Council, and chaired Borromeo's Financial Committee. He is married to the former Dolly Holmes and has seven children.

Mary Kutchback: Under the instruction of Borromeo's Sister Mary Angela Glassmeyer, Mary Bizelli Kutchback learned to play the piano and organ while a student at Borromeo School. At the age of eleven she began playing the organ in church. She has continued as organist through the change from Gregorian chants to congregational music, two church renovations, and numerous pregnancies. Mary Kutchback has played for both the Children's Choir and the Adult Choir, and presently provides music on school days for the children's Mass. She is married to David Kutchback.

Lucy Rauch: A graduate of the Academy of the Sacred Heart, Duke University, and St.

Henry Elmendorf

Henry Elmendorf in Rome with Cardinal John Carberry for the 1978 installation of Pope John Paul II.

Louis University School of Law, Lucy Rauch has worked as an assistant prosecutor in St. Charles and currently serves the public as the first female full circuit judge in the county. She directs the Bicentennial Restoration Committee, serves on the Home and Health Board of the St. Joseph Health Center, the Salvation Army Board, and is one of the first female members of the Rotary Club.

Reinhart Stiegemeier: One of the city's foremost proponents of historic preservation, Stiegemeier moved to town from a nearby farm at the age of seven. He founded the South Main Street Historical District, which helped maintain the area's nineteenth century character and prevented the demolition of some of its buildings. He was one of the original members of the St. Charles County Historical Society. Stiegemeier provided many photographs and other assistance for the writing of this history. He died in 1991.

Weber family: Brothers Aloys, Clem, Edward, Francis, Joe, and Leo, their wives and numerous children, have been staunch supporters of the parish for many years. The brothers still farm north St. Charles county. Each spring they and many other local farmers observe Rogation Days by attending Mass and having their seeds, machinery, and fields blessed. The Webers have been active in the Ushers Club, and have two sisters who are professed religious. Many dozens of Weber children have attended Borromeo School and Duchesne High School. Twenty-five Weber families currently belong to the parish.

Note: Though many have served St. Charles Borromeo over the years in nearly countless ways, space does not allow that all receive herein the recognition they deserve for their generous contributions. The parish nevertheless salutes these numerous unsung angels.

Pastors of St. Charles Borromeo

Priests of Various Orders

1. Pierre Joseph Didier, O.S.B. 1792-1794
2. Charles Leander Lusson, O.A.R. 1798-1804
3. Joseph Marie Dunand, O.C.S.O. . . . ca. 1811-ca. 1814
4. Benedict Richard, O.S.B. 1818-1820
5. John Acquaroni, C.M. 1820-1822

Jesuits

1. Peter J. Verhaegen 1826-1828
2. John B. Smedts 1828-1833
3. Charles Van Quickenborne 1833-1835
4. Judocus Van Assche 1835-1836
5. John B. Smedts 1836-1843
6. Peter J. Verhaegen 1843-1844
7. Leonard Nota* 1844-1845
8. Theodore De Theux 1845-1846
9. John Schoenmakers 1846-1847
10. Francis X. De Coen 1847-1849
11. Joseph Aschwanden 1849-1850
12. Francis X. De Coen 1850-1851
13. Peter J. Verhaegen 1851-1857
14. Peter Tschieder 1857-1858

15. Peter J. Verhaegen 1858-1868
16. John Roes 1868-1879
17. Joesph Zealand 1879-1882
18. Victor Van der Putten 1882-1885
19. Adrian Sweere 1885-1888
20. Henry Baselmans 1888-1889
21. Joseph Rosswinkel 1889-1895
22. Joseph Meuffels 1895-1897
23. Constantine Lagae 1897-1911
24. Joseph Rielag 1911-1919
25. Stephen McNamara 1919-1926
26. Henry Ehrhard 1926-1932
27. William Sommerhauser 1932-1944
28. Lawrence Cusack 1944-1949
29. James Fallon 1949-1957

*Leonard Nota may have been sent temporarily.

Transferred to Diocesan Clergy, May 10, 1957

1. Michael P. Owens 1957-1988
2. Paul Zipfel 1988-1989
3. Richard Tillman 1989-

Epilogue

The restored church is a far cry from the rude log building where the earliest residents of St. Charles worshiped. At first glance, today's parishioners may seem to have nothing in common with the uneducated, poverty-stricken trappers and rowers from Louis Blanchette's day, but a strong thread of faith connects the generations.

In the past 200 years, the people of St. Charles Borromeo have spoken a rough form of French, Indian dialects, German, and English. They have lived in tents and vertical log cabins, brick Victorian houses and modern tract homes. They have hunted and trapped, grown corn and wheat, operated small businesses, and worked for Fortune 500 companies. Some have fought native Americans, others were native Americans. Through the years there have been disagreements, especially during the Civil War. The congregation has included slaves and slaveowners, corporate officers and manual laborers, Democrats and Republicans. And yet, in spite of their many differences, the people of the parish have come together for 200 years to worship the same God and to advance their common faith.

They have not always gotten along with their spiritual leaders, but they have pulled together and accomplished much. They have attracted hardy souls like Peter Verhaegen and Philippine Duchesne, John B. Smedts and Felix Verreydt. Through the guidance of these and other European missionaries, St. Charles shed its old reputation as a wayward place. It has proven a fertile ground for vocations, and has sent its priests and religious to corners of the world as remote as St. Charles once was.

The territory of the parish once stretched past the Rocky Mountains toward the Pacific Ocean; now it encompasses a small portion of St. Charles city and county. St. Charles Borromeo people are rich as well as poor, upper middle class and lower middle class. Although the parish now has fewer young people than it has had for several decades, it boasts many families that have belonged for over a century. St. Charles Borromeo inspires a quality of loyalty unknown in youthful parishes.

In the beginning, laymen ran the parish. The congregation agreed to give up this direct leadership in the 1820s. Over a century and a half later, the laypeople of St. Charles Borromeo are reasserting their responsibility to the Church and to each other. At the same time, they have lost nearly all of their teaching Sisters, and no longer enjoy the luxury of having five or six priests in residence. How St. Charles Borromeo responds to these and the many other challenges looming ahead in its third century depends, as always, upon the faith and cooperation of its people.

Abbreviations

AA	Archives of the Archdiocese of St. Louis	MHS	Missouri Historical Society
BLC	Abraham P. Nasatir (ed.), *Before Lewis and Clark*	MMC	Minutes of Mothers Club
		PD	Louise Callan, *Philippine Duchesne*
DHS	Duchesne High School	*PDWP*	Catherine Mooney, *Philippine Duchesne: A Woman with the Poor*
HASL	John Rothensteiner, *History of the Archdiocese of St. Louis*	*RACHS*	*Review of the American Catholic Historical Society*
HD	*Historia Domus*	SCB	St. Charles Borromeo
HDOM	*Historia Domus,* translation by James O'Meara	SCBA	St. Charles Borromeo Archives
HM	Louis Houck, *History of Missouri*	SCCHS	St. Charles County Historical Society
HSC	*History of St. Charles, Montgomery and Warren Counties, Missouri.*	*SFF*	Gilbert Garraghan, *St. Ferdinand de Florissant*
JA	Jesuit Missouri Province Archives	*SMV*	Lawrence Kinnaird (ed.), *Spain in the Mississippi Valley, 1765-1794*
JMUS	Gilbert J. Garraghan, *The Jesuits of the Middle United States*	*SRM*	Louis Houck (ed.), *The Spanish Regime in Missouri*
JR	Reuben G. Thwaites (ed.), *The Jesuit Relations and Allied Documents*	*SSH*	Louise Callan, *The Society of the Sacred Heart in North America*
JRPH	John Killoren and others, *Jesuit Roots and Pioneer Heroes*	*SWV*	Abraham P. Nasatir (ed.), *Spanish War Vessels on the Mississippi, 1792-1796*
MCBC	Minutes of the Church Building Committee		

Notes

Preface

1. "I have seen nothing more . . ." *JR* 59: 141.
2. "in order that I may . . ." *JR* 59: 143.
3. "because most of the time . . ." Rui to O'Reilly, Oct. 29, 1769, *SRM,* 1: 63.
4. "and all the districts . . ." O'Reilly to Piernas, Feb. 17, 1770, *SRM,* 1: 76.
5. "that the dominion. . . ." O'Reilly to Piernas, Feb. 17, 1770, *SRM,* 1: 76.
6. On the powers of lieutenant governors, see Archibald, "From 'La Louisiane' to 'La Luisiana': The Imposition of Spanish Administration in the Upper Mississippi Valley."
7. On Spanish taxes, see Holmes, "Spanish Regulation of Taverns and the Liquor Trade in the Mississippi Valley," in McDermott's *The Spanish in the Mississippi Valley.*
8. Unzaga's report appears in *SRM,* 1: 114-120.
9. Spanish harvest figures are found in *SRM* 1: 326, 2: 143.
10. Meurin's letter appears in Rothensteiner's *HASL* 1: 120.
11. Records of Gibault's (and Meurin's) sacramental acts are kept in the archives of the Old Cathedral.
12. "attending so many villages. . . ." Gibault to Bishop Jean-Olivier Briand, Oct. 1769, see *HASL* 1: 130-131.
13. "has four villages. . . ." *HASL* 1: 155.
14. The Oct. 13, 1789 agreement to build a log church is kept in the archives of the MHS.
15. "where they intend constructing. . . ." see *BLC* 1: 132.
16. "There is no doubt. . . ." Pérez to Miró, Sep. 10, 1790, *SMV* 2: 378.
17. Biographical information about the early priests who may have ministered to St. Charles before 1791 comes mainly from Ekberg's *Colonial Ste. Genevieve, SRM,* and *BLC.*

Part I

Chapter 1

1. "The inhabitants of the small hills. . . ." Pérez to Miró, Sep. 10, 1790, *SMV* 2: 378.
2. "As patron of the said town. . . ." *SMV* 2: 377.
3. The unidentified source in the SCB file of the JA is an unsigned handwritten account of the early days of the parish. Jesuit historian Gilbert Garraghan may have been the author.
4. see Conway's lecture, page 14.
5. Sommerhauser's partially completed manuscript is kept in the SCB file at the JA.
6. "In accord with the Señor . . . ." Carondelet to Bajamar, July 25, 1792, *SMV* 3: 67-68.
7. "I also gave a passport . . . ." Trudeau to Carondelet, Ap. 30, 1795, *BLC* 1: 324.
8. "St. Charles is too distant. . . ." Trudeau to Carondelet, Sep. 26, 1795, *BLC* 1: 350.
9. "it would be difficult. . . ." from Collot's *A Journey in North America:* 277.
10. "This town is already too big. . . ." and other material on Gayoso de Lemos's visit comes from *SWV:* 127- 128, 305-

308, 336-337.

11. Some of de Finiels' impressions of St. Charles appear on page 74 of his *An Account of Upper Louisiana.*

12. For more on the slavery of both blacks and Indians before 1804, see Winstanley Briggs' "Slavery in French Colonial Illinois."

13. "because they are obliged. . . ." Trudeau to Carondelet, Jan. 15, 1798, *BLC* 2: 543.

14. for more on Blanchette, see Ben Emmons' article.

15. "who gives himself to drink. . . ." Delassus to Stoddard, *Billon's Annals of St. Louis* 1: 366.

16. Most of the information about early parishioners comes rom Billon's *Annals, SRM, HM,* and SCBA.

Chapter 2

1. For background on tensions between Creoles and "Americans" see Jay Gitlin's "'Avec Bien de Regret.'"

2. " . . . there is in the very atmosphere. . . ." from John E. Kirkpatrick's *Timothy Flint:* 111.

3. " . . . they live in a perfect state. . . ." and other information on St. Charles appears in *Journals of the Lewis and Clark Expedition* 2: 241-244.

4. "I know these clergymen well. . . ." Stoddard to Dearborn, June 3, 1804, *BLC* 2: 742.

5. see *HASL* 1 for more on Maxwell and Flynn.

6. "On my arrival I. . . ." *RACHS* 26: 340-341.

7. "He is a sprightly. . . ." see *HASL* 1: 226.

8. For more of Dunand's reports, see *RACHS* 26: 329-346 and 27: 45-64.

9. Details on Flaget's visit can be found in *SFF* 116-118.

10. The original pleading is on file at the MHS. The JA contain a few related documents.

11. Information on parishioners comes from Billon's *Annals, SRM* and *HM.* For more on Antoine Janis and Marie Louise, see Ekberg's *Colonial Ste. Genevieve,* 227-229.

Chapter 3

1. "It is simply astonishing. . . ." *PDWP* 110.

2. Dubourg's plan for a "Seminary for female education" in in St. Charles is kept in the SCB file, JA.

3. "a tomb in which. . . ." *PDWP* 122.

4. "Monseigneur Dubourg, who looks. . ." *PD* 273.

5. "The town is partly visible. . . ." *PD* 271.

6. "exorbitant," see *PD* 273.

7. "seven small rooms. . . ." *PD* 278.

8. "the village is willing. . . ." *PD* 273.

9. "Mr. Richard. . . ." *HASL* 1: 301-302.

10. "he went off. . . ." *PD* 305.

11. "When we complain to the bishop. . . ." *PD* 278.

12. "These children. . . ." *PD* 278.

13. "Their laziness. . . ." *PD* 284.

14. "Bishop Dubourg has said. . . ." *PDWP* 129, translation by Mooney.

15. "As to cloister. . . ." *PD* 289.

16. "So many difficulties. . . ." *PD* 280.

17. "They have already hauled. . . ." *PD* 295.

18. "As we are in a time. . . ." *PD* 296.

19. "The section north. . . ." *PD* 288.

20. "They all . . ." Verreydt memoirs, JA.

Part II

Chapter 4

1. "The Father Rector. . . ." *PD* 399.

2. For Mother Duchesne's letter re whooping cough: *PD* 399.

3. "St. Charles is a town. . . ." *JMUS* 1:

206-207.

4. "I do not hear. . . ." *JMUS* 1: 207.
5. "The churches of St. Charles. . . ." *JMUS* 1: 208.
6. "I have the pleasure. . . ." *JMUS* 1: 209
7. "The church is to be roofed. . . ." *JMUS* 1: 211
8. "The facade was of. . . ." *JMUS* 1: 211.
9. "On the 12th. . . ." *JMUS* 1: 212.
10. "Our dearest Brother. . . ." *JMUS* 1: 217.
11. "Do not think of. . . ." *SSH* 224.
12. "In order to keep down. . . ." *SSH* 229.
13. "The people of St. Charles. . . ." *SSH* 231.
14. "Mr. Proux. . . ." Lucille Mathevon to Monsignor, Feb. 10, 1833, AA, Sacred Heart file, translation by Sara Gaylor.
15. "When a storm. . . ." *SSH* 233-234.

Chapter 5

1. For more on St. Louis cemeteries, see UMSL's Archaeological Survey, Interim Report to the Bureau of Support Operations of the St. Louis Police Department, Mar 21, 1990: "The 'Old Catholic' Cemetery at Jefferson and Mill Streets."
2. "The city of St. Charles. . . ." Lucille Mathevon to Monsignor, Aug 7, 1833, AA, Sacred Heart file, translation by Sara Gaylor.
3. "This section is being. . . ." *SSH* 237.
4. Statistical reports from the parish for certain years in the 19th century are kept at AA, SCB file.
5. A large collection of the parish's deeds, rentals, and other legal documents is in the SCB file of the JA.
6. Information on parishioners comes in part from Bryan's *Pioneer Families of Missouri.*
7. Jesuit biographical material throughout the book comes from *JRPH, JMUS,* and the JA.

Chapter 6

1. For more on the anti-Catholic movement of the mid-19th century, see Faherty's *Dream by the River.*
2. "The town of St. Charles. . . ." *HDOM,* 15.
3. "These were damp, dingy. . . ." from an unsigned, handwritten account, JA, SCB file.
4. Census information is from SCCHS.
5. "Another nuisance. . . ." *HDOM,* 17.
6. "In the beginning. . . ." *HDOM,* 21.
7. "a spacious house. . . ." *HDOM,* 21.
8. "A railroad was. . . ." *HDOM,* 16-17.
9. "A lady living with. . . ." *HDOM,* 25.
10. "spreading good books. . . ." *HDOM,* 23.
11. "The Civil War. . . ." *HDOM,* 20.
12. "seem to go at will. . . ." Michael Fellman's *Inside War,* 169. Other Civil War material is from the files of the SCCHS.
13. The best sources on Rebecca Younger are Marley Brant's *The Families of Charles Lee and Henry Washington Younger,* and the author herself.
14. For more on James Bridger, see *JMUS* 2: 86-87, 101; Cecil Alter's *Jim Bridger,* 156, 185, 218, 240-241, 258-259; and Hiram M. Chittenden's *Life, Letters and Travels of Father Pierre Jean De Smet,* 1483-1485, 1488-1489.

Part III

Chapter 7

1. "This year the church. . . ." *HDOM,* 26.
2. "In consideration. . . ." from an unsigned handwritten account addressed to Jesuit historian Gilbert Garraghan, JA, SCB file.
3. "the ground previously owned. . . ."

translated by the author, page 29 of a section of *HD* possibly written by John Roes and not translated by O'Meara, JA, SCB file.

4. "by the exercises. . . ." *HDOM,* 51.
5. "Seeing such a. . . ." Unsigned letter to Garraghan, JA, SCB file.
6. "Our new house. . . ." *HDOM,* 51.
7. "This year also. . . ." translated by the author, pages 28-29 of the same section cited above in note 3 to Chapter 3, Part 1.
8. "To this school. . . ." *HDOM,* 26.
9. "Many parents are careless. . ." *HDOM,* 27.
10. Biographical information is from *HSC.*

Chapter 8

1. All centennial quotes are from the program featuring Conway's lecture.
2. Biographical material comes from *HSC.*

Chapter 9

1. Information in "Modernizing the Facilities" comes from *HD* and from Father Lagae's ledger book of improvements, 1898-1911, SCBA.
2. All quotes in "New Entertainments and Special Events" comes from *HD* and from Lagae's ledger book, SCBA.
3. For more on Charles Charroppin, see *JRPH,* 95-99.

Part IV

Chapter 10

1. " . . . there was an angry . . ." and other details of
the storm, see *St. Charles Cosmos-Monitor,* July 8, 1915.

2. "We lighted a blessed candle . . ." Sister M. Flaget to Mother General, July 7, 1915; Loretto Archives.
3. "at least the same . . ." page 2, MCBC, JA, SCB file
4. "over a stretch . . ." and other information on the nature of the storm, Hayes to Chief of U.S. Weather Bureau, Washington, D.C., July 13, 1915, SCBA.
5. "We won't know the result . . ." *HD,* July 14, 1915.
6. " . . . believing that you are . . . "SCB Finance Committee to Brother Knights, July 20, 1915, SCBA.
7. "allowing all the old . . ." MCBC, July 28, 1915, SCBA.
8. "secured the good will . . ." *HD,* July 30, 1915.
9. "the city teamsters . . ." *HD,* Aug. 23, 1915.
10. "Workmen excavating . . ." *Cosmos-Monitor,* Sep. 8, 1915.
11. "Deo Gratias" *HD,* Oct. 2, 1915.
12. "to collect among the farmers" *HD,* Nov. 9, 1915.
13. "the difference in the . . ." MCBC Jan. 16, 1916, SCBA.
14. "thank God, but little . . ." *HD,* Apr. 14, 1916.
15. "that the corner . . ." MCBC, Mar. 23, 1916, SCBA.
16. " . . . with a day's wages . . ." *HD,* Ap. 30, 1916.
17. "It is a sheer . . ." *HD,* May 15, 1916.
18. " . . . agent for the . . ." *HD,* June 26, 1916.
19. "Brick masons could . . ." *HD,* June 30, 1916.
20. "some negroes hauled . . ." *HD,* July 29, 1916.
21. for details of Grafton explosion and Ueberle's accident and death, see *Cosmos-Monitor* Oct. 11 and 18, 1916.
22. "had some trouble . . ." *HD,* Oct. 5, 1916.
23. "A splendid sight." *HD,* Feb. 10, 1917.

24. "The ceremonies carried out . . ." *Cosmos-Monitor,* May 30, 1917.
25. "The euchre this evening . . ." *HD,* Feb. 5, 1918.
26. "Before retiring . . ." *HD,* Mar. 30, 1918.
27. "By order of an ordinance . . ." *HD,* Oct. 10, 1918.
28. "About noon . . ." *HD,* Nov. 7 & 11, 1918.
29. "We are to send . . ." page 6 MMC, SCBA.
30. "he had a plan . . ." MMC, p. 11, SCBA.
31. "Each child to bring . . ." MMC, p. 7, SCBA.
32. "a social as well as . . ." MMC, P. 17, SCBA.

Chapter 11

1. "Fr. McNamara left . . ." *HD,* Aug. 26, 1926.
2. "It was deemed . . ." *HD,* Sep. 6, 1926.
3. "first one for . . ." *HD,* Sep. 6, 1926.
4. "I called on . . ." Ehrhard to Fr. William Sommerhauser, Ap. 17, 1941, JA.
5. "The scenes were pathetic," *HD,* Dec. 23, 1931.
6. "At 8 p.m. . . ." *HD,* Aug. 18, 1932.
7. "for some years past . . ." *HD,* Aug. 17, 1932.
8. "have been acting . . ." *HD,* Aug. 19, 1932.
9. "that the Notre Dame . . ." *HD,* Aug. 18, 1932.
10. " . . . the church was crowded . . ." *Cosmos-Monitor,* Mar. 13, 1934.
11. "mushy", "dainty . . ." Sommerhauser to Fr. Provincial, June 30, 1940; Closed Houses, File 67, JA.

Chapter 12

1. "Parishioners . . . were. . . ." *Cosmos-Monitor,* Aug. 5, 1944.
2. Information on the building of DHS comes from the DHS file of SCBA.
3. "We have directed over . . ." Nov. 6, 1953 proposal of Thomas R. Finn and Associates; DHS file, SCBA.
4. "It is for us . . ." *Greater St. Charles Central High School Campaign News,* Mar. 28, 1954; DHS file, SCBA.

Part V

Chapter 13

1. Biographical material on diocesan priests comes from AA.

Chapter 14

1. "No boundary lines . . ." Rielag to Archdiocese, Sep. 23, 1914, AA, SCB file.
2. "Many elderly people . . ." Archdiocese of St. Louis Committee for the Ministry & Life of Priests, Parish Data Form—1969; AA, SCB file.
3. For more on St. Philippine's canonization and related events: *St. Louis Post-Dispatch,* Aug. 23, 1987; *St. Louis Review,* July 1 and 15, 1988; *St. Louis Post-Dispatch,* July 3, 1988.

Bibliography

Books

Alter, J. Cecil. *Jim Bridger.* Norman: University of Oklahoma Press, 1962.

Beers, Henry Putney. *French and Spanish Records of Louisiana: A Bibliographical Guide to Archive and Manuscript Sources.* Baton Rouge: Louisiana State University Press, 1989.

Billon, Frederic L. *Annals of St. Louis in its Early Days Under the French and Spanish Dominations, 1764-1804.* St. Louis, 1886.

Brant, Marley. *The Families of Charles Lee and Henry Washington Younger: A Geneological Sketch.* Liberty, Mo.: Clay County Division of Historical Research and Development, 1986.

Breslow, Lori. *Small Town.* St. Charles, Mo.: The John J. Buse Historical Museum, 1977.

Bryan, Wm. S. and Robert Rose. *A History of the Pioneer Families of Missouri.* Baltimore: Geneological Publishing, Co., 1984.

Callan, Louise. *Philippine Duchesne: Frontier Missionary of the Sacred Heart, 1769-1852.* Westminister, Md.: Newman Press, 1957.

_____, *The Society of the Sacred Heart in North America.* New York: Longman, Green and Co., 1937.

Chittenden, Hiram M. and Alfred Talbot Richardson. *Life, Letters and Travels of Father Pierre Jean De Smet, S.J., 1801-1873.* 4 vols. New York: 1905.

Collot, Georges-Victor. *A Journey in North America.* 2 vols. Paris: Arthur Bertrand, 1826.

Drummond, Malcolm C. *Historic Sites in St. Charles County, Missouri.* St. Charles, Mo.: Harland Bartholomew and Associates, 1976.

Ekberg, Carl J. *Colonial Ste. Genevieve: An Adventure on the Mississippi Frontier.* Gerald, Mo.: Patrice Press, 1985.

Ekberg, Carl J., and William E. Foley, eds. *An Account of Upper Louisiana by Nicolas de Finiels.* Columbia: University of Missouri Press, 1989.

Faherty, William Barnaby. *Dream by the River: Two Centuries of Saint Louis Catholicism, 1766-1967.* St. Louis: Piraeus Publishers, 1973.

Fellman, Michael. *Inside War: The Guerilla Conflict in Missouri During the Civil War.* New York: Oxford University Press, 1989.

Foley, William E. *The Genesis of Missouri: From Wilderness Outpost to Statehood.* Columbia: University of Missouri Press, 1989.

Garraghan, Gilbert J. *The Jesuits of the Middle United States.* 3 vols. New York: America Press, 1938.

_____, *Saint Ferdinand de Florissant: The Story of an Ancient Parish.* Chicago: Loyola University Press, 1923.

History of St. Charles, Montgomery and Warren Counties, Missouri. St. Louis: National Historical Company, 1875.

Houck, Louis. *History of Missouri.* 3 vols. Chicago: R. R. Donnelley, 1908.

_____, ed. *The Spanish Regime in Missouri.* 2 vols. Chicago: R.R. Donnelley, 1909.

Killoren, John J., and NiNi Harris, Nancy Merz, David J. Suwalsky, Thomas J. Nickolai, and William Barnaby Faherty. *Jesuit Roots and Pioneer Heroes of the Middle West.* Florissant, Mo.: St. Stanislaus Jesuit Historical Museum, 1988.

Kinnaird, Lawrence, ed. *Spain in the Missis-*

sippi Valley, 1765-1794. 3 vols. Annual Report of the American Historical Association for the Year 1945. Washington, D.C.: Government Printing Office, 1946.

Kirkpatrick, John Ervin. *Timothy Flint: Pioneer, Missionary, Author, Editor, 1780-1840.* Cleveland: Arthur H. Clark Co., 1911.

McDermott, John Francis, ed. *Private Libraries in Creole St. Louis.* Baltimore: Johns Hopkins University Press, 1938.

_____, ed. *The Spanish in the Mississippi Valley, 1762-1804.* Urbana: University of Illinois Press, 1974.

Melville, Annabelle M. *Louis William DuBourg: Bishop of Louisiana and the Floridas, Bishop of Montauban, and Archbishop of Besancon, 1766-1833.* 2 vols. Chicago: Loyola University Press, 1986.

Mooney, Catherine M. *Philippine Duchesne: A Woman with the Poor.* New York: Paulist Press, 1990.

Moulton, Gary E., ed. *The Journals of the Lewis and Clark Expedition.* vol. 2. Lincoln: University of Nebraska Press, 1986.

Nasatir, Abraham P., ed. *Before Lewis and Clark: Documents Illustrating the History of Missouri, 1785-1804.* 2 vols. St. Louis: St. Louis Historical Documents Foundation, 1952.

_____, ed. *Spanish War Vessels on the Mississippi, 1792-1796.* New Haven: Yale University Press, 1968.

Olson, Edna McElhiney. *Historical Saint Charles, Missouri.* St. Charles, Mo., 1967.

Rothensteiner, John E. *History of the Archdiocese of St. Louis.* 2 vols. St. Louis: Blackwell Wielandy Co., 1928.

Spalding, Martin J. *Sketches of the Life, Times, and Character of Benedict Joseph Flaget, First Bishop of Louisville.* Louisville, Ky.: Webb & Levering, 1852.

Thwaites, Reuben Gold, ed. *The Jesuit Relations and Allied Documents.* vol. 59, *Travels and Explorations of the Jesuit Missionaries in New France, 1610-1791.* Reprint. New York: Pageant Book Co., 1959.

Articles

Archibald, Robert R. "From 'La Louisiane' to 'La Luisiana': The Imposition of Spanish Administration in the Upper Mississippi Valley." 11, no. 1 (Summer 1990): 25-37.

Briggs, Winstanley. "Slavery in French Colonial Illinois." *Chicago History* (Winter 1989-1990): 67-81.

Callahan, Ann. "An Unknown Pioneer." *The Maryville Magazine* (May 1952): 23-27.

Conway, James J. "Historical Sketch of the Church and Parish of St. Charles Borromeo, St. Charles, Missouri: A Lecture." Presented October 16, 1892 at Centennial celebration of parish.

Emmons, Ben L. "The Founding of St. Charles and Blanchette, its Founder." *Missouri Historical Review* 18 (July 1924): 507-520.

Flick, Ella M. E., ed. "Diary of the Reverend Father Marie Joseph Dunand." *Review of the American Catholic Historical Society* 26, 328-346; 27, 45-64.

Gitlin, Jay. "'Avec Bien de Regret': The Americanization of Creole St. Louis." *Gateway Heritage* (Spring 1989) 2-11.

Holmes, Jack D.L., "Spanish Regulation of Taverns and the Liquor Trade in the Mississippi Valley." In *The Spanish in the Mississippi Valley, 1762-1804,* edited by John Francis McDermott. Urbana: University of Illinois Press, 1974.

University of Missouri—St. Louis. "Archaeological Survey, March 21, 1990, Interim Report." Prepared for Bureau of Support Operations, St. Louis Police Department: "The 'Old Catholic' Cemetery at Jefferson and Mill Streets: A Preliminary Assessment Based on Excavations and Record Searches."

Collections and Papers

Archivo General de Indias, Seville, Spain
Audiencias
Papeles de Cuba (Cuba Papers)
Archdiocese of St. Louis Archives, St.
Louis, Mo.
St. Charles Borromeo file
Society of the Sacred Heart file
Society of Jesus file
Emmons Title Company, St. Charles, Mo.
Historic New Orleans Collection, New Or-
leans, La.
Microfilm of Archivo General de Indias,
Cuba Papers
Jesuit Missouri Province Archives. St. Louis,
Mo.
St. Charles Borromeo Collection
Felix Verreydt memoirs
Consultors' Minutes
Missouri Province Catalogues
Closed Houses, File 67
Lovejoy Library, Southern Illinois Universi-
ty — Edwardsville McDermott, John
Francis. Mississippi Valley Research Col-
lection.
Missouri Historical Society, St. Louis, Mo.
American State Papers, Public Lands
Hunt's Minutes
St. Charles Archives
Missouri State Archives, Jefferson City, Mo.
Livres Terriens
*St. Charles County Surveys, Inventory Book
3170.*
Old Cathedral Archives, St. Louis, Mo.
St. Charles Borromeo Archives, St. Charles,
Mo.
Sacramental records
Historia Domus, various years
Historia Domus, O'Meara translation, cov-
ering 1823-1872 minutes of various
parish groups, clippings, journals
St. Charles County Historical Society, St.
Charles, Mo.
St. Charles Borromeo papers
Civil War papers
Circuit court docket abstracts

City and county census records
School Sisters of Notre Dame Archives, St.
Louis, Mo.
Sisters of Loretto Archives, Nerinx, Ky.
Society of the Sacred Heart, National
Archives, St. Louis, Mo.
State Historical Society of Missouri,
Columbia, Mo.
Sanborne's Fire Insurance Maps of St.
Charles, various years from 1886-1929.

Newspapers

St. Charles Cosmos-Monitor
St. Charles Daily Banner News
St. Charles Journal
St. Charles Post-Dispatch
St. Louis Post-Dispatch
St. Louis Register
St. Louis Review

Interviews

Mary K. Austerschmidt
Douglas Boschert
Helen Briscoe
Father Arthur Bromschwig
Father Donald Buhr
Sister Mary Arthen Casson, S.S.N.D.
Irene Dryden
Henry and Ethel Elmendorf
Chauvin Emmons
Father Bob Gettinger
Sid Ginger
Jack Gould
Jack and Emily Heck
Richard Johannesman
Joyce Heck Lange
Queen Miller
Kathleen Netsch
Lorraine Pund
Elizabeth Rauch
Barbara Schwendeman
Father Richard Tillman
Charleen Ueberle
Joe Weber
Billye and Eugene Williams
Madeline Wilmes

Index